D0926762

COMMUNALISM:

FROM ITS ORIGINS TO THE TWENTIETH CENTURY

BOOKS IN PRINT BY KENNETH REXROTH

CONTINUUM BOOKS / HERDER AND HERDER:

The Alternative Society
With Eye and Ear
American Poetry in the Twentieth Century
The Orchid Boat: The Women Poets of China
    with Ling Chung
The Elastic Retort: Essays in Literature and Ideas

NEW DIRECTIONS:

The Phoenix and the Tortoise
The Collected Longer Poems of Kenneth Rexroth
The Collected Shorter Poems of Kenneth Rexroth
100 Poems from the Japanese
100 Poems from the Chinese
Love and the Turning Year:
    100 More Poems from the Chinese
Pierre Reverdy: Selected Poems
New Poems: Love Is an Art of Time
100 More Japanese Poems
Bird in the Bush
Assays
An Autobiographical Novel
Beyond the Mountains

UNICORN PRESS:

Sky Sea Birds Trees Earth House Beasts Flowers

CITY LIGHTS:

30 Spanish Poems of Love and Exile

PYM RANDALL PRESS:

100 French Poems

UNIVERSITY OF MICHIGAN PRESS:

Poems from the Greek Anthology

AVON BOOKS:

The Classics Revisited

COMMUNALISM:

FROM ITS ORIGINS TO THE TWENTIETH CENTURY

KENNETH REXROTH

A CONTINUUM BOOK · | ·
THE SEABURY PRESS · | · NEW YORK

The Seabury Press
815 Second Avenue
New York, N. Y. 10017

Design by Lynn Braswell

Printed in the United States of America

Library of Congress Cataloging in Publication Data

Rexroth, Kenneth, 1905—
    Communalism: from its origins to the twentieth century.

    (A Continuum book)
    1. Collective settlements—History. I. Title.
HX626.R48   335'.9   73-17882
ISBN 0-8164-9204-2

for Carol and Merisa,
who did the hard work

CONTENTS

INTRODUCTION

Prior to 1918 the word "communism" did not mean Left Social Democracy of the sort represented by the Russian Bolsheviks, a radical, revolutionary form of State socialism. Quite the contrary, it was used of those who wished in one way or another to abolish the State, who believed that socialism was not a matter of seizing power, but of doing away with power and returning society to an organic community of non-coercive human relations. They believed that this was what society was naturally, and that the State was only a morbid growth on the normal body of *oeconomia,* the housekeeping of the human family, grouped in voluntary association. Even the word "socialism" itself was originally applied to the free communist communities which were so common in America in the nineteenth century.

People who believe in libertarian communism can be grouped roughly under three general theories, each with its old masters, theoreticians, leaders, organizations, and literature. First there are the anarchists in a rather limited variety: communist-anarchists, mutualists, anarcho-syndicalists, individual anarchists, and a few minor groups and combinations. Second, the members of intentional communities, usually but by no means always religious in inspiration. The words "communalism" and "communalist" seem to have died out and it would be good to appropriate them to this group, although the by now too confusing word "communist" actually fits them best of all. Third, there are the Left Marxists, who prior to 1918 had become a widespread movement challenging the Social Democratic Second International. It was to them the Bolsheviks appealed for support in the early days of their revolution. Lenin's *The State and Revolution* is an authoritarian parody of their ideas. They in turn have called it "the greatest pre-election pamphlet ever written. "Elect us and we will wither away." Against them Lenin wrote *Leftism: An Infantile Disorder*. There is a story that, when the Communist International was formed, a delegate objected to the name. Referring to all these groups he said: "But there are already communists." Lenin answered: "Nobody ever heard of them, and when we get through with them nobody ever will." Today these ideas are more influential than they ever have been.

East Germany, Poland, Hungary, Czechoslovakia, each of the revolts against the Russian power has taken the same form as the first, the revolt of the Kronstadt sailors in 1921—free soviets, workers' councils, neighborhood committees, and peasant communes—the same social forms that were so common in the first years of the Spanish Civil War in Barcelona and in the countryside in Catalonia and Andalusia. In no instance have these revolts been reactionary, anti-communist. The slogan "Back to Free Enterprise" has never been raised. The fact is that once a society has been converted to the bureaucratic State capitalism of the Bolsheviks with the *Communist Manifesto* and *The State and Revolution* taught to all school children, a society, when it rejects the power structure, has no place else to go. The only possible fulfillment of Official Communism is free communism. Like capitalism before it, Marxism as a policy of the ruling class contains within itself the seeds of its own destruction. In Yugoslavia, where a Communist Party did manage to break free from Russian hegemony, the march toward ever greater workers' participation in industry, political and economic devolution, and federated communes has been irresistible. The Yugoslav Communist Party may be what Milovan Djilas calls it, the new ruling class; but for that class to withstand the Russian pressure, it must continuously grant concessions to insure popular support, and these concessions of course take place within an ideological context common to both the bureaucracy and the workers—a commitment to "communism."

Since the Great Cultural Revolution in China a similar process had been going on, but from the top down. The Chinese Communist Party is trying to create and preserve at all levels of an immense population the social relations of the first two years of the Russian Bolshevik revolution, not by democratic methods but by the most rigid, coercive authoritarianism.

This is the situation in the so-called socialist half of the world: in the capitalist half, ideological development is much further advanced, but the practical results are blocked by a power structure inherited from the industrial and financial organization of nineteenth-century capitalism. Tendencies toward decentralization, and initiative at the point of production, are masked by the outworn juridical apparatus. It is in the freer areas of the social interpersonal relations of individuals, away from factory or governmental bureaucracy, that the revolutionary developments are most apparent. Effective attack on the State and the economic system requires power, and the State, which is simply the police force of the economic system, has, so far, all the effective power. Demonstrations or Molotov cocktails are equally powerless before the hydrogen bomb. This is why the important changes are taking place in what the youth revolt calls "life style." And this is why their elders of both Old Left and Right accuse them of parasitism. Communes seem to the older generation as much luxuries of late capitalism as the immensely profitable exploitation of music—or drugs.

As concentration and depersonalization increase in the dominant society, as the concentration of capital increases with the takeover of ever larger businesses by conglomerates and international corporations, as more and more local initiative is abandoned to the rule of the central State, and as computerization and automation narrow the role of human initiative, in both labor and administration, life becomes ever more unreal, aimless, and empty of meaning for all but a tiny elite who still cling to the illusion they possess initiative. Action and reaction—thesis and antithesis—this state of affairs produces its opposite. All over the world we are witnessing an instinctive revolt against dehumanization. Marxism proposed to overcome the alienation of man from his work, from his fellows, and from himself by changing the economic system. The economic system has been changed, but human self-alienation has only increased. Whether it is called socialism or capitalism, in terms of humane satisfactions and life-meaning it is the same East and West. So today the present revolt is not primarily concerned with changing political or economic structures but is a head-on attack on human self-alienation as such.

The alternative society which is the form of this revolt has largely come about instinctively. Two centuries of

revolutions have exhausted the options. There is no
place else to turn. It is right that ecology should have become so enormously popular at this juncture. It is not just that man is
destroying the planet on which he lives, and driving
himself toward extinction by mining his environment
and reducing all business enterprise to the form of an
extractive industry. The human race is a certain kind of
species, developed in a specific environment, with
specific relations internally, man to man, and exter-
nally to other species. Had this situation not existed, the
human race had not evolved, and had it not continued
within a narrow range of modification, man would have
become extinct. The present relation of man to his environment and man to man has become so unlike the
optimum necessary for the evolution of the species that
humanity as we know it cannot endure. In such a situation a demand for readjustment is as instinctive as the
reaction of an invertebrate animal subject to electric
shock. This is what all the schools and tendencies of the
libertarian and communal tradition have in common, a
primary emphasis on man as a member of an organic
community, a biota, in creative, non-exploitative relationship with his fellows and his environment. The
communist-anarchists Élisée Reclus and Peter Kropotkin were both geographers and, if anyone was, they
were also the founders of the science of ecology.

Before the eighteenth century man had to collaborate
with his environment to survive. Even so the disappearance of the great mammals, who flourished until
after the end of the Ice Age, has been blamed on human
hunters, then a very small portion of the biota indeed;
and deforestation, slash-and-burn agriculture, and the
salting up of irrigated lands have destroyed whole
civilizations. With the onset of the industrial and scientific age business enterprise has tended more and more

xiv · | · COMMUNALISM

to treat the planet as a mine rather than a farm and to treat human resources in the same way. It is now obvious that if the human race continues on this course it will not last beyond the end of the century. The workings of the economic system have produced, in true Marxist fashion, many of the phenomena of communalism and anarchism. Most obvious is the tremendous growth throughout the Western world of communal living itself. With the runaway inflation of a moribund Keynesian economy, thousands of young people, particularly young people with children, find it impossible to preserve the standard of living they had encountered in a middle-class affluent society and are able to escape real poverty only in small communes. Meanwhile, the kind of life lived in stately homes, and twelve-room apartments, has ceased, and these places are taken over by groups who share expenses and responsibilities—moving always ahead of the redevelopers' wrecking ball. As urban life becomes too expensive, distraught, and filthy—as well as dangerous—and as tax money goes to war rather than to community life, more and more people flee the city and set up rural communes on the old-fashioned sixty to two-hundred-acre general farms which can no longer compete with industrialized agriculture.

One could not ask for a clearer relationship between economics and what Engels used to call the "superstructure." It is true that such communes at present are in a sense humane parasites on the dehumanized dominant society, but the assumption is that at least the rural ones may survive when the dominant society breaks down in chaos and nuclear war. To become economically independent the communes would have to develop an economy of their own as a systematic devolution of the ever more concentrated dominant economy. This would require an entirely different standard of living, in the fundamental sense of an entirely different scale of life values. But this, of course, is what is slowly taking place.

Almost all the problems which face the development of an alternative society have been realized and discussed in theory somewhere in the libertarian tradition. Friedrich Engels made the contrast *Socialism —Utopian or Scientific.* The scientific socialism of Marx and Engels was supposed to demonstrate almost mathematically that socialist revolution was inevitable and that therefore the duty of the revolutionary was to collaborate with history and never ask where, when, why, how, or what. Any attempt to answer those questions beforehand was "utopian." But history has produced only more of the same and called it socialism. By not answering the fundamental questions beforehand, by not having a plan for what a new society should be, Marxism has turned out to be not very far removed from "revolution for the hell of it." Today we realize that social change must move toward a rather clearly envisaged future or it will move toward disaster. It is either utopia or catastrophe.

As the technology has moved past a critical point, a point at which quantity changes into quality, as water turns into steam, it becomes ever more incompatible with the social structures, especially the power structure of nineteenth-century industrial and financial exploitation. The same kind of contradiction between social forms and economic content is occurring as in the eighteenth and early nineteenth centuries when capitalist methods of exploitation burst through the crust of feudal and mercantile forms. Although the existing tendencies of the capitalist system and of the State are to use the ongoing technological revolution for purposes of ever greater industrial, administrative, and political concentration, the real potential of these changes moves in the opposite direction. Over wide areas of the economy it becomes increasingly possible xvi · | · COMMUNALISM

to begin a radical devolution and decentralization of production. At the same time labor power, in the sense of brute muscular energy, declines in importance; and it is questionable if today it would be possible to construct a model of economic theory in which, as in the economics of Marx and Ricardo, labor power in that sense was the sole or even the primary source of value.

If the aim of production was life-enhancement and not profit, it would be quite possible to begin now to make more and more kinds of work easy, interesting, and creative. Notoriously already, certain kinds of monotonous work—assembly-line production of automobiles, old-fashioned mining, and so forth—are suffering from a breakdown of morale on the job and from an inability to recruit sufficient workers at full production. Drug use in Detroit is almost as common as it was in Vietnam and for similar reasons—the rejection of an intolerable way of life.

The demand for change in the way of life presses continuously against the blockage of obsolete social structures and, in cases where the power structure can permit it, overthrows and breaks through them. The special economic marriage peculiar to the nineteenth and early twentieth centuries has become obsolete as a cog in the machinery of production. (It was beginning to do so when Ibsen wrote *The Doll's House.*) The present political, economic, and religious systems offer no meaningful alternative. As a result, a sexual revolution is taking place surpassing the wildest dreams of feminists and the free lovers of the old anarchist movement. Over twenty years ago a woman friend of mine remarked: "There's an Emma Goldman in every car parked along the beach tonight." Today the demand is for, not random and promiscuous relationships, but ones with a new kind of interpersonal and personal significance. As these relationships become common they are profoundly modifying the social structure.

Not so long ago an anarchist life style was confined to a tiny minority of self-conscious bohemians and revolutionaries. Bohemianism is the subculture of the alienated. Unknown in previous societies, it grew up with capitalism itself. William Blake and William Godwin and their circles are roughly contemporary with the French Revolution and the onset of the industrial age. It has been said of bohemia that it is a parasitic utopia whose inhabitants live as if the revolution were over; or again, that the bohemian foregoes the necessities of the poor to enjoy the luxuries of the rich. What this simply means is that from the beginning capitalism secreted, as a kind of natural product, a small, slowly growing class of people who flatly rejected its alienation and lack of meaning. Even in the hard days of primitive accumulation of capital, the system was so inefficient that it was possible to live a different kind of life in its interstices, if one was lucky, well, usually self-educated, and born above the level of dire poverty. Today interstices have opened up everywhere in an affluent society. The fact that thousands of people can desert the industrial capitalist economy and live by making pots or batiks or leather work or strumming guitars may seem superficial and trivial. It is not. The problem is to reorganize the economy so that the automobiles are made in the same way.

Today everyone knows that a major war would result in the extermination of the human race, but that nevertheless as long as any of the existing political or economic systems continue the impossible war is certain to come eventually. The two largest conflicts since the Second World War, in Korea and Vietnam, broke down in a complete collapse of morale. Without war the economic and political systems produce the same kind of demoralization. The symptoms of the collapse of the civilization are all about us, and they are far more pronounced than they were in the last years of the Roman

Empire. Yet not all of these symptoms are necessarily pathological. The contemporary world is being pulled apart by two contrary tendencies—one toward social death, one toward the birth of a new society. Many of the phenomena of the present crisis are ambivalent and can either mean death or birth depending on how the crisis is resolved.

The crisis of a civilization is a mass phenomenon and moves onward without benefit of ideology. The demand for freedom, community, life significance, the attack on alienation, is largely inchoate and instinctive. In the libertarian revolutionary movement these objectives were ideological, confined to books, or realized with difficulty, usually only temporarily in small experimental communities, or in individual lives and tiny social circles. It has been said of the contemporary revolutionary wave that it is a revolution without theory, anti-ideological. But the theory, the ideology, already exists in a tradition as old as capitalism itself. Furthermore, just as individuals specially gifted have been able to live free lives in the interstices of an exploitative, competitive system, so in periods when the developing capitalist system has temporarily and locally broken down due to the drag of outworn forms there have existed brief revolutionary honeymoons in which freer communal organization has prevailed. Whenever the power structure falters or fails the general tendency is to replace it with free communism. This is almost a law of revolution. In every instance so far, either the old power structure, as in the Paris Commune or the Spanish Civil War, or a new one, as in the French and Bolshevik Revolutions, has suppressed these free revolutionary societies with wholesale terror and bloodshed.

COMMUNALISM:

FROM ITS ORIGINS TO THE TWENTIETH CENTURY

I

The Neolithic Village

The idea that early man had gone through a long stage of primitive communism is by no means confined to Marx and Engels, Lewis Morgan, Tylor, and the orthodox anthropologists influenced by Darwin in the late nineteenth century. It is shared by all the classical historians from Greece to China and is part of the mythological history of almost all cultures. This much is self-evident. People who hunt and gather cannot be anything but communist. Even in the most favorable environments the land can only support a very small number of people in any one group who live only by taking what nature is able to offer. Division of labor is minimal—hunting for the man, gathering for the woman. A few men may be more expert in chipping flints; a few women more expert in dressing skins. Here and there an individual may have more intense religious experiences than others in a small band.

Sometimes these primitive specialists may have become known over fairly wide areas. We have archaeological evidence for paleolithic "flint factories" in the form of great heaps of chips and rejects, and for trade in finished flints over long distances. It is improbable that extensively painted caves like Lascaux or Altamira were of interest only to the few people in the locality. Presumably they were religious centers to which many bands came from a wide territory. Also it is difficult to believe that the very high degree of skill shown in many paleolithic painted caves was not the result of specialization. Altamira and Lascaux were painted by artists. It is true, of course, that modern Stone Age peoples show almost as widely diffused artistic talent as do kindergarten children. It is the specialization demanded by society which destroys aesthetic response and artistic ability.

This is about the limit of the division of labor possible in a hunting and gathering society, and to survive no individual can be too specialized. The women gathering bulbs must be able to cope with any animal, herbivorous or carnivorous, they encounter; and it is obvious *prima-facie* that the artists of Altamira had a thorough anatomical knowledge of the animals they painted. In a hunting and gathering society it is impossible to accumulate much of a surplus. The mammoth rots away before he can be eaten up. Rodents make off with the store of roots and wild grain—we have no archaeological evidence for grain pits and other methods of storage before the advent of "incipient agriculture."

In such a society it is impossible for class structure to arise. Although it is an unwarranted assumption that present hunting and gathering peoples are exactly like their and our paleolithic ancestors, nevertheless the ecology is determinative—form follows function. They are without exception "communistic"; they cannot be anything else.

Until recent years archaeologists have not been too familiar with anthropological studies of surviving hunting and gathering peoples. Most of them live even today surprisingly well while having to do surprisingly little work—which is one reason why they refuse to become civilized. This continues to be true in spite of the fact they have been segregated into lands nobody else wants—the Bushmen into the Kalahari Desert in Africa; Blackfellows into the deserts of Central Australia, or the dense jungles in Northwest Australia; others into the wildernesses of Malaysia, India, Ceylon, South America, and other parts of Africa. Very often they live alongside people who practice slash-and-burn agriculture in the jungle; and the hunters and gatherers seem to have fully as adequate and a far more varied diet.

John Muir has estimated that the pine nuts of the one-leaf piñon in the open forests on the western slope of the Sierras gave the Piutes more calories per acre than the corn plots of the Iroquois. In California, west of the Sierras, the harvest of acorns, buckeye, roots, and seeds, as well as small game, mostly rabbits, supported the densest Indian population on the continent. Several tribes which had once practiced big-game hunting or agriculture, abandoned these pursuits when they entered California's natural abundance. Most of this largesse has disappeared, destroyed by modern grazing and agriculture. The highly nutritious camass bulb whose blossoms once made the western meadows look like lakes, and the wild seeds rich in protein of the original perennial grass cover, are both gone forever, but still today it would be perfectly possible for a family of five to live by fishing and harvesting of a few oak trees and some wild plants.

Natural foods were almost as abundant in the deciduous forests of Eastern America and Northern Europe, which is why an exclusive dependence on agriculture took so long to evolve. This forest life produced a peculiar power structure. In California, power simply dissolved in abundance that offered no Archimedes' fulcrum. In the deciduous forest, power came to be internalized in the organization of warfare as a sport and in the exploitation of the bearers of what culture there was—the women. The men were hunters and warriors and held on by force to a way of life that was a kind of revival of the paleolithic big-game hunters. The women were the weavers, basketmakers, potters, dressers of skins, food gatherers and agriculturalists, even porters and builders when the camp was moved—and were beaten for their pains. The conquest of civilized Europe by peoples with a forest background established this ethic, especially amongst the ruling class, where it endures today.

Paleolithic and neolithic are out-of-date terms, but it is still not too widely realized that chipped flint tools are by and large better for the work they were called upon to do than are polished stone ones, and chipped flint for many purposes survived all through the neolithic. Polished stone came in with agriculture (chipped flint microliths remain better for sickles) and with the use of a far wider range of stones, especially hard metamorphic rocks like quartzite which do not have regular fracture.

Social stratification in the village economy of early agriculture was never more than at arm's length. The war leader or shaman was immersed in the community and subject to it. Only with large-scale systematic agriculture and irrigation and the urban revolution do specialists, castes, and classes become remote from one another.

The typical early agricultural community is Jarmo on the edge of the Persian plateau, twenty-five small houses, possibly one hundred and fifty people. However, at Jericho, at a spring in the Palestinian desert, there seems to have been a town even before there was agriculture. In the valleys above the Mesopotamian plain, social stratifications, class, and status appear in the grave goods of the burials during the transition from village to town, contemporary with small-scale systematic irrigation, free-threshing cereals, woolly sheep (that is, deliberate breeding of domestic plants and animals), and the plow, soon to be ox-drawn; but the towns were still widely separated. With large-scale irrigation and cities man ceased to be in ecological balance with the biota. An accelerated imbalance becomes apparent in the flourishing of weeds and the salting of irrigated land. This resulted in a political dynamism in which life became ever more "unnatural" in internal and external relations.

Towns and cities developed in the richer lands opened up by the new technology in the Mesopotamian plain. In the piedmont valleys the ancient villages were left to the old ways. By 4000 B.C. village life in the Near and Middle East was established in all of its essentials as it was to endure until the mid-twentieth century. The State would remain a distant reality and impinge on village life only in a violent role—in war, in the collection of taxes, and, rarely, in the pursuit of a major criminal.

In Europe the "megalithic religion" that produced monuments like Stonehenge seems to have preceded the rise of towns. The deciduous slash-and-burn culture produced a priestly class and a widespread cult at a technologically more primitive level than in the Mediterranean world, as witness the history of Mayan civilization.

In village life religion took the form of group activity in which the entire community participated: the rites of spring and harvest, group marriage in the fields, clay "mother goddesses" with exaggerated sexual characteristics in domestic shrines. With the growth of towns religion became a ceremonial cult in which the populace participated as spectators or, at best, marchers in procession.

Agricultural surpluses permitted the growth of specialist craftsmen. In the early priestly states of Mesopotamia we find records of highly organized communities—herdsmen, craftsmen, fieldworkers, scribes—all united in a kind of religious syndicalism. Eventually priests and warriors took advantage of the increased specialization to develop a rigid caste structure topped by imaginary crafts supposedly vital to survival, and then to force the peasant to contribute more work to support this superstructure. Here was the origin of alienation: in work for a distant authority and in unpaid labor. But this early alienation was overcome by supernatural and patriotic sanctions and never reached the degree, even with slavery, that it did under industrialism. The results of work remained clearly visible. The peasant way of life always produces tangible goods from this closest of all work with nature. As long as the results of work are visible, work preserves some creativity and is not psychologically destructive. Of course the early craftsmen and scribes did not suffer from this primitive alienation at all, quite the reverse, and we have abundant literature praising their way of life.

As agriculture developed and became the principal means of livelihood, larger buildings began to appear, as we see in some of the ruins in upland Iraq and Iran. Some have hearths every five meters or so and may have been family dormitories like the long houses of the

Iroquois. Others have none and perhaps served as assembly halls or early temples, although they lack altars. A few have a single large hearth and may have been communal dining halls. To judge from the evidence of the earliest agricultural societies that we know, at Jericho and on the Persian plateau, for instance, life still must have been almost as communistic as amongst hunting and gathering people. The neolithic revolution—agriculture, domestication of plants and animals, weaving, pottery, polished stone tools and weapons, sedentary village communities—altered life profoundly. Still the archaeological evidence is that the division of labor and the class structure were little more developed than they had been in the paleolithic. The community was still small; the structure was still communalistic; but the surplus admitted a greater degree of specialization. Where such societies still existed into modern times we find potters, weavers, shamans, shamanesses, medicine men, tool-makers, and sometimes, especially in Africa, professional artists. But we do not find individuals who live by power over their fellows. Exploitation of man by man and by the State come in together with the second revolution, the urban revolution—the development of towns and agriculture over wide areas. Kings, priests, and a caste of traders appear together with the first small cities, as do warfare with organized armies, large-scale irrigation, and, a little later, writing.

We think of the civilizations of the late neolithic and early Bronze Age as having left primitive communism far behind. As a matter of fact, most of them were what we would call today State socialist. This term is often applied to the Inca civilization of Peru. What might be called the myth of Chinese civilization, not just Confucianism, but the whole universe of discourse in which

Chinese political and economic theory operate from the beginnings to the present day, is what, if we were to translate it into Western terms, we would certainly call State socialist.

Communistic societies survive well into the neolithic revolution both historically and amongst people in that stage of development today. The most immediately obvious are the Pueblo Indians of the American Southwest. These are people speaking various languages and with differing historical antecedents and they lie within the radiation zone of the highly structured civilizations of the Mexican plateau. Nevertheless they all share a passionately guarded communal life which they have managed to protect even until now against the onslaughts of Spanish missionaries and American free enterprise. In some the communal ethic is more apparent than in others. The Zuni may well be the most homogeneous people on earth. Some Pueblos are yielding to the enveloping American civilization and becoming at best a kind of human zoo for tourists; and others are disintegrating altogether. Even where the economic life of the community has become largely Americanized, it is still the community with its councils and committees that rules, however riven by conflicts between the old ways and the new. Similarly the religious life of the Pueblos is not controlled by an exploiting caste of priests but is in the hands of traditionally sanctioned groups, to at least one of which everyone in the community belongs.

Perhaps it was religious brotherhoods such as the Pueblo communities which made the transition to the monasticism which we find in most of the later city and nation state civilizations. A monastic order is by definition a communistic, usually authoritarian, religious society. We know that there were such societies in Egyptian civilization; there were thousands of what we would call monks in great centers such as Heliopolis, in the Aztec, Mayan, and Peruvian civilizations of the New World, in Mesopotamia at least after Sumeria, and possibly earlier, and of course India. The only major civilization in which monasticism does not seem to have arisen was the Chinese before Buddhism. Life amongst the servitors in the temples in pre-Exilic Palestine must have been organized on something like monastic principles. The remarkable thing is that we know almost nothing about these communities. Even Egypt with its enormous mass of surviving records provides us with little direct evidence. Our evidence comes from Herodotus and other Greek and Roman historians. We know close to nothing whatever about the Druids. It is disputed if they even existed as an organized religious brotherhood. The life and teachings of early monasticism are the province of the occultists who have certainly made the most out of them. Perhaps it is characteristic of such communities that they are in fact occult. Their way of life and their teachings are kept secret from the general population, even though they are, in the great "hydraulic civilizations," to use Wittvogel's term, part of the State apparatus.

In Greece and post-Exilic Israel such communities are both occultist and alienated, or at least at cross-purposes with their dominant societies. The early Pythagorean brotherhood is shrouded in the legends of late Hellenistic neo-Pythagoreanism and neo-Platonism. There seem to be few facts ascertainable. The early followers of Pythagoras seem to have been a non-celibate monastic community devoted to the study of primitive science, especially to a mathematical mysticism, with no belief in the myths and cults of ordinary Greek religion, and with an authoritarian, caste-structured, communalistic theory of society which survives

in a highly modified form in Plato's *Republic*. At first
they seem to have taken no part in the usual political
life of the communities in which they lived in Magna
Graeca, in the instep of the Italian boot. The famous
fragment attributed to Pythagoras, "wretches, utter
wretches, keep your hands from beans!" is supposed
not to refer to diet, but to democratic politics—the
Greek citizen voted yes or no with white and black beans.
In the course of time the Pythagorean brotherhood became political and controlled several cities, most
notably Cortona and Metapontum. Eventually people
rose against them and they were massacred. How much
of all this is history and how much is legend, it is
impossible to say; but it is remotely possible that for a
few years in a few communities, a polity vaguely like
Plato's *Republic*, but far more simple, actually existed.

2

Essenes, Therapeutae, Qumran

Until recent years our knowledge of religious communist groups in the classic period was quite limited. We knew almost nothing of the life of the Egyptian temple monks although it is certain that the power of the organized priesthoods was almost as great as that of the pharaohs and at certain times, notably the priesthood of Amon in the XVIII Dynasty in the sixteenth century, dominated the throne and disposed of pharaohs at will. The famous "heretic king," Ihknaton, was more a rebel against the Amon priesthood than he was a monotheist. No more is known of the lives of the various Greek and Roman religious brotherhoods or the Persian Magi. The most information we have is about the Essenes, the communist religious cult or lay monastic movement amongst the Jews; but that amounts to little more than brief descriptions in Philo, Josephus, and Pliny. With the discovery of the Dead Sea Scrolls and the community at Qumran in the desert hills above the Dead Sea, which was almost certainly the same as Philo's Essenes, we can form a pretty clear picture of the life of a communist religious sect around the beginning of the Christian era. From an anthropologist's point of view the most outstanding characteristic of this life is that it was a highly ritualized return to the life of the primitive village community and was a conscious revolt against the life of the city, or even town, and the attendant priestly temple structure and militaristic kingship.

On these brief materials provided by Pliny, Josephus, and Philo, with echoes but little augmentation in the Church fathers, an immense structure of speculation was raised, particularly in the nineteenth century, by writers influenced by the higher criticism of the Bible and by Liberal Protestantism. The Essenes were supposed to have been Buddhists or Magi or Pythagoreans or members of an occult, eremitical Egyptian cult. It was hypothesized that Jesus was an Essene; even more, John the Baptist. Since all three classical authors were commonly read by theologians and learned religious laymen from the Renaissance on, their picture of the Essenes' rule of life probably had a considerable influence on the rule of life of the more literate, strict Pietist sects. In the nineteenth century, the most balanced speculation on the relations between the Essenes, John, Jesus, and the first Christians was Ernest Renan's. His ideas were to have great influence on the picture of primitive Christianity held by most radical socialists after the publication of his *Life of Jesus*.

In 1947 seven scrolls of leather were found by Bedouin shepherds at approximately the spot described by Pliny. In the course of the next ten years a dozen caves surrounding the ruins of a settlement on the Wadi Qumran produced scrolls and fragments in abundance—more than five hundred manuscripts—

and the settlement itself was carefully excavated. The Essene community was removed from the realm of speculation and fantasy. The discoveries included large parts or fragments of almost all the books of the Old Testament and apocryphal and pseudepigraphic writings, commentaries, hymns, apocalyptic and prophetic writings peculiar to the sect, and an extensive and detailed *Manual of Discipline* or monastic rule. By and large the accounts of the three classic authors were substantiated. There are variations only in detail, with two important exceptions. First of all there are many skeletons of women in the Qumran cemetery. Either the sect was not celibate, or it was divided into a celibate order and an association of married laymen such as we still find in the Franciscans. Inside the community enclosure the archaeologists discovered large numbers of carefully buried jars filled with the bones of sheep, goats, and cattle, each animal buried individually. There can be little doubt that these are the remains of the sacrificial feasts of the community, so that Josephus's statement is to be understood as meaning that the Essenes rejected the sacrificial cult of the temple at Jerusalem and carried on one of their own (as the Falasha of Ethiopia do today). This is important because it means that the Essene community did not consider itself just a stricter Jewish sect but a new Jerusalem which would replace the old.

The scrolls and the excavations expand the picture of the community given by the classic authors in very specific ways, over and above minor disagreements. The community was organized according to the strictest order. At the top was the so-called Teacher of Righteousness, followed by the priests and Levites, and below them the rank and file, each of whom had his place in the elaborate hierarchical structure. In spite of this structure the community was a complete democracy. In theological matters the authority of the priests seems to have been absolute, but the governing council consisted of twelve laymen and three priests, patterned on the government of Israel in the Wilderness, and the decisions of this council were subject to the meeting of the entire community in which every man had a vote. The theology of the community was a kind of apocalypticism, millenarianism, chiliasm, a rigorously eschatological interpretation of life and history.

Apocalyptic has been called spoiled prophecy. The prophetic books of the Old Testament envisage the fulfillment of the purpose of God in history in the normal development of this world. The apocalyptic writings of the Old and New Testaments and their respective apocryphal additions look forward to the end of history, the rule of this world, in cataclysm, and to the advent of a supermundane kingdom of God beyond history. Millenarianism is the belief in the advent of this kingdom as the fulfillment of time—the thousand years mentioned in Revelation 20 during which holiness is to be triumphant throughout the world, when Christ the anointed Messiah will reign on earth with his saints. Chiliasm is the belief in the theocratic kingdom as such, and the belief that the present community of the faithful should model themselves on the future kingdom. In an eschatological world-view all morals and ethics, every scale of values, personal or historical, are oriented toward, and organized by, the expectation of final cataclysm, judgment of the world, and advent of the transhistorical kingdom.

In immediate expectation of the apocalypse great possessions, status, power, become meaningless, and the chiliastic, millenarian community practices a strict community of goods, the sharing of voluntary poverty. Labor is reduced to its simplest terms—to the agricultural labor of the early village community and its attendant necessary crafts, all made easier by the technology taken from the dominant—and doomed—society. These three characteristics of the Essene community at Qumran were certainly not original. Many aspects of their theology, the coming war of the Sons of Darkness and the Sons of Light, for instance, are to be found in Persian religion. But Qumran is now the community about which we know not just the most, but in fact a great deal. The existence of similar communities throughout the Near East around the time of the Christian era is still largely speculative. Whatever their antecedents, these outstanding characteristics of the Essenes were to remain the distinguishing marks of almost every communalist sect from then on, and were, in a secularized form, to be perpetuated in the revolutionary movements of the nineteenth century, utopian, communist, anarchist, and socialist.

Philo of Alexandria, the Jewish neo-platonic (more or less) philosopher who wrote in the first decades of the Christian era, gives the earliest accounts of the Essenes in his book *Quod Omnis Probis Liber Sit* and in the *Apologia pro Judaeis*. The latter work is lost but the Essene passage is quoted by Eusebius of Caesarea. Philo says in the former:

The Essenes are totally dedicated to the worship of God. They do not offer animal sacrifice. They flee the cities and live in villages. Mostly they work in the fields. Others practice peaceful crafts. They do not hoard money or buy and rent land. They live without goods or property. They never make weapons or any objects which might be turned to evil purpose. They engage in no commerce. They have no slaves and condemn slavery. They avoid metaphysics, logic, and all philosophy except ethics which they study in the divinely given ancestral laws of the Jews. Every seventh day they keep holy and do no work but spend their time in religious assemblies seated strictly according to their rank, and listen to the exposition of their sacred books explained according to the ancient symbolical system. They study piety, holiness, justice, the sacred law, and the rules of their order, all leading to the love of God, of virtue, and of men, to which ends their lives are completely devoted. They refuse to take oaths and never lie. They believe that God is the cause only of good, never of evil. They treat all men with equal kindness and live together in a communal way. No one man owns his house. Their homes are always open to visiting members. They keep one purse and one budget. They eat together in a common meal and take their clothes from a common store. They care for the sick, the young, and the aged.

So much for the *Quod Omnis Probis Liber Sit.* In the *Apologia pro Judaeis* Philo adds:

They live in a number of towns in Judaea and also in villages in large companies. There are no children amongst them. [This is in contradiction to his other statement.] Their variety of occupations makes them self-sufficient. Those who earn wages "in the world" turn their money over to the common fund. They do not marry.

Philo ends this account with four paragraphs of diatribe against women, marriage, and children which are usually assumed to reflect his own attitude, not that of the Essenes. Some paragraphs of his description apparently describe life in the communities of the order; others that of associates like Franciscan tertiaries who live in the world.

In *De Vita Contemplativa*, which is doubtfully attributed to Philo, there occurs a description of an Egyptian community similar to the Essenes—the Therapeutae. They lived in Alexandria, each member in a separate hut, with a tiny chapel for prayer, something like the arrangement of the medieval Carthusians, and met at sunrise and sunset for community prayer, and once a day for a common meal. The most ascetic members ate only every other day, and a few only once a week. On the Sabbath, they met for more extended religious service, which included a sermon. On the major Jewish holidays, especially Pentecost, they began at sunset on the eve of the Holy Days with an ascetic but ceremonial feast, a sermon, prayers, and the antiphonal chanting of psalms and singing of hymns (between the separated men and women), and choral dancing in imitation of Moses and Miriam at the Red Sea. Facing the sunrise they prayed that the Light of Truth might illumine their minds and then returned to their solitary cells for study and contemplation.

This is the only original account of the Therapeutae, and because of its resemblance to the early monasticism in the Egyptian desert, it attracted great attention from early Christian writers, many of whom believed that Philo and the Therapeutae were Christians of the apostolic age. In the nineteenth century they were often equated with the Essenes, but they seem to have been far more ascetic, city-based, and to have practiced only a minimum of community life. If we accept the account of *De Vita Contemplativa* at face value they would seem to be a Jewish communal monastic sect influenced by Egyptian religion and the practices of the communities of priests and priestesses at the great temples, especially that of Heliopolis, as the Essenes were undoubtably influenced by Persian religion. Philo does not say how they made a living. The implication is that they held all goods, which were very few indeed, in common, and lived on alms. Light and the sun play a large role in the brief account. For instance, "they took care of the needs of nature only under the cover of darkness" so that they would not offend the sun. This emphasis alone would connect them with possible ritual taboos of the Heliopolitan temple, as well as with the "light metaphysics" of Philo, and this Persian philosophical concept would haunt the more mystical communalist sects down to the present time. "By Light, Light," in the words of Philo himself.

The Jewish historian Flavius Josephus wrote *The Jewish War* between A.D. 70 and 75. In it he says:

The Essenes are celibate but adopt children and raise them in the order. They give all their property to the order and live a common life without poverty or wealth. They regard oil as a defilement and do not anoint their bodies. They always wear white garments. Their treasurers and other officers are elected by the whole community. They neither buy nor sell amongst themselves. Each man gives to whoever needs it and receives in return whatever he requires. [From each according to his ability to each according to his needs.] They get up, pray in the sunrise, work until about 11 A.M., bathe, clothed in loin cloths, in cold water, and go to their communal dinner of bread and one dish of food. Before and after eating a priest blesses the food and says a prayer. Afterwards they all give thanks to God, lay aside the garments which they have worn for the meal, since they are sacred garments, [says Josephus significantly,] and work until sunset, and then go to supper in the same manner as they had dined. Most of their actions are ordered by their administrators but aid and pity to others are permitted individual initiative. They do not take oaths. They study their ancient books and the herbs and minerals that heal sickness. A postulant for the order waits outside one year and is tried and tested. If he is accepted he is given a hatchet, a loin cloth, and a white robe [as in the Pythagorean brotherhood]. For two years he serves a novitiate and can take part in the purificatory rites. If he passes this trial period he is accepted into the order, admitted to the common meals, and for the only time in his life swears his loyalty to the order in the most solemn of oaths. Those guilty of the most serious faults are expelled and, still bound to their oath, perish for lack of food. Justice is dispensed in assemblies of the whole community, not less than a hundred. Not only do they do no work on the Sabbath; they do not light a fire, move any object, or go to the toilet. One use of their axes is to dig themselves a latrine and they move their bowels covered with their robes. During the Roman war they were brutally tortured, but bore their pains impassively, and refused to blaspheme or to eat forbidden food. They believe in the immortality of the soul, that the good go to the Islands of the Blessed and the bad to Hades. Some of them, studying their sacred books, become expert at predicting the future.

As an addendum Josephus mentions that there is another order of married Essenes. In the *Jewish Antiquities* he notes that they send offerings to the temple in Jerusalem but do not take part in the sacrifices there or enter the temple precincts but offer sacrifice amongst themselves. He estimates that there are over four thousand Essenes who live the common life.

The seventeenth chapter of the fifth book of *The Natural History of Pliny the Elder* in Philemon Holland's translation made in 1601 says:

Along the west coast [of the Dead Sea] inhabite the Esseni. A nation of all others throughout the world most admirable and wonderful. Women they see none: carnall lust they know not: they handle no money: they lead their life by themselves, and keepe companie onely with date trees. Yet neverthelesse, the countrey is evermore well peopled, for that daily numbers of straungers resort thither in great frequencie from other parts: and namely, such as be wearie of this miserable life, are by the surging waves of frowning fortune driven hither, to sort with them in their manner of living. Thus for many thousand yeers (a thing incredible, and yet most true) a people hath continued without any supply of newbreed and generation. So mightily encrease they evermore, by the wearisome estate and repentance of other men. Beneath them, stood sometime Engadda, for fertilitie of soile and plentie of datetree groves, accounted the next citie in all Iudaea, to Ierusalem. Now, they say, it serveth for a place onely to interre their dead. Beyond it, there is a castle or fortresse situate upon a rocke, and the same not farre from the lake of Sodome Asphatites. And thus much as touching Iudaea.

Near the caves where the Dead Sea scrolls were discovered there was an extensive ruin, Khirbet Qumran, which had been visited by archaeologists but never explored. In 1951 excavations began and it was soon obvious that they were uncovering the community buildings of the sect that had hidden the scrolls. There were no living quarters. The members must have lived in tents and huts and in the caves in the nearby cliff. There were silos, storehouses, a bakery, a mill, a kitchen, a laundry, workshops, pottery kilns, and an elaborate waterworks, an aqueduct from the nearby Wadi Qumran, and cisterns which supplied tanks and bathing pools. The sacred water was a most important factor in the life of the community in this waterless land. There was a scriptorium where their sacred books were copied and an assembly hall and a refectory for the common meal. Two miles south of Khirbet Qumran excavations began in 1956, on the sight of Ain Feshkhah, and uncovered the agricultural center where those who worked in the fields and palm groves and cared for the herds lived and worked. Today we can form a clearer picture of this life and beliefs and cult practices of the Qumran community than of almost any other in the distant past.

Rather significantly, the Essenes chose the site of an early Iron Age fortified village and opened up its old irrigation works. They were returning to the village life that had preceded Hellenistic and even Hebrew culture. Such was their beginning. Their end is dramatically obvious. All the buildings are marked by fire and scattered over the ground are the iron arrowheads of the Roman Tenth Legion which in A.D. 76–78 marched through the desert exterminating the Jewish sectaries, pacifists, Essenes, and fighting Zealots alike. Over and over again the Qumran documents refer to the Teacher of Righteousness and his persecution by and long struggle with the Wicked Priest. There is probably more dispute about these two figures than anything else in the scrolls. Was the former the founder of the sect and the Wicked Priest a specific high priest? Was the Teacher of Righteousness the name of an office in the community and the Wicked Priest a symbol for the hierarchy at the Jerusalem temple—the establishment? Are they cosmogonic and apocalyptic figures whose warfare is in heaven? Probably all three, depending on the particular text. We should remember that it is not only the life of Christ that is treated this way; it is the general tendency of Jewish religious thought to project history onto the screen of the heavens. One thing the Teacher of Righteousness is not, and that is the Messiah; and the long dispute as to whether he anticipates Christ or is Jesus Christ himself is misconceived.

The elaborate hierarchical structure of the Qumran community is not just one of religious initiation or group order. It is military. The common term for the "local chapters" and settlements of the community is usually translated "camps." Not only did Khirbet Qumran with its tents and huts surrounding the buildings on the site of an old fort look like a military camp; it was one, the general headquarters of the salvation army engaged in a holy war, the war of the Sons of Light against the Sons of Darkness. In that war each man had one place and no other in the ranks—"'Tis the final conflict; let each stand in his place." This marshalled army was thought of as fighting along with and paralleling the order of the hosts of heaven. This is why the secret names of the angels are part of the initiation of the novice. The battle was going on in eternity, in time the community was standing at attention awaiting the order to engage the enemy. History would come to an end with the winning of the holy war and the establishment of the messianic kingdom.

The sacramental character of the communal meal as an outward physical sign of an inward spiritual reality is obvious, but it differs radically from the Christian Eucharist, at least as that first appears to us at the end of the first century. It is an anticipation of the messianic banquet celebrating the victory in the holy war and the inauguration of the new kingdom. The meal begins with the blessing of bread and wine by a priest and by the lay administrator, who are referred to in the liturgical texts as the Priest Messiah, the descendant of Aaron, and the King Messiah, the descendant of David. The Sons of Light, the victorious army of the Lord, are seated at the table, each in his ordained place. Twice a day each member of the community is permitted to live in the *eschaton,* the end of time.

The camp at Qumran was not only the camp of the Army of the Future, it was the camp of the Army of the Past, of Israel in the Wilderness, and of the conquest of Canaan. Again, the hierarchical structure duplicated that of Israel at the beginning of significant history, the time of the giving of the Covenant and the Law. The governing council is modeled exactly on that of the Exodus, the lay "kings of the twelve tribes," and the three high priests. History repeats itself, but on a transcendent plane.

Many of the disputes over the Qumran documents are generated by careful choice of words to translate key terms. Some people translate *'esah* as "church." Dupont-Sommer translates it as "party." This enables him to speak of the Party of the Community and the Councils of the Party but this of course could be pushed further, to make a comparison which is obvious— "soviet" means council—and we can complete the quotation with a Bolshevik version of the International: "The international soviet shall be the human race." This way lies not madness but certainly crankiness.

Apocalypse is a disappointed prophecy—true, but what does that mean? It means that apocalypticism arises when the historical conditions become apocalyptic, when there is no way out. The Qumran Essenes were not wrong. Although the holy war did not come, both the old and new Israel were defeated. And the tradition was established and with it a new way of life. As Renan said, Christianity was an Essenism which succeeded—more or less.

3

The Early Church, Monasticism

Ever since Christianity became a church, as we understand the word, a power structure, the doctors of the Church have played down or denied the communal nature of early Christianity. On the other hand, social radicals have made much of it, and of the early Church's close connections, or even identity, with the Essenes. An unprejudiced reader, uninvolved in this controversy, reading the New Testament for the first time, would certainly form the impression that primitive Christianity was communist and that its "communal life" endured throughout the ministry of Paul, and, if he were to read them, on through the time of the apostolic fathers. The statements in Acts are indisputable.

Acts 2.44–47:

And all that believe were together, and held all things common; and sold their possessions and goods, and parted them to

all men, as every man had need. And they, continuing daily
with one accord in the temple, and breaking bread from house
to house, did eat their meat with gladness and singleness of
heart, praising God, and having favor with all the people. And
the Lord added to the church daily such as should be saved.

Acts 4.32–37 and 5.1–10:

And the multitude of them that believed were of one heart and
of one soul: neither said any of them that ought of the things
which he possessed was his own: but they had all things
common. And with great power gave the apostles witness of
the resurrection of the Lord Jesus: and great grace was upon
them all. Neither was there any among them that lacked: for
as many as were possessors of lands or houses, sold them, and
brought the prices of the things that were sold, and laid them
down at the apostles' feet: and distribution was made unto
every man according as he had need. And Joses, who by the
apostles was surnamed Barnabas, (which is, being interpreted, the son of consolation,) a Levite, and of the country of
Cyprus, having land, sold it, and brought the money, and laid
it at the apostles' feet.

But a certain man named Ananias, with Sapphira his wife,
sold a possession, and kept back part of the price, his wife also
being privy to it, and brought a certain part, and laid it at the
apostles' feet. But Peter said, Ananias, why hath Satan filled
thine heart to lie to the Holy Ghost, and to keep back part
of the price of the land? Whiles it remained, was it not thine
own? and after it was sold, was it not in thine own power?
Why hast thou conceived this thing in thine heart? thou hast
not lied unto men, but unto God. And Ananias, hearing these
words, fell down, and gave up the ghost: and great fear came
on all them that heard these things. And the young men arose,
wound him up, and carried him out, and buried him. And it
was about the space of three hours after, when his wife, not
knowing what was done, came in. And Peter answered unto

her, Tell me whether ye sold the land for so much? And she
said, Yea, for so much. Then Peter said unto her, How is it
that ye have agreed together to tempt the Spirit of the Lord?
behold, the feet of them which have buried thy husband are
at the door, and shall carry thee out. Then fell she down
straightway at his feet, and yielded up the ghost; and the young
men came in, and found her dead, and, carrying her forth,
buried her by her husband.

This narrative is given in full because it is the crux. It
certainly leaves no doubt whatever that the apostolic
Church was communalist. Both the Epistle of James
and the Epistle of Jude fit best into this context and it is
significant that both documents claim to be by brothers
of the Lord. Scattered through the Pauline epistles are
remarks which can be interpreted as antagonistic to the
communalist life of the so-called "Jerusalem Church"
of which James, the brother of Jesus, was supposed to
have been the bishop, or even in later accounts "bishop
of bishops." When the attack on the celebration of the
Eucharist as part of the common meal of the whole
Christian community began, the key passage was
I Corinthians II.20–22, in which St. Paul seems, or certainly can be made to seem, to reject the practice.

Those early heresies, the Ebionites and Nazarenes,
which preserved the communal life rejected the
Pauline epistles and claimed direct descent from James
and the Jerusalem Church, practiced a Jewish life,
obeying the Old Law as well as the New, and have often
been called Essene-Christians. "Ebionites" means
"poor men," and the term "Nazarene" may have been
employed for an Essene-like sect even before the ministry of Jesus.

Eusebius, Hippolitus, and Origen, who were already
beginning to etherealize the eschatology of the Gospels,

remark on the extreme millenarianism of the Ebionites. They seem to have lived in separate communities and, like the Essenes, took frequent baths of purification. The pseudo-Clementine *Homilies* and *Recognitions* are usually attributed to them and the curious can read their ideas there. Centuries later the Mennonites would refer to the Clementine *Homilies* and *Recognitions* as primitive Christian authorities authenticating their own beliefs. We read in the early fathers of various other heretical communist sects but we know almost nothing about them. There does seem to be a general tendency amongst those who split from the Church over doctrinal matters also to reject its worldliness and to revive the communalism of the apostolic Church. These heresies come and go all through the centuries before the estabishment of the State Church by Constantine and definition of its dogmas in the ecumenical councils called by the emperor. The remarkable thing about the Ebionites is that they survived as communities in the marginal lands of the Near East until they were absorbed or overrun by Islam in the seventh century.

In the Orthodox Church communism was taken away from the laity and made a privilege of the monks, but monasticism is simply authoritarian, celibate communism. Christian monastic communities first appear in the deserts of Egypt and then of Syria, Palestine, and Sinai—in the same kinds of place as the Essene community at Qumran and the Essene-like Egyptian Therapeutae described by Philo. In Toynbee's terms these monastic communities could be described as "successor states" to the Essenes.

The earliest monks known to us were hermits who did not live in organized communities but, as it were, in loosely associated hamlets, on the edges of the desert above the Nile in Lower Egypt. Curiously they do not seem to have always been celibate. Many of them lived with a female companion, a *soror mystica*. What this means we have no way of knowing but the practice survived in the eremitical life and reappears in the early Irish Church.

St. Pachomius is said to have established the first organized monasteries in Upper Egypt. Although the earlier hamlets of hermits must have had some kind of community, they apparently did not live together, much less share meals and work in common or live by rule. All these factors in the monastic life were introduced by Pachomius and from his foundations, which eventually came to number seven thousand people in his lifetime, descend all future orthodox monastic orders.

The significant thing about St. Pachomius is that he had been an officer in the army of Constantine. Organized monasticism appears as a reflex of the State Church. Even under the most tolerant emperors the Christian communities had been at cross-purposes with the dominant society. Christians were still awaiting the Second Coming. Although the most extreme chiliasm was dying out amongst the orthodox as the years went by, and the apocalypse receded from the immediate to the remote future, the Church was still the community of the remnant that would be saved, antagonistic in all its values to those of secular society. The apostolic life was held binding on all its members, although the early communism was abandoned for a simple community of people forced to live in the world. In practice the Gospels' constant insistence on charity led to a considerable measure of "communism of consumption." Pre-Constantinian monasticism was simply a more extreme form of the life of the ordinary Christian. Due to the fact that it was not governed by any communal discipline it tended to push ascetic practices to ever greater extremes.

With Constantine's establishment the very nature of the Church and the entire concept of the kingdom changed. The Church ceased to be a remnant, but thought of itself as coterminous with society itself. Its bishops became part of the state structure. Its theological disputes were settled by councils of state attended by functionaries appointed by the emperor. Its congregations became parishes fixed in place, its bishops administrators of a given territory. The apostolic and Pauline organization of intervisitation, correspondence, and wandering missioners ceased. All the future monastic rules were to have paragraphs condemning wandering monks and preachers. The contrast is so great that it is easy to see why future heretical and Protestant sects would come to look on the established Church as an organization for the suppression of Christianity and its heads—emperor or pope—as Antichrist.

The apostolic life, said the established Church, was a council of perfection meant only for those with a special vocation—monks and nuns. In the future the term "religious" would be applied to them only, in distinction to the laity. Since the dynamism of the apostolic life was so great that if it were allowed to run loose in society it would bring down both established Church and empire, or for that matter any worldly polity, then or now, it was necessary to isolate this dynamism. Organized monasticism was a method of quarantining the Christian life. This is why the Church has always insisted that monasticism be celibate. There have been only a very few religious orders which have associated monks, nuns, and married people in one community, and they were only created to counteract heretical associations. Lay monasticism, a community of families holding all things in common, living a life modelled on that of the apostles, unavoidably becomes a counter-culture, a remnant awaiting the coming of the messianic kingdom.

Time and the emperor postponed the Second Coming to the remote future—the established Church *is* the kingdom. These ideas are usually attributed to St. Augustine, but they are only worked out in systematic detail in his *City of God,* and are adjusted there to the collapse of the empire in the West. It is significant that Augustine's master, St. Ambrose, still believed, or half-believed, in the communism of the apostolic life, while Augustine not only preached against it, but denounced again and again the merging of the Eucharist in the *agape*, the community meal. The two most important rites of the Christian cult ceased to be communal functions and were reorganized and directed toward support of the State religion. The Eucharist became a sacrifice performed by the priest in which the laity participated only as praying spectators. The important meaning of the insistence on infant baptism was that it tied the lay family to the parish, to the territorial administration —as in the future both the Anabaptists on the one side, and Luther and the Catholics on the other, were to insist, each for different ends.

In areas remote from the control of Church and Empire like Ireland and, to a lesser degree, Britain, or both remote and heretical like the Nestorian Church, which left the Roman for the Persian Empire, monasticism was both more eremitical and more socially effective, both on the Church and on the surrounding secular society, Christian or pagan—an apparent measure of the quarantine established by St. Pachomius, St. Basil, and St. Benedict.

The social effectiveness of organized monasticism was due to the founders' insistence upon work, an insistence that increased from Pachomius to Basil to Benedict. The early monks of the desert must have been parasitic on the ordinary Christian community. Considering where they lived, there is no other way they could have supported themselves. They devoted themselves to prayer, meditation, fasting and other austerities. St. Pachomius's foundations were governed by an elaborate rule. The members lived in dormitories instead of separately in caves and huts and had their meals and prayers in common. The abbot of the motherhouse was the superior of all the other convents whether of men or women, appointed their superiors, visited them periodically, and presided at a general chapter held annually at the motherhouse. As tightly organized a system as this would not appear again until the Benedictine reforms in the early Middle Ages. Time not spent in prayer was spent in work. Each monastery had its own farmlands and craft workshops and was largely self-sufficient. In other words, they achieved a large measure of "communism of production." Pachomian monasticism flourished until the Muslim conquest of Egypt, when it entered into a long decline; and it is now almost extinct except in Ethiopia.

St. Basil owed his advance from scholar to priest, and from priest to bishop and monastic founder, to his forcefulness as a polemicist against the Arian heresy which was threatening the integrity of Church and empire. The monastic life in Greece and Asia Minor had largely been eremitical and not subject to any discipline either in way of life or in theology. St. Basil adapted the rule of the Pachomian monks to the conditions of the patriarchate of Constantinople and established the type that would prevail to this day in Eastern Orthodoxy. Originally there was great insistence in the rule on work and on strict obedience to Orthodox doctrine. As time went on monasticism in the East became more and more parasitic economically. The monks lived on land that they did not farm but left to peasants on shares and hired laborers, while they devoted themselves to prayer and contemplation. Perhaps due to this rather hothouse atmosphere, the heresies, schisms, and enthusiastic movements which have arisen in Orthodoxy have originated in the monasteries. Eventually there would arise monastic cities like Mount Athos, not at all self-supporting, isolated from, yet parasitic on, lay society. Monasticism in the Western empire was the creation of Benedict of Nursia. Although the entire meaning and purpose of the monastic life as he conceived it was prayer and contemplation centered around the "work of God," eight "hours" of the Divine Office when the community solemnly chanted psalms, sang hymns, and prayed together in chapel, there was in fact a much greater emphasis on work in the field, in shops, in copying manuscripts, than in Eastern monasticism. The reason for this is simple. What had been the Roman Empire in the West was in ruins. Cities were being deserted, land went out of cultivation, population declined unbelievably, to perhaps a fifth of what it had been under Marcus Aurelius, and the appurtenances of civilization, namely, literature and the arts, ceased to be produced by the secular society. Irish monasticism was a special exception, unlike any other, with probably pre-Christian sources.

The Benedictines cleared forests, drained land that had gone back to marsh, reorganized peasant cultivation, carved and painted religious statues and pictures, and copied manuscripts, mostly religious, but some also of the classic culture of Rome. Many monastic leaders in the West were quite conscious of their role as preservers of civilization. Cassiodorus founded a monastery devoted to saving the literary heritage of Latin civilization. In the case of the Benedictines the "quarantine" of organized monasticism had a reverse effect. The secular society had broken down in chaos. Within the monasteries civilization survived in what was really a garrison state, protected by supernatural sanctions, within the barbaric secular state.

Each Benedictine monastery was an entity unto itself. There was no central administration. Early Benedictinism was not a religious order in the later sense of the word. The reason for this too was simple. Centralization requires ease of communication and communication had broken down. The Benedictine rule is in some ways stricter than that of Basilian or of Pachomian monasticism but it is still more rational, more flexible, and more communitarian. The abbot functions as the president of the chapter, the council of monks in which all the professed have a vote. The monks are vowed to obey the rule and the abbot and therefore the rule is not easy to change, but the abbot rules as the head of a kind of democratic centralism. Decisions are subject to discussion and vote, but once made must be obeyed absolutely. There are officers in charge of all the various activities of the community, whether in the fields, the workshops, the hospital, the kitchen, or the scriptorium and library, and each overseer is subject to the control of the abbot and the chapter.

Unlike the Essenes at Qumran or the earliest monks, the Benedictines did not look upon themselves as a saved remnant, antagonistic to a world doomed to perdition. Quite the contrary; they were called to save the world in the most literal sense. Not only were they called to save and rehabilitate a shattered civilization, but they thought of themselves as called to spread the Gospel to the heathens beyond the limits of the former empire. The Benedictines, together with the Irish monks of the Rule of St. Columba, inaugurated a second wave of missionary activity, after that of the early Church, and were responsible for Christianizing Middle Europe and Scandinavia. The strategic importance of such missionary activity as a defense of Latin civilization was obvious.

The Benedictine rule and bylaws and administrative measures are a priceless deposit of information on the techniques and the problems of a communal fellowship in dynamic relationship with a disorganized society. Unfortunately, although some Church historians have thought otherwise, the example of the Benedictine life seems to have had little direct effect on later communalist religious groups, whether heretical sects or movements wthin the Church.

There is only one religious order of any importance which included priests, monks, nuns, and married people all living in one community, usually a village with a monastery at one end, a nunnery at the other, and the lay people in between. This was the order founded in England by St. Gilbert of Sempringham. It never spread beyond England, although its example influenced a very few small continental foundations. Since the Church had always feared such an organization it is strange that the Gilbertines seem to have had very little influence on society and were not in any way connected with the lay monasticism which was to become so popular on the continent on the eve of the Reformation, specifically the Béghards and Béguines, the Brethren of the Common Life, and the *Gottesfreunde* or Friends of God.

This dynamic relationship was to come with the friars, especially the Franciscans. It is significant that St. Francis himself always refused ordination to the priesthood. Both Franciscans and Dominicans were lay-oriented. The proper name of the Society founded by St. Dominic is the Order of Preachers and the Franciscans were dedicated to preaching, hearing confessions, and to manifest poverty both as a virtue in itself and as

a witness to the world. The life of St. Francis, like that
of Pope John XXIII, is a perfect example of what hap-
pens to the Church when it accidentally permits a person who models his life closely on that of the historical
Jesus to attain a position of influence or power.

The Dark Ages and the early Middle Ages are remarkably free of large-scale millenarian and communist sects and heresies. The Benedictine solution
seems to have been effective in satisfying the demand
implicit in Christianity for a life of apostolic community
and poverty. The doctrine of St. Augustine that the
Church itself was the kingdom seems to have been almost universally accepted. There was a pandemic of
millenary fever as the literal millennium, the year one
thousand, drew near;* but when it passed without the
end of the world, millenarianism died out, and in those
days it did not take the form of separate sects claiming
to be the "saving remnant" but affected the entire population. From the fall of Rome to the twelfth century the
spiritual energies of men went to building medieval
civilization itself with little diversion. The so-called
"medieval synthesis" was a remarkably self-contained
structure in the history of cultures, and as it was growing it was able to absorb all the possible activities of its
society. The Church was not just coterminous with society; society was coterminous with the Church. As in
primitive cultures, Catholicism was an anthropological
religion, one method of defining society.

The only important heresy, that of the Paulicians-
Bogomiles-Cathari-Albigenses was not a heresy at all,
but a different religion, Gnostic and Manichaean. That
is, it was Oriental and pre-Christian in origin, and concerned with the progress of the soul through the stages

---

* Many modern historians deny this happened except in the imagination of nineteenth century historians who thought it *must* have.
The evidence is slight at best.

of a cosmogonic drama, a progress abetted by the knowledge of occult mysteries. It was very far from communistic and only incidentially millenarian. The judgment, the fire, and the kingdom were internalized as stages in the salvation of the soul. The Albigensian church was governed by an elite of illuminated adepts and where it could, as briefly in Bulgaria, was quite willing to become an established church. When it threatened to become so in the south of France it was suppressed in the bloodiest of all Crusades—which took the form, significantly, of a territorial war.

Gnosticism was never totally suppressed, and vestiges of occult mysteries turn up here and there in the heresies of the later Middle Ages, but they remain occult, difficult to trace, and never important in any popular movement except possibly the Brotherhood of the Free Spirit. This did not prevent the Church from seeing Cathari everywhere, all through the later Middle Ages and the Reformation. But in fact dualist, Manichaean, or Gnostic doctrines are exceedingly rare in the evidence, although there is no way of proving or disproving the latter-day occultists' claims that they were an esoteric teaching confined to the inner elites of various heretical movements.

Certainly as we survey the many tiny heretical groups that got in trouble with the authorities from the tenth to the twelfth century, it is possible to see emerging an orthodoxy of the heterodox, a consensus which would later form a body of doctrine characteristic of the more radical offshoots of the Reformation, of which the Taborites, the Anabaptists, and the more extreme sectaries of the English Civil War are perfect examples. For instance, eight different sects denied the existence of purgatory and the efficacy of prayers for the dead. The baptism of children was rejected by fifteen such groups; the reality of the humanity of Christ, by four; the resurrection of the body, by three. The sacrament of the

Lord's Supper was abandoned, either as communion or sacrifice, in twelve separate cases. Almost all heretics denied the doctrine of transubstantiation, which was still only in the process of definition in the Church itself. Prayers to and veneration of the saints were likewise denied. Auricular confession was rejected by an indefinite number, although many groups practiced public confession to the congregation, as in the early Church. There are nine cases of vegetarianism, ten or more admissions of the practice of free love, group sex, or ceremonial orgies, and a far larger number of unsubstantiated accusations. Catharist and Gnostic influence led some to the rejection of the Old Testament, but most groups placed greater emphasis on it than did the Church, and a few followed the letter of the Jewish law. Without exception they all rejected the authority of the established Church and condemned its clergy for simony, adultery, pederasty, ignorance, and hypocrisy.

Only a very few are known to have practiced the apostolic community of goods. Outstanding was the community of Monteforte, a castle in the archdiocese of Milan. When the archbishop discovered their existence, he had them all arrested and brought to Milan to trial. The entire population of the castle and its domain had been converted by a man we know only as Giardo. Led by him, the more articulate defendants turned their trial into a propaganda demonstration for themselves, and so we have a fairly complete record of their beliefs. They did not believe in a priesthood or in sacraments, but lived lives guided and sanctified by the indwelling of the Holy Spirit. They were vegetarian and ate nothing which had been begotten by sexual intercourse. Those who could lived in strict chastity with their spouses, or did not marry. When the archbishop asked how, if every one lived so, the human race could perpetuate itself, Giardo replied that when men had become pure they would reproduce asexually like bees. The elders of the group kept up a continuous chain of prayer, replacing each other night and day. They interpreted the Trinity allegorically—the Father as Creator, the Son as the soul of man, beloved of God, and the Holy Spirit as the divine wisdom in each human soul. From the countess and nobles to the lowliest peasant they practiced a complete communism and lived a largely self-sufficient life, independent of the surrounding economy. They claimed to have brethren all over Europe. They also held a belief, peculiar to themselves, that to be saved they must die in torment. They were so convinced of this that if one of them started to die a natural death, he called upon the others to torture and kill him. The archbishop set up a cross and a stake and demanded that they choose between submission to the Church and death by fire. Only a few chose the cross. Almost all went joyfully to their deaths.

This was only the second official execution for heresy in the Western Church. It had been preceded by that of a group of heretics in Orléans about 1015. They seem to have been Gnostics, more Gnostic in fact than the Cathari, and what we would call today upper-class bohemian intellectuals. They were accused by a spy, who had been initiated for the purpose of exposing them, of ritual sexual orgies and the worship of devils. As far as we know they did not practice community of goods nor was this an accusation at all common in the heresy trials of the early Middle Ages.

An important factor in later heresy was the spread of knowledge of the Bible, especially after it had been translated into the vernacular. The appeal to the communism of the apostles was an appeal to the Bible, and the sole authority of the Bible was not an important factor in early heresy. The un-Christian wealth of the Church was. It took only a slight familiarity with the

Gospels and epistles read at Mass to realize that if Christianity was the patterning of one's life on the life of Christ and his disciples, then the Church was literally Antichrist, shorn up of its apocalyptical personification as the great evil figure, Antichrist. The accusation was certainly just. Nothing was more dangerous to the power of the established Church than the little bands of laymen devoted to voluntary poverty, Bible study, and good works that began to flourish in the twelfth century in northern Italy, eastern France, the Rhineland, and Bohemia.

In 1176, a generation before St. Francis, one Peter Waldo, a wealthy merchant of Lyons, sold all he had and gave it to the poor and gathered together a group of pious laymen who wished to return to the apostolic life of poverty and evangelism. Soon they were in communication with other little groups and the movement grew rapidly. Pope Alexander III approved their vow of poverty and placed them in obedience to their local bishops, who in most cases forbade them to preach, for simply by living an apostolic life they were challenging the clergy as representatives of the apostles. When the bishop of Lyons forbade them to preach they decided to obey God rather than man and were excommunicated and expelled from the city and three years later condemned by Pope Lucius III and the Council of Lyons in 1184.

So began the heretical sect of the Waldenses or Poor Men of Lyons which spread rapidly over Europe to become the largest and most widespread of any medieval heresy. Tirelessly persecuted by the Church, and the object of several Crusades, they were eventually driven into the mountain valleys of Lombardy, Savoy, the Tyrol, and Bohemia and Moravia, where they managed to survive down the centuries. The Czech Waldenses were absorbed into the Taborites or the Czech Brethren. The Lombard Waldenses were discovered by the Reformers and became the special care of English Protestants after the massacre immortalized in Milton's sonnet, and a minor object of Cromwell's foreign policy. They are still in existence in the same mountain valleys and in recent years have established chapels in some of the cities of northern Italy. The original Poor Men of Lyons practiced community of goods and at various times embattled groups of Waldenses returned to a kind of siege communism. But through all the doctrinal changes of the sect down the centuries they never abandoned the practice of voluntary poverty. They were originally accused only of refusing to take oaths, bear arms, or approve of capital punishment. Eventually, they came to believe that any layman not in a state of mortal sin could consecrate the bread and wine of communion, rejected the sacrifice of the Mass, and denied that the papal Church was the Church of Christ, insisting rather that it was the scarlet woman of the apocalypse and that none of its special teachings or practices could be followed without sin.

During the Reformation in the sixteenth century the Waldenses were extensively proselytized by the reformers and doctrinally became assimilated to the main body of Protestantism in its Swiss Calvinist form. Throughout the nineteenth century English Protestants, led by a Colonel Beckwith, who settled amongst them, spent considerable money building schools, hospitals, churches, and other social services in their communities. Although doctrinally they differ little from the Swiss Protestants to the north of them, the entire feeling of their mountain villages is different. Although they no longer practice communism they are not acquisitive or competitive. They remain much poorer than they need be and live by a social ethic of mutual aid, cooperation, and close spiritual unity, not unlike the settlements of strict Mennonites or Amish in America.

4

Eckhart, Brethren of the Free Spirit

St. Francis is not only the most attractive of all the Christian saints, he is the most attractive of Christians, admired by Buddhists, atheists, completely secular, modern people, Communists, to whom the figure of Christ himself is at best unattractive. Partly this is due to the sentimentalization of the legend of his life and that of his companions in the early days of the order. Many people today who put his statue in their gardens know nothing about him except that he preached a sermon to the birds, wrote a hymn to the sun, and called the donkey his brother. These bits of information are important because they are signs of a revolution of the sensibility—which incidentally was a metaphysical revolution of which certainly St. Francis himself was quite unaware. They stand for a mystical and emotional immediate realization of the unity of being, a notion foreign, in fact antagonistic, to the main Judeo-Christian tradition.

"I am that I am"—the God of Judaism is the only self-sufficient being. All the reality that we can know is contingent, created out of nothing, and hence of an inferior order of reality. Faced with the "utterly other," the contingent soul can finally only respond with fear and trembling.

If God is immanent in the world and if the unknowable Trinity has in its Second Person become the comrade of man, the world is charged through and through with joy. "And honde by honde then shulle us take/ And joy and bliss shulle we mak/ For the Devil of Hell man haght forsak/ And Christ Our Lord is made our mate," as it says in the Middle English poem by some anonymous Franciscan. This is not a matter of doctrine. The Alexandrian and the scholastic philosophers of the Church had worked out a sensible relationship of the deity to the world. It is a matter of religious sensibility.

Many others before him had called for a return to the life of the historical Jesus and his companions, but no one before St. Francis had preached that life, both the life of Christ and the Christ-like life, as one of intense abiding joy. When late in his own life St. Francis, entranced in prayer, was to be marked on the hands and feet and side with the stigmata, the wounds of the crucifixion, it was during a transport of pure joy.

Had St. Francis been a philosopher or preacher, and simply taught the virtues of a life made new, he would have been only another out of so many, and his words would have been subject to dispute, modification, or denial. But he lived the new life, more intensely than anyone else and with an always manifest joy, and he gathered a band of companions who shared and also manifested that life.

It would seem to have been the sheerest accident that the Church accepted him and the pope permitted the foundation of his order. There were other little bands of poor men trying to live the life of the Gospels in the same years but they were condemned. Had Peter Waldo encountered only slightly more sympathetic officials in the hierarchy of the Church he might have superseded St. Francis. Certainly his original message was a much safer one. The Church permitted the establishment of the Franciscan order because it met an immediate need. Heretical movements were springing up everywhere at the end of the twelfth century; and the old monastic organization, although it had undergone two drastic reforms, could not meet the need of which these movements were a symptom. Not only had Benedictine monasticism become wealthy and its abbots part of the power structure, but its relationship to society had become reversed, centripetal. The secular world existed for it, not it for the world. Franciscanism was dynamically centrifugal, outgoing, to use the contemporary slang, as of course had been the Gospel itself.

Central to the evangelism of St. Francis was his notion of poverty as a virtue. He began his religious career by giving away literally everything he had, clothing himself in a ragged robe and preaching to the poor. Poverty had been a form of ascetic penance like fasting, a disciplining of the soul. To the hermit in the desert the point of poverty was that it was painful. To St. Francis it was a joyful way to live.

To the first great Franciscan theologian and philosopher, St. Bonaventure, the virtue of poverty was secondary, as a means to the primary virtue of charity. To St. Francis poverty was the condition of interior perfection. It was the pure, transparent glass, unclouded by the distractions of possession, through which the soul can see God, not darkly, but face to face. In Giotto's great mural St. Francis marries Poverty, the handmaid of the Lord. "Behold the handmaid of the Lord." The

Virgin Mary was the handmaid of the Lord and in the mystical Franciscanism of St. Francis and the later Franciscan Spirituals poverty came to mean the perfect receptivity of the soul to God—"be it done unto me according to thy word."

This is a very inflammatory evangel to preach to the poor and does anything but make them content with their lot. The powers of State and Church were self-evidently sunk in opulence and luxury and always greedy for more—which could of course come only from the labor of the poor. Although the Christianity of St. Francis might be called immediate Christianity, Christianity without eschatology, without apocalypse, it did in fact internalize the eschatology of the Gospels. The Last Things were now in the immediate relationship of man to man and man to God. So his audience could form a simple, if logically frail conclusion. If the saving remnant were poor, the poor were the saving remnant. Around the unity of being in the joy of revelation, a unity made possible by virtue of poverty, and reinforced by community, would revolve the heretical movements of three hundred years.

When he founded his order St. Francis had envisaged a little band of utterly devoted comrades, a group small enough for perfect communion, agreement of principle, and identity of aim. There were only twelve brothers when Pope Innocent III approved the order and its first rule in 1209. Ten years later it had spread all over Europe and to the Holy Land. The whole body no longer met at the tiny Church of the Portiuncula at Assisi, but were represented by delegates, central administrative officials, and provincial authorities. But the original gospel of St. Francis was incompatible with delegated authority and long before the death of the founder, powerful factions had begun to advocate change in the

original principles. The Order of Friars Minor was re-
peating the history of Christianity itself.

One of the commonest clichés of American politicians
and businessmen is "I just model my life on the Sermon
on the Mount," something they obviously have never
read. The Sermon on the Mount and the original gospel
of St. Francis represent an etherealized and internalized apocalypticism, an eschatological ethic. It has
been called an impossibilist ethic, and so it is in the
sense that no social order since the invention of organized religion and politics could stand if it were put
into practice.

St. Francis was aware of what had happened and as
he was dying he wrote a testament insisting on the pre-
servation of the literal principles of the original rule and
forbidding any appeal to the pope to change them. But
the order had ceased to be a comradeship of poverty and
joy, a communion, and had become an institution,
spread to the farthest reaches of the Western world and
one of the principal bulwarks of the papacy and of the
power structure of the Church. He was no sooner dead
than the order did appeal to the pope and his testament
was set aside and poverty was defined in purely symbolic, legalistic terms. The order was permitted to use
property through trustees appointed by the pope. Then
began a struggle which would last for two generations
within the order, and then be continued outside of it,
and finally outside of the Church, to restore the original
life of mystical poverty.

The faction that wished to restore obedience to St.
Francis's original rule and testament were known as
Zealots or Spirituals. They were probably never more
than a sizable minority in the order. The majority were
moderates or Conventuals who stood between them and
the faction, originally led by Elias of Cortona, who

wished to change the order into just another monastic institution with rank, power, and great properties. The struggle would not be resolved until John XXII permitted the formation of the Observants, who were allowed to practice a modified poverty, a poor and scanty use of property. Meanwhile many of the Spirituals were driven deeper and deeper into antagonism to the main body of the order and finally into a separate movement, the Fraticelli, who were condemned as heretics.

Since they were unable to win over a majority of the order, the Spirituals early began to appeal to the laity, and to form third-order groups owing allegiance solely to them. The popular influence of the Spirituals grew as the Conventuals became more and more worldly and finally corrupt. By Chaucer's time the order of Friars Minor was thought of as being corrupt, as having failed to practice its promise to society, and it had thus become a common butt of satire. The lay followers of the Spirituals seem to have been most common in Provence where they were gathered in small organized communities and where they were first called Béguines. The term was probably derived from the Albigenses, and the memory of the older heresy and the destruction of Provençal culture and the Crusade against it certainly contributed to the growth of the movement.

In the meantime a new and explosive ingredient had entered into the ideology of the Spirituals and their followers. Administratively cornered and hopeless of changing the establishment, they turned to apocalypticism.

In the previous century Joachim of Fiore (c. 1132–1202), a Cistercian abbot, had written a series of expositions of the apocalyptic books of the Bible. He divided the history of humanity into three periods: the age of the Father, under Jewish Law; of the Son, under the Gospel; and the coming age of the Holy Spirit, when all law would pass away, because all men, immersed in contemplation, would act only according to the will of God, a kind of utopia of contemplative monks, the everlasting Gospel of an everlasting Sabbath. This rather simple picture was enormously elaborated by an immense pseudonymous literature attributed to Joachim and written mostly by Spirituals.

The convergence of the Christ-like life of St. Francis and the apocalypticism of Joachim was like the mixture of oxygen and hydrogen. Before St. Francis, and in the established Church after him, the historical Jesus played little role in medieval religion. Christ was a ritualized figure only briefly human in the crib at Christmas and on the cross on Good Friday. Spiritual Franciscanism, like all the movements which would descend from it, was intensely evangelical and it was made possible by the growth of literacy, specifically through the reading of the Bible and devotional literature in the vernacular. Poverty was the central issue in the struggle with the order and the papacy. To the Spirituals poverty was not only the life of Christ and his apostles, and the joy and innocence of St. Francis; it was a foretaste of the bliss of the kingdom that would come at the end of apocalypse. St. Francis and later Peter John Olivi, a Franciscan commentator on the Book of Revelation, became actual figures of the apocalypse: St. Francis, the Angel of the Sixth Seal, Oliver the Angel with the Face like the Sun. When the papacy condemned first the doctrine that Christ and the apostles lived in absolute poverty, then that which said poverty was essential to the Franciscan rule, and then the Spirituals as such, the pope became Antichrist.

The Spirituals, the Béguines of Provence, and the Fraticelli did not believe that Christ and the apostles held their goods in common; they believed they held none. The poverty of these mendicant Franciscans thus was absolute. They lived from day to day by begging. Since the injunction to poverty in the rule was obviously the foundation stone of the order, John XXII was patently wrong and so the pope could err. This was one of the most important and enduring results of the controversy.

The use of wealth held from the pope by trustees for the order appointed by him meant he had at his disposal the credit of a reserve fund of immense wealth, and in its exile at Avignon the papacy was continuously borrowing money. In his final bull on the controversy John XXII broke the connection within the Church and the Gospel and promulgated the doctrine of the sanctity of property as such. The Church was ranged on the side of property and power, lordship, explicitly in so many words, as had never been done before. In the course of the argument between John XXII and the philosopher William of Occam, and the expelled head of the order, Michael of Cesena, originally a Conventual, the disputants raised some fundamental questions. If the use but not the ownership of property was permitted, what about money? What about the bag of Judas? The disputants struck close to the meaning of money, property as such in its pure form. Again, if property is evil, whoever holds property and permits its use is to that extent un-Christian. The users are parasitic and guilty of complicity. Therefore a truly Christian society would abolish property altogether. By standing against the creation of a religious order devoted to total poverty and self-sacrifice, evangelism, the growing popularity of mysticism, and the laity's demand for community life devoted to such objectives, the Church had locked itself into an impasse.

The continuous papal suppressions and the prohibition of the formation of any new religious order by the Fourth Lateran Council had the effect of smashing globules of quicksilver and resulted in the metastasis of mystical communities of laymen free of ecclesiastical control or even knowledge throughout society. Communities and meetings became entirely secret and their beliefs occult. The Béguine communities spread over Europe, but especially along the Rhine and in northern France, where the women were known as Béguines and the men as Béghards. Many of these were communities of lay people who wished to live together and devote their lives to prayer, contemplation, common labor, and begging. Some became simply poorhouses, others conventicles of mystical piety, but all through them, moving like the cells of a new growth, were the Brethren of the Free Spirit.

The doctrines of the Brethren of the Free Spirit go back to the heresies of the first century of Christianity. By mystical contemplation, they taught, man can become united with God, so united he is God, and therefore rises above all laws, churches and rites made by God for common man, and can do whatever he wishes. United with God it is impossible for the mystic to sin, therefore he can do whatever he wants. Theft, lying, especially sexual license, are permitted; prayer and all religious observances are useless. This is a kind of mirror image in a clouded and distorting glass of the morality and ethics of mysticism, and it is not peculiar to Christianity. At the same time, Sufis preaching the same doctrine were being persecuted and crucified in Persia. Hinduism, Buddhism, contemporary American Zen have all produced the same distortion.

It was easy for the Brethren of the Free Spirit to quote texts like St. Augustine's "Love and do what you will" and St. Paul's "Where the spirit of the Lord is, there is liberty" (II Cor. 2.17), and the mystical theology of the great Rhenish mystics Meister Eckhart, Tauler, and Suso. In addition there was the occult, erotic mysticism of the spiritual alchemists. Arnold of Villanova and other leaders of the new spirituality were alchemists.

The Brethren of the Free Spirit did not set themselves up as an organized movement but functioned as a diffused body of esoterics, content to operate within the Church and the movement of lay mystical communities. They left few records behind except in the charges of their enemies and in testimony elicited under torture in their trials. From the Gnostics to the Mormons, the Church has always accused those she considers heretics of being guilty of orgies of unbridled sexuality. The Brethren of the Free Spirit seem to have actually indulged in such practices; the testimony is unanimous and this aspect is always central. It is impossible to tell whether these orgies were simply pastimes or rites in a cult of erotic mysticism. They seem to have been extremely common.

For a century popes, bishops, and inquisitors were busy condemning them and hunting them down. They managed to exist in the allegedly closed society of the later Middle Ages because in fact it was not all that closed. In the incoherent, unpoliced cities of the Rhineland and the Netherlands it was easy for a community to take over a house and pretend to be a legitimate association of pious laymen devoted to prayer, Scripture-reading, and work. The only danger was from informers, and once an informer was admitted under vows to what the Church considered diabolism he was at least guilty of complicity.

This was the principal problem facing the Church, separating the wheat from the tares. The fifteenth century witnessed a tremendous growth of religious associations and communities outside the regular religious orders. If the Church had not tolerated them, there would have been, as there was eventually, wholesale revolt. As the life and preaching of St. Francis had represented an alteration in the sensibility, so the new communities represented another. This sensibility was given literary and theological form in the writings of the Rhenish mystics, all of whom, at one time or another, came in conflict with the Church and had propositions drawn from their teachings condemned. Nor has any of them ever been granted the title of saint and only two are "blessed"; and though greatly popular, they are even today still only tolerated. The doctor of the new mysticism was Meister Eckhart.

Parallel with the growth of scholastic philosophy the Church had developed orthodox, systematic, mystical theology. Beginning with St. Bernard of Clairvaux, (1090–1153), the relentless opponent of Abélard, continuing through Hugh and Richard of the Paris monastery of St. Victor, to the Franciscan St. Bonaventure (1221–1274), the great mystical doctors of the Church had resisted the steady Aristotelianization, actually secularization, of the scholastic philosophers. Their roots were in the neo-Platonism of St. Augustine, the visionary writings attributed to St. Paul's disciple Dionysius the Areopagite, and to John Scotus Erigena, the latter's neo-Platonic disciple and translator, who lived in the time just after Charlemagne.

All had striven to resolve the dilemma posed by the mystical experience. That experience carries with it its own conviction of unquestionable reality. The mystic in his realization of God feels the indisputable power of empiric fact. Christian doctrine says that God created the world out of nothing. Man is utterly contingent, God utterly omnipotent and self-sufficient. How can any experience bridge this gap? In one way or another all the great orthodox mystics dismiss this ultimate problem of knowledge by making the knowledge of God in the soul primary. The knowledge of the reality of the world stems from it. As St. Bonaventure describes the ascent of the soul to God by love through the ladder of creatures, at the end the soul discovers that the last rung was the first, the *scintilla animae,* the spark of God in the soul which itself is not only the faculty of mystical knowledge but partakes directly of the divine Being. This process is only given a more emotional and intensely devotional tone by the impassioned rhetoric of St. Bonaventure. It is basic and explicit in the epistemology of Richard of St. Victor and more or less implicit in St. Bernard. Of course, it also goes back to Plato himself and is the subject of his dialogue with Phaedo. It is knowledge of God which enables knowledge of ideas. This central tradition of mystical theology was never to have its orthodoxy questioned because it always seemed to operate within the context of developing scholasticism. But the true situation was quite the other way around. Its exponents had a purely Christian tradition, or at least, so everyone thought, on their side, whereas the Aristotelianizers had to defend their introduction of pagan and Arabic secular philosophy. So even St. Thomas Aquinas and Duns Scotus were placed on the defensive.

Behind Meister Eckhart and his descendants lay another tradition peculiar to the Rhineland. Beginning with St. Hildegard of Bingen in the early twelfth century, and Elizabeth of Schönau, Elizabeth of Hungary, Countess of Thuringia in the thirteenth century and Mechthild of Magdeburg, this tradition was carried on by women, and was characterized by visionary experiences, emotionalism, erotic imagery, and passionate criticism of the abuses of the Church and the corruption of the papacy. Most of them wrote in the vernacular and are numbered amongst the most important of the founders of German literature. To judge from the visions from which she made paintings, St. Hildegard suffered from migraine and saw the intense light patterns which are symptomatic of that affliction. As her descendants, all these women give special prominence to the light mysticism which goes back through St. Bonaventure at least to the first-century Jewish neo-Platonist Philo, and which well may be based on constantly recurring visions of light which are the aura of the mystical experience itself. St. Mechthild's *The Flowing Light of the Godhead* is one of the most beautiful works in the German language. Saturated with light mysticism and erotic symbolism, her poems, with only slight alteration, could be turned into songs of the most extreme romantic love.

The older mystical theology had grown up in the monasteries amongst learned and contemplative men. Rhenish mysticism flourished in the Béguinages and other semi-monastic communities of devout women associated in poverty, work, prayer, and meditation. Its teachers were just over the edge of orthodoxy from the least heretical of the Brethren of the Free Spirit. The testimony of the often patently insane and unfortunate enthusiasts trapped and tortured by the Inquisition is, to put it mildly, highly suspect. Even in the records of trials we have only one case in which a house of Béguines was given over to sexual orgies, that of the so-called Sisters of Schweydnitz. It was probably true, but it reads like the assembly-belt productions of modern pornography. Often the inquisitors seem to have been engaged in a war against women. One of the Béguines' constantly reiterated "crimes" is the performance of the rites of the Church in their chapels and confession to each other, practices forbidden to women.

There is, in fact, only one questionable document of the entire movement of Béguine mysticism, presumably influenced by the heresy of the Brethren of the Free

Spirit. Margaret of Parete was tried and burned in Paris in 1311 and accused of teaching that when the soul was consumed with the love of God it partook of God's being and could do anything that the sensual body desired. In recent years the manuscript of her book, *The Mirror of Simple Souls,* has been discovered and printed. As would be true of Meister Eckhart and his successors the interpretation by the Inquisition is based on an equivocation. She taught that at the seventh stage of the illumination, the culmination of a process of seven stages which goes back in mystical literature to the very earliest time and is described in perfectly orthodox fashion, the soul becomes united with God. By His grace it is freed from sin. It realizes the whole Trinity and loses its own identity, and so it ceases to be able to sin. It lives from then on entirely in the love of God as one of the seraphim. It needs no Church, priesthood, or book. Its knowledge is direct participation in God's knowledge. It cannot sin because its will is God's will; poverty, prayer, sacraments, asceticism, penances, fasts, become of no importance to the soul, lost in God, where deprivations and symbols can have no existence. The soul uses them only to pay an indifferent tribute to nature, to the world, and to the religious community.

It is easy to see how just the slightest shift of emphasis could change this teaching to a justification of the immoralism attributed to the Brethren of the Free Spirit, or of the hysteria which was later to break loose in the revolutionary commune of the Münster Anabaptists. But in Margaret of Parete the emphasis lies the other way, as it does wherever we have bona fide documentation by the heretical mystics themselves. Of course from the point of view of the Catholic Church she is heretical enough.

Margaret of Parete was burned and soon forgotten.

But the influence of Meister Eckhart is stronger today than it has been in hundreds of years. Eckhart met the problems of contingency and omnipotence, creator-and-creature-from-nothing by making God the only reality and the presence or imprint of God upon nothing, the source of reality in the creature. Reality in other words was a hierarchically structured participation of the creature in the creator. From the point of view of the creature this process could be reversed. If creatureliness is real, God becomes the Divine Nothing. God is not, as in scholasticism, the final subject of all predicates. He is being as unpredicable. The existence of the creature, in so far as it exists, is the existence of God, and the creature's experience of God is therefore in the final analysis equally unpredicable. Neither can even be described; both can only be indicated. We can only point at reality, our own or God's. The soul comes to the realization of God by knowledge, not as in the older Christian mysticism by love. Love is the garment of knowledge. The soul first trains itself by systematic unknowing until at last it confronts the only reality, the only knowledge, God manifest in itself. The soul can say nothing about this experience in the sense of defining it. It can only reveal it to others.

This is the neo-platonic way of negation taught by St. Augustine. But the neo-platonic deity lies beyond reality and cannot be said to exist in the same sense. Eckhart, so often accused of dualism, is actually an extreme monist, yet there is a subtle difference between his theory of being and the pantheism of someone like Spinoza. Since reality for Eckhart is dense, there is no gap between the internal process of God, the Trinity, and the world of his creation. The Godhead engenders the Son at the same time or in the same moment of eternity as the creation of the world. So far with a little

straining Eckhart's teaching can be adjusted to orthodoxy, but the co-eternity of the Son and the world,
his critics were quick to point out, is heresy.

"In the beginning was the Word," says St. John, "and
all things were made by him and without him was not
anything made that was made." The begetting of the
Word is a dual process—internal and external—God's
knowledge of himself and the creation by Knowledge,
the Logos, of the world. Creation is the garment of the
uncreate.

Although in his Latin treatises Eckhart is rigorously
intellectualistic—the soul ascends to God by knowledge, or rather, realizes God in the inmost recesses of
self, and being, both absolute and contingent, is
equated with knowing—in his popular sermons in German, preached mostly to Dominican nuns and congregations of Béguines, he adopts the long familiar language of the theology of the heart. "The soul," he said,
"to become the bride of God, must become in all things
womanly, a virgin wife, free of all attachment, so that it
can conceive Jesus in the soul and bring forth fruit."
The union of love is total and has its end only in itself.
Love is not desire striving to satisfy a want; but it is the
fullness of being shared by the soul in God. Prayer, good
works, alms, are worthless unless they flow from a will
completely consumed with the love of God and totally
submissive to his will. Where Eckhart thought it was
appropriate to his audience that he discuss his theology
in terms of willing rather than knowing he was perfectly willing to do so. It is from his popular sermons
that much of the later passionate mysticism of his descendants stems, to culminate in the spiritual nuptials
of Ruysbroeck.

What is the primary datum of Eckhart's knowledge of
existence? It is the unpredictable, indescribable reli-

gious experience itself, a transcendental *Cogito ergo sum,* the Jehovah that said his name was "I am that I am." As has been pointed out in recent years, if the word "God" with all its excess baggage, and what Whitehead called "metaphysical complements," is abandoned as misleading, Eckhart's mysticism is practically indistinguishable from the pure religious empiricism of Buddhism; and philosophically from the soul, the *Atman,* as perspective participation in *Brahman,* the ground of being, of the *Upanishads* and Vedanta; and from the Sufism of ibn-Arabi.

Each soul is in its final recesses a spark of the Uncreated Light, the source, the spring, from which all reality flows and which it can reach by contemplation. Here is the beginning of a doctrine of the Inner Light which would be characteristic of the mystical sects from this time on, and which is central to the theology of Quakerism. From Eckhart also descends the practical aspect—Quietism. The religious experience is one of ever-increasing stillness. "Stand in awe and sin not; commune within your own heart in your chamber and be still."

Eckhart's mysticism sounds like a very lonely business—one would think that it would dissolve not only the Church and its cult, but all communal religious experience altogether. On the contrary, it set in train a widespread development of the community life. The Friends of God, the Brotherhood of the Common Life, and similar groups of both priests and laymen spread rapidly over the Rhineland, the Low Countries, Western Germany, and Bohemia. It was as though the Church were developing antibodies as orthodox as prolific to combat the infection of the Brethren of the Free Spirit. Of course the teaching of Eckhart was not orthodox at all. It was only adjusted to orthodoxy where possible.

Toward the end of his life the archbishop of Cologne took proceedings against him. He appealed to Pope John XXII and in 1329, two years after his death, twenty-eight of his propositions were condemned. Once again we find John XXII, the worst of the popes, standing against the demands of the most devout of the Christian communities for a richer spiritual life than could be provided by the decadent medieval establishment.

5

John Wycliffe, The English Peasants' Rebellion

Each of Eckhart's descendants, Johann Tauler, Henry Suso, Jan van Ruysbroeck, strove to adjust his mystical theology to strict orthodoxy but none of them succeeded. Even Thomas à Kempis's *Imitation of Christ,* the most popular devotional manual ever written in the West, and the only universally known exposition of the religious sensibility of the Brethren of the Common Life, is to this day not accepted without qualification by Roman Catholics. Tauler was to have a great influence on Luther, who was to popularize the *Theologica Germanica,* a collection written or edited by an unknown disciple of Tauler's. By the time we get to Nicholas of Cusa the tradition has become completely divorced from and antagonistic to medieval philosophy. Nicholas of Cusa's *Of Learned Ignorance* is Eckhart reinterpreted in Renaissance terms. With Jakob Boehme's (1575–1624) complex theosophy we have moved into a world entirely foreign to Catholicism and Lutheranism.

To this day, Quakers and Mennonites and similar groups insist that they are neither Catholic nor Protestant, but belong to an older church that goes back to the life of the apostles and that emerges again in history in the two centuries before Luther. This is true. We should think of this great wave of spirituality in Northern Europe not as something new, but as the rediscovery of something old; not as a body of doctrinal, mystical theology, and least of all in terms of the sensational episodes of the history of its struggle with the pope and the Church, but as a way of life. In every city there were little groups of people meeting together in one another's homes, or in large rooms barren of decorations and images, living together in communes in town houses or in seclusion in the country. Most of them still went to Mass on Sundays and to confession at Easter. But their religious life was centered on their own meetings, where they sat quietly listening to the readings of the Scriptures and their exposition, praying together spontaneously or sitting quietly waiting for the Inner Light, the movement of the Spirit. Behind all the conflicts and controversies, persecutions, trials, burnings, and wars, this way of life would go on. The apocalyptic men and the apocalyptic events would rise up, flourish in the melodramas of history, and then pass away, to be absorbed in the quiet life of the apostolic communities.

By the middle of the fourteenth century the tensions generated by the profound economic and social changes of the ending of the Middle Ages were becoming unbearable, yet the shell of the old way of life grew ever tighter and harder. The objective situation grew steadily worse. England was convulsed with the War of Roses, an internecine struggle of the aristocracy over

the control of the wool trade. There were peasant revolts everywhere. The papacy was in captivity in Avignon to the French king. Eventually there would be two
popes, each claiming the throne, and finally three.
Rome was left to decay and Italy was overrun with war-
ring armies of Guelphs and Ghibellines, papalists and
imperialists. In the middle of the fourteenth century the
Black Death struck Europe and killed off a third or more
of the population. The resulting economic and social
dislocation, especially the rise in prices and the scarcity
of labor, accelerated the breakdown of the feudal system. Meanwhile the new empire of the Ottoman Turks
was spreading steadily up the Balkan peninsula until at
last it would reach the walls of Vienna, control the
Mediterranean Sea, and threaten to overwhelm Chris-
tendom. From the Black Death to the end of the Thirty-
Years War, three hundred years, Western Europe would
be in continuous turmoil.

The first explosion occurred in Bohemia, with the
preaching of John Hus (c. 1369–1415), his burning by
the Council of Constance, the growth of a schismatic
Bohemian Church, and the Hussite Wars. Except for
the Albigensian crusade, religious conflict had been
local, even individual. In Bohemia it became a national
movement involving large-scale military conflicts, and
here for the first time religious communism ceased to
be a matter of small, often clandestine, intentional
communities and came to involve whole towns and territories.

Since John Hus was charged by the Council of Constance with preaching doctrines of the English heretic
John Wycliffe, we should first go back and discuss Wycliffe, even though the accusations of the Council were
unjust. John Wycliffe (c. 1329–1384) was the first of the
Reformation leaders rather than the last of the
medieval heretics. He spoke to the entire English na-

tion, not to an obscure clandestine sect. Although he began as a philosopher and theologian, his concerns finally became largely political. He was not a personal leader but a preacher and writer. He claimed no special revelation and preached no apocalypse. His revolutionary ideas were developed rationally from the accepted terms of scholastic realism. Most of his active life was spent as master of Balliol College at Oxford and after he was expelled, or rather, after he retired to his parish at Lutterworth, he continued to write and publish and died in full communion with the Church. He was by no means a spokesman for social revolution, although his followers and popularizers of his ideas, the Lollards, were blamed for the Peasants' Rebellion of 1381. He was himself the spokesman, not of the poor or the working class, but of the great magnates, the lords, the king, and the State power against the Church. Although many of his ideas became part of the creed of Protestantism, they have little to do with the apocalyptic and communal movements that challenged the power of both State and Church and strove to establish a society modeled on the community of the apostles.

For Wycliffe the Bible was the sole authority in all matters religious or secular. He held a peculiar notion, derived from his extreme scholastic realism, of the Bible as the earthly embodiment of the uncreated word of God, an eternal Bible in heaven which reflected as in a mirror the second person of the Trinity, the Logos, the Word. This is a Muslim idea, the uncreated Koran, and appears in Wycliffe for the first time in the West. Although it ceased to be held in so extreme a form, this notion does go far to explain the bibliolatry of English Protestantism. Wycliffe too was responsible for the first complete translation of the Bible into English. Its effect was such that the Church forbade unauthorized bibles in English and eventually, for a time, the private possession of vernacular bibles of any sort.

Wycliffe believed that the Church should be completely subject to the State and should be disendowed by force of the temporal power and should then have no temporal, or even religious, possessions, much less temporal power. The religious orders should be abolished. All ministers and priests should preach. Preaching was more important than Mass. There was no scriptural authority for Mass as a sacrifice in which Christ was present sacramentally. Oral confession was unnecessary. The sacraments were invalid if administered by a priest in mortal sin, and so too was the authority of the hierarchy. No sinful pope should be obeyed. Since according to Wycliffe the clergy generally were in mortal sin by definition, the entire structure of the Church fell to the ground.

Wycliffe's preaching of disendowment took a strictly practical turn. In a petition to Parliament his followers pointed out that if the Church were deprived of its property and reduced to evangelical poverty it would be possible to finance fifteen new earldoms, fifteen thousand knighthoods, fifteen universities, one hundred almshouses, and fifteen thousand new ministers of the Gospel, with twenty thousand pounds left over for the royal treasury. This was a theology ready to the hand of Henry VIII. It was hardly a movement of folk mysticism or spirituality, but the beginning of a struggle for power between the two ruling classes of the Middle Ages.

Wycliffe by no means condemned secular wealth. "Secular men may have wordly goods enough without number . . . so that they get them truly, and spend them to God's honor, and the furthering of truth, and help of their Christian brethren, and that they suffer not Antichrist's clerks to destroy secular lordships, and rob their tenants feigned jurisdiction of Antichrist." The property of the king, the great lords, and the wool barons and merchants has become holy, and the pope, archbishops, and abbots Antichrist. Directly over the question of the new form of property Wycliffe was historically correct—England would owe its great leap forward in the development of capitalism to Henry VIII's secularization of the wealth of the Church.

Wycliffe was too early on the scene, however. The State and the great lords were not prepared to embark on so revolutionary a program. The Holy Inquisition had been banned from England and the English Church was more independent of the pope than most, especially during the Avignon papacy when the pope seemed to most Englishmen a vassal of the French king. After the Peasants' Rebellion and Wycliffe's death, his followers, the Lollards, were increasingly persecuted. The State eventually established its own inquisition. As literacy in the movement declined, popular Lollardry came to appeal more and more to a decision by force, postponed of course until a time when the Lollards themselves had sufficient power. And so they became directly subversive, not because they were apocalyptics, struggling for the millennial kingdom, but because they demanded a political revolution in the relations of Church and State. This is the first pre-Reformation movement of which this is true, and it in part accounts for the political character assumed immediately by the Hussite revolt in Bohemia. Lollardry went on all through the Wars of the Roses, always providing the throne with a ready-made justification for economic attacks upon the Church.

Amongst the Lollards, as is the case with any such movement, there were more extreme radicals. It is true that once in all his writings Wycliffe had briefly justified a communist society. He had said first in his *De Civili Dominio:* "All good things of God ought to be in common. The proof is as follows: every man ought to be in a state of grace. If he is in a state of grace he is lord of the world and all it contains. Therefore every man ought to be lord of the whole world. But because of the multitudes of men this will not happen unless they hold all things in common." But this is in Latin and in a learned treatise, and Wycliffe immediately went on to say that history since the sin of Adam had lead to authority and the unequal distribution of wealth in which all good Christians should acquiesce, as long as it is in the hands of laymen. This is the standard orthodox treatment. If all men were in a state of grace, wealth and poverty would not exist.

The English Peasants' Rebellion of 1381 began as a spontaneous eruption in Essex, a mass protest of yeomen against increasingly heavy taxes, and what today would be called deflationary measures with which the State was attempting to overcome the high wages and inflation which had resulted from the Black Death a generation before. The peasants were revolting against the attempts of the nobles to destroy the feudal status of the yeoman and reduce him to a serf. The rebels elected Wat Tyler as their leader and he appointed Jack Straw his chief lieutenant. As the revolt spread they captured towns and castles in Essex and Kent and eventually took over London. It was not until they sacked the archbishop's palace and liberated the prisoners in the episcopal prison that they liberated John Ball, called a Lollard, but more likely a millenarian heretic of the old style. William Morris's *A Dream of John Ball* has made Ball famous and given him a greater role in the revolt than in fact he actually had.

The official demands of the peasants presented to the

king were simple and practical enough. In essence they were demanding the abolition of feudal dues and obligations and the substitution of wage labor and the drastic reduction of taxes. That they were not inspired by Wycliffites is shown by their sacking and burning of the great palace in Savoy of John of Gaunt, long the patron of Wycliffe.

John Ball on the other hand is famous for his distich, "When Adam dalf and Eve span, Who was then a gentilman?" The historian Jean Froissart quotes what he says was a typical sermon of John Ball's, delivered before the insurrection and for which he had been put in prison:

Ah, yes good people, the matters goeth not well to pass in England, nor shall not do till everything be common, and that there be no villages nor gentlemen, but that we may be all united together, and that the lords be no greater masters than we be. What have we deserved, or why should we be kept thus in servage? We be all come from one father and mother, Adam and Eve: whereby can they say or shew that they be greater lords than we be, saving by that they cause us to win and labour for that they dispend? They are clothed in velvet and camlet furred with grise, and we be vestured with poor cloth: they have their wines, spices and good bread, and we have the drawing out of the chaff and drink water: they dwell in fair houses, and we have the pain and travail, rain and wind in the fields; and by that that cometh of our labours they keep and maintain their estates: we be called their bondmen, and without we do readily them service, we be beaten; and we have no sovereign to whom we may complain, nor that will hear us nor do us right. Let us go to the king, he is young, and shew him what servage we be in, and shew him how we will have it otherwise, or else we will provide us of some remedy; aid if we go together, all manner of people that be now in any bondage will follow us to the intent to be made free; and when the king seeth us, we shall have some remedy, either by fairness or otherwise.

Thomas Walsingham in his *Chronicle* quotes a sermon of Ball's—in indirect discourse:

In the beginning all human beings were created free and equal. Evil men by an unjust oppression first introduced serfdom against the will of God. Now is the time given by God when the common people could, if they only would, cast off the yoke they have borne so long and win the freedom they had always yearned for. Therefore they should be of good heart and conduct themselves like the wise husbandman in the scriptures who gathered the wheat into his barn, and uprooted and burnt the tares which had almost choked the good grain; for the harvest time was come. The tares were the great lords, the judges and the lawyers. They must all be exterminated, and so must everyone else who might be dangerous to the community of the future. Then, once the great ones had been cut off, men would all enjoy equal freedom, rank, and power, and share all things in common.

This is all that we really know of Ball. At the height of the revolt the young king met with Tyler and Jack Straw twice and eventually granted the abolition of serfdom, all feudal services, the removal of all restrictions on freedom of labor and trade, and a general amnesty for the rebels. At the second meeting the rebels were dispersed. Wat Tyler was killed and the rebellion suppressed. John Ball, Jack Straw, and one hundred and ten others were executed. The promises of the king were revoked. The last rebels were hunted down in East Anglia and the revolt died away with no immediate effect.

The Peasants' Rebellion was much more articulate and apparently led by better educated men than similar uprisings in France and Flanders. In it we can see the beginning of a pattern that was to be repeated many

times. There is a popular uprising against the economically moribund feudal relationships. It takes the form of
the demand for free labor and free markets of
capitalism. The revolt gets out of hand and turns into a
general uprising against the rich. In its course it throws
into prominence ex-priests and others who preach the
advent of a religious revolution, the coming of the
apocalypse and the millennium. They are not part of the
main body of the revolt but parasitic upon it and when
the revolt is suppressed, and even more if it is successful, they are executed. However, there is a certain continuity. Since the apocalypticists are the most passionate preachers and propagandists, their words are remembered and passed on and provide fuel for the next
revolt.

6

Hus, The Hussite Wars, Tabor

It is easy to be misled by the melodramas of revolution. Although it is true that history moves by leaps through critical points when quantity changes into quality, as water turns into steam, one does not have to be a conservative to realize that fundamental economic change takes place over a very long time and against the resistance of massive inertia. The English Peasants' Rebellion with its clear demand for the abolition of a feudal economy took place in 1381. It was just three hundred years later, with the accession of William of Orange to the throne, a relatively quiet event which the English rightly call the Great Revolution, that the most important elements of a feudal economy were finally done away with. Even so, feudal rituals and unimportant relics linger to this day.

Nevertheless, all over Europe the profound economic, political, and religious crisis at the end of the fourteenth century meant that feudalism as an intact and total,

workable system, identical with society itself, had
broken down. This is most apparent in the crisis of the
Church. Economic relations between laymen were already changing, but those of the Church were purely
feudal and its property lay like a great obstructive mass
of frozen capital in the way of the development of a new
economy. The Church had ceased to be simply the religious expression of society itself, and heresy, which
had previously been—with the exception of the Cathari
in Provence—confined to obscure tiny bands of eccentric enthusiasts, was springing up everywhere. Half-
conscious revulsion, shared by almost everyone, with
the inadequacy and corruption of the Church was becoming conscious and turning into mass movements.
   Nowhere was this more true than in Bohemia. In
modern times, as part of the Austro-Hungarian Empire,
and then as Czechoslovakia, Bohemia has not played a
central role in European history. This was not true at
the end of the Middle Ages. The king of Bohemia ranked
as the first of the electors of the Holy Roman Empire.
King Wenceslaus IV was Holy Roman Emperor and his
family were in key positions and ranked as one of the
two or three most important ruling houses of all Europe.
His brother Sigismund was King of Hungary. The University of Prague, founded in 1348, was still the only
university in the empire, and its influence spread
throughout all of Central Europe and the borderlands to
the east.
   From the mission of Sts. Cyril and Methodius in 862
in Moravia until the early years of the tenth century
Bohemia was Greek Orthodox in religion and was taken
into the Roman Catholic Church by King Vaclav (St.
Wenceslaus). In the fourteenth century Bohemia included Moravia, Silesia, and Upper and Lower Lusatia
and was the dominant power of central Europe. The
bulk of the population was Slavic—the modern Czechs

and Slovaks—but the ruling class was mostly German. There were German settlements scattered throughout the country and the northern borderlands were almost entirely German. The Church was one of the wealthiest and most corrupt in Europe. Over half the land belonged to the hierarchy and the religious orders. The bishops and great abbots led the luxurious lives of lay lords. Most of them were German, while the lower clergy were largely Slavic; and often the two classes did not speak each other's language.

Due to the fact it was the seat of the empire, Bohemia was ridden with the political intrigues and corruption resulting from the conflict of emperor and pope. The upper class was extremely wealthy. Prior to the discovery of America the mines of Bohemia were the principal European source of silver. To a lesser degree the country produced lead, gold, and copper. This wealth was most unequally distributed, concentrated at the top of the upper classes, while below them the ordinary people lived in a Slavic peasant economy and were only a little better off than their fellows in Poland and White Russia.

Wenceslaus IV was involved in a struggle with the electors and the great lords of the empire and was finally deposed. He refused to accept the election of Rupert, Elector Palatine, but finally consented to that of his brother, Sigismund, King of Hungary, and then devoted himself to dissipation and conflict with both the lay and ecclesiastical lords of Bohemia. The papacy had just returned from Avignon to Rome and almost immediately gone into schism, with the French and Spanish supporting Clement VII who went back to Avignon; England and the empire, including Bohemia and northern and central Italy, Urban VI. Their royal patrons did not prove very generous with money and both papacies became almost bankrupt and were forced to use every method, especially the sale of indulgences, to raise money. A powerful movement amongst the theologians of Europe, led by Jean Gerson, Chancellor of the University of Paris, and Pierre Cardinal d'Ailly, and including eventually even most of the cardinals, began to agitate for a solution of the problem by way of a general council of the whole Roman Catholic Church. The Council of Pisa in 1409 elected Alexander V, but Benedict XIII in Avignon and Gregory XII in Rome refused to resign, so there were three popes. When Alexander died after ten months, Baldassare Cossa, a layman and retired pirate, was crowned John XXIII (after hasty ordination as a priest the night before) and, under the protection of the Emperor Sigismund, immediately became involved in almost continuous warfare in Italy, with the resulting drive for a new sale of indulgences to finance his crusades.

At this point the long maturing and explosive situation in Bohemia came to a head. The Emperor Charles IV and Wenceslaus had encouraged a measure of religious freedom and anti-papalism in Bohemia. The Inquisition was kept out of the country and a number of Wycliffite and Lollard preachers from England and Waldenses from Lombardy, the Jura, and the Alps migrated to Bohemia. The king established in Prague a chapel for popular preaching, dependent upon his patronage directly, and independent of the archbishop or any monastic order. This was the Bethlehem Chapel, where sermons were given in both Czech and Latin, and where, at the time with which we are concerned, King Wenceslaus and Queen Sophia usually attended services in preference to those in the cathedral. There had been a succession of reformist preachers for over a generation, largely under the influence of Wycliffe, and popular dissent in Bohemia had moved far to the left. Rejection of the papal claims, transubstantiation, infant baptism, communion in one kind for the laity, and the denunciation of the simony, nepotism, and luxury of the Church were common. In 1402 John Hus was appointed rector of the University of Prague. Before then he had been dean of the philosophical faculty and a well-known preacher in Czech at the Bethlehem Chapel. In terms of the religious struggle which was maturing in Bohemia he was not even a middle-of-the-road man, but a conservative. He had defended Wycliffe's teachings, but not in themselves in most cases, simply the right of the Wycliffites to be heard, although he had translated Wycliffe's *Trialogus*. Wycliffe was a scholar and theologian, Hus a preacher and pastor. His own writings were, considering the theological turmoil, and the profound crisis in the Church, surprisingly orthodox. Yet in the next five years he was in almost continuous trouble with the ecclesiastical establishment, not because of any theological heresies (such ideas were far over the head of the archbishop, who had been a soldier before he was appointed to the post), but for his denunciations of the manifest abuses in the Church.

During the preparations for an ecumenical council to heal the great schism, elect only one pope, and reform the Church, King Wenceslaus, Hus, and the Czech clergy and people remained neutral, but the German hierarchy sided with Gregory XII. In the ensuing conflict the king issued an edict giving three votes to the Bohemians and only one to the Bavarians, Saxons, and Poles combined, a reversal of the previous order of the governing board of the university. The archbishop immediately moved to the attack and secured the condemnation of Lollardry and all of Wycliffe's books by Pope Alexander V and another papal bull prohibiting preaching in all independent chapels.

Hus continued to preach and was excommunicated

by the archbishop, whereupon he appealed to the new pope, John XXIII, who was soon to prove himself one of the most corrupt and depraved in the history of the papacy. Pope John XXIII not only upheld the archbishop but laid the city of Prague under interdict as long as Hus continued to preach. At the same time the pope flooded Bohemia with peddlers of indulgences to finance his crusade against King Ladislaus of Naples. Hus and the more radical reformers denounced the sale of indulgences. Hus's situation in Prague eventually became untenable and he went into exile in the countryside very near to where the revolutionary commune of Tabor was later established. There he spent two years writing, and published his principal work, *De Ecclesia.*

In 1414 the newly convoked Council of Constance invited Hus to come and defend himself from the charges of heresy which had been lodged against him by the archbishop's faction. The Emperor Sigismund gave him safe-conduct, promising that whatever judgment was given by the Council, he would be allowed to return safely to Bohemia, where, if he were to be found guilty of heresy, his case would be at the disposal of King Wenceslaus. This was a subterfuge to entice him to Constance. Shortly after he arrived John XXIII appointed a commission to examine the charges. The safe-conduct was withdrawn by the emperor. Hus was imprisoned. Then began the agonizing process of theological whipsawing.

Hus was first accused of holding a long list of Wycliffite and Waldensian doctrines, most of which he denied. The list was changed; and although he again denied that he had held most of these tenets he was required to abjure them all. He refused to abjure doctrines which he had never held. Finally a new list, taken largely from *De Ecclesia,* was submitted to him. Most of these he was able to interpret in an orthodox manner, but his interpretations were rejected. The important items were those in which he condemned the corruption, abuses, and despotism of the Church and denied the authority of both evil popes and evil secular rulers. His principal prosecutors were Jean Gerson and Pierre d'Ailly, who were merciless in their attacks upon him, but who themselves, while the Council was still in session, had just helped to depose John XXIII for simony, heresy, fornication, and pederasty. The trial was marked by incredible disorder and shouted abuse on the part of the holy fathers in council assembled. Most of the time Hus could not be heard and submitted his answers to the charges in writing after the sessions. At his final condemnation he seemed unable to believe the outrageous injustice of the proceedings and was still pleading for permission to defend himself when he was condemned, stripped ceremonially of his priestly vestments, turned over to the civil power, his betrayer, the emperor, and taken away to be burned.

Hus was without doubt the noblest, as he was the first, of all the great reformers. He was also the most conservative. It never entered his mind to found a sect. He only desired to reform the Church without basically altering either its structure or its theology. The ideas which he really held, and even many of which he was falsely accused, differed little from the doctrines and reforms proposed for the first Vatican Council which had been expected by many to rehabilitate the Church, but which, due to pressure from the papal Curia, refused even to consider the matter.

Hus also differed very little from Gerson and d'Ailly, but that little was important. Hus stood by his conscience. He refused to deny what he believed to be the truth, to affirm untruths, or to denounce himself for ideas which he had never held. Gerson and d'Ailly stood for authority. They wanted his submission to judgment regardless. Obedience for them was more important than truth. What this means of course is that they believed that the Church was founded on obedience and the truth came afterwards. In a sense they were right. George Bernard Shaw's argument in his preface to *Saint Joan* is correct, although more applicable to Hus than to Jeanne d'Arc. Although the greatest moral theologians of the Roman Catholic Church have always said that conscience was primary, this has never been true in practice. St. Joan, John Hus, St. Thomas More, all died for their consciences even though More's conscience bade him prefer the authority of the pope to that of King Henry. A completely authoritarian structure demands obedience, not as a choice of the individual will following the dictates of conscience, but simply obedience regardless. If the sanctity of the individual soul and the primacy of its willing were made the foundation of moral action, all authoritarian structures would eventually be eroded away.

Hus was a man of the center, hardly a radical, far indeed from being a communist, but as he was being maneuvered to his death in Constance, Bohemia was rising in revolt, at first against the betrayal of the emperor and the injustice of the Council and eventually against the Church, the empire, and medieval civilization itself. The death of this conscientious man precipitated the first national revolution in Western history.

When the news of Hus's execution reached Prague, reform and unrest turned into revolution. Nobles, king, queen, and people, Slavs and many of the Germans, were united in condemnation of the act of the Council and the treachery of Emperor Sigismund. The nobles had written earlier demanding Hus's release, and after his execution four hundred and fifty-two nobles from all parts of Bohemia and Moravia assembled in an

emergency congress and answered the Council's condemnation of Hus and of the Bohemian practice of giving communion to the laity in both kinds, bread and
wine, with the sternest condemnation of their own.
They refused to recognize any of the Council's decrees
and refused to obey the new pope unless he were a
moral man and acted according to the will of God, a
refusal they extended to the entire hierarchy. Theological decisions they vested in the University of Prague
and they agreed to allow free preaching on their own
estates. The Council answered by burning Hus's associate Jerome, who had first abjured and then, moved
by Hus's martyrdom, recanted his abjuration; and by
summoning all the signers of the nobles' manifesto and
implicitly the king and queen and the heads of the university to Constance to stand trial for heresy.

With the blessing of the Council, Sigismund gathered
an army to invade Bohemia. The Council disbanded in
April 1418 without resolving the deadlock except by
wholesale excommunications and interdicts. In 1419
King Wenceslaus attempted a restoration of followers of
the Council to office in the Church and university and
packed the town council with anti-Hussites. As the pro-
testing populace demonstrated outside the town hall
their opponents pelted them with rocks. Under the
leadership of Jan Zizka, the Hussites invaded the town
hall, threw the burgomaster and several councillors out
the window, and tore them to pieces in the streets.
When the news was brought King Wenceslaus he was
seized with an apoplectic fit and died a few days later.

This first Defenestration of Prague marked the beginning of open warfare. Germans and conciliarists,
usually the same, were expelled from their estates and
offices all over Bohemia. For a short time there was
fighting in Prague between the small army of foreign
mercenaries loyal to the queen and the Hussites led by

Zizka who captured the castle Vysehrad which dominated the city. The nobles arranged a truce. The citizens restored the castle and Zizka and the army of the
more radical reformers left Prague for Pilsen, the
center of German power in its area. They were unable to
hold Pilsen and went from there, fighting their way
south, to form a new settlement to which the name of
Tabor, the hill of the Transfiguration of Christ, was
given. Armies of the papal Crusade were invading
Bohemia and Moravia from several directions and on
June 30, 1420, they united in the siege of Prague. All
parties of the Hussites met in council and presented the
pope with four demands known henceforth as the Articles of Prague, a minimum program which remained
non-negotiable throughout the Hussite Wars and the
settlement fifteen years later:

I.   The word of God shall be preached and proclaimed freely
throughout the kingdom of Bohemia by the priests of the Lord.

II.   The sacrament of the most holy Eucharist shall be freely
administered in both kinds, bread and wine, to all faithful
believers not in mortal sin as it was instituted by the word of
Our Saviour.

III.   The secular power over riches and worldly goods which
the clergy possesses contrary to Christ's teachings, to the prejudice of its office, and to the detriment of the secular arm,
shall be taken from them and they shall be reduced to the
evangelical rule and apostolic life of Christ and his disciples.

IV.   All mortal sin and especially all public ones and others
contrary to God's law shall in every rank in life be properly and
reasonably prohibited and destroyed by those whose office it
is. These include fornication, murder, lying, theft, usury,
superfluous evil, and superstitious arts among the people, and
among the clergy all simoniacal charges for priestly services
and all immorality, profane behavior, and contentiousness.

This was not only a minimum program on which everyone could agree, except for that as yet small number who did not believe in the sacrament of the Eucharist at all; it was also a program which went back to the earliest movements of dissent in Western Europe and was common to practically all of them. It became the entire program of the right wing of the Bohemian reformers, who laid special emphasis on the right of the laity to communion in both kinds and who were henceforth known as Utraquists (or "both-ists") or Calixtines (for chalice). The great importance of this demand was an inheritance from the early days of Christianity in Bohemia when it had been evangelized by Greek Orthodox missionaries, and the Orthodox practice of communion of both kinds may well have never completely died out. There was nothing in these demands which was not theologically compatible with the strictest Roman Catholic orthodoxy. But the third and fourth were totally incompatible with its practice, or for that matter with that of any established church. Implicit too was the heretical doctrine that obedience is not owed to immoral clergy and their sacraments were invalid; but nowhere was this conviction spelled out.

The emissaries of the pope and the emperor refused even to discuss the Articles of Prague and continued the siege. Zizka defeated and utterly routed their army in a great battle. From then on papal and imperial forces invaded the country again and again, every time to be defeated with great slaughter, except on those occasions when their armies turned and ran without fighting.

It has often been said that the French Revolution invented the national army, the *levée en masse* of a whole people. Its true inventor was Jan Zizka. Although the Taborites formed the nucleus of a permanent fighting force, each crusade of the emperor and pope united the great majority of the Czech people. Zizka introduced remarkably modern methods of highly drilled combat, and the Taborite army was the first to use artillery systematically as a major tactical arm. The invasion attempts were answered by raids deep into enemy territory, and in the early days loot was an important part of the income of Tabor. Zizka was never able to gain complete control of the German-owned mines or the city of Pilsen which remained a Romanist redoubt. Initially the majority of the workers who were Slavs rose in revolt but they were put down by German mercenaries and at Kutna Hora sixteen thousand Taborite priests and their followers were killed by being thrown into the mines.

Zizka began his career blind in one eye and an arrow eventually blinded the other. His last battles were fought when he was totally blind. He died in 1424 of the plague on the eve of a planned conquest of Moravia and Silesia and his place was taken by Procopius who defeated the Germans in two great battles in 1427 and who spread the counter-attack of the Bohemian armies to Austria, Hungary, Silesia, Saxony, Brandenburg, the Palatine, and Franconia.

The Taborite armies ceased simply to raid enemy territory and began to conquer it, that is, to leave garrisons in the towns and castles which capitulated. Revolutionary Bohemia threatened to control all of Middle Europe. Pope Martin V called a general council at Basel in 1431 to launch yet another Crusade, which again went down in overwhelming defeat. Emissaries of the pope, the emperor, and the Council began secret negotiations with the Utraquists, who were in no sense economic or social revolutionaries and who were only in the most uneasy alliances with communist Tabor. The Taborites themselves had been unable to win over the peasantry and had first introduced forced requisition of food for the army and the cities and then their own form of semi-feudal exactions. More than fifteen years of continuous victories had gone by and the army itself was degenerating and filling up with adventurers from all over Europe. Eventually the Taborites were isolated and defeated on May 30, 1434, near Lipany in Bohemia when thirteen thousand out of an army of eighteen thousand were killed, and both Procopius the Great and his chief lieutenant, Procopius the Little, fell in battle.

The Utraquists, Pope Alexander VI, and the Emperor Sigismund agreed to negotiate on the basis of the Articles of Prague and in 1436 they were accepted by all parties in a modified and ambiguous form which permitted optional use of the Roman rite in the mass. The Bohemian National Church lasted as a kind of Uniat church, like those of the Orthodox rite in communion with Rome, until after the battle at White Mountain in 1620 in the Thirty Years War. It was then suppressed and the complete Roman obedience re-established. The Utraquists themselves captured Tabor in 1452 and the militant Taborites were forced into an underground existence to re-emerge as the Anabaptists and the other radical sects of the Reformation begun by Luther. The pacifist and more purely religious communists began the Unitas Fratrum, also known as the Czech Brethren, Moravian Brethren, or United Brethren, who endure to this day. The Hutterites also trace their ancestry back to Tabor.

The continuous imperial and papal crusades forced a broad united front upon the disparate groups of the Bohemian reformation and revolution. Whenever the outside pressure relaxed, this unity broke down in factionalism which sometimes reached the point of armed conflict. These divisions were along clearly defined ethnic and class lines.

Most of the German nobles and wealthy merchants and mine owners were Romanists. Many of them left the country. Others managed to hold out in small enclaves which were never incorporated into the revolutionary Bohemian state. The reason was that there was no revolutionary Bohemian state, no single, unified political entity coterminous with Czech lands. The Czech nobles and magnates and some Germans formed the right wing of the Utraquist party along with the archbishop and Queen Sophia. For them the Articles of Prague were not a minimum but a maximum program. Once they had secularized the property of the Church they became socially conservative, quite content with their feudal privileges modified by monopolies and franchises not unlike the English upper class in Henry VIII's time.

At the beginning of the revolution, with the first siege of Prague, political power passed largely into the hands of the artisan class. Except for certain crafts, like the goldsmiths, these people were almost entirely Czech and allied with them were petty Czech nobles like Jan Zizka and most of the not very sizable lower middle class. They were militant Utraquists. For them the Articles of Prague were a minimum program. This loose alliance was anti-papalist and had no desire to see a restored Roman Catholicism, but envisaged a free Catholic Church in which the pope would be only the bishop of Rome, the first amongst equals. They rejected the Roman doctrine of transubstantiation and most of their clergy held to the Wycliffite doctrine of remanence, namely, that the bread and wine remained unchanged after the consecration and that Christ's body and blood were present only spiritually, "as in a mirror." They also rejected the idea that the Mass was a sacrifice and interpreted it as essentially a spiritual communion, a congregational act. They rejected the feudal economic and social structure; but since developed capitalism, even in its mercantile form, still lay in the future, they were indefinite about what to put in its place. Politically they were democrats, although leaders like Jan Zizka slowly reintroduced the leadership of an educated elite of clergy, petty nobles, and well-to-do educated citizens.

The fifteenth century was a time of inflation and economic instability, most especially in Bohemia, and there had grown up in Prague a large unemployed class, as well as a semi-criminal underworld. They, along with the working poor, formed a *Lumpen* proletariat which was always ready for riot and which acted as a steady drag toward the extreme left.

As time went on, and news of the revolution in Bohemia spread across Europe, sectarians and heretics migrated to Prague—at first from nearby Bavaria, the Tyrol, and the Rhineland, and eventually from as far away as Lithuania, England, and even Spain. One of the leaders of the Oreb brotherhood was an English Lollard, Peter Payne. After the establishment of the communes of Tabor and Oreb, this migration became a flood. Every eccentric and religious psychotic in Europe seems to have headed for Bohemia. In 1418 forty refugees from Lisle and Tournai arrived in Prague fleeing from the violent persecution in their homeland. These were the first of the Picards, Pikarti as they were called, who gave their name to the most extreme forms of the revolt.

The Bohemian revolution produced a reaction in the rest of Europe not unlike the red hunts and white terrors of the twentieth century. Everywhere heretics and schismatics who had been tolerated or ignored as inconsequential by the State were hunted out and burned, or lynched by mobs. Those who could fled to Bohemia where they believed the earthly paradise was in the process of realization. All these different elements went to form the class of those who have nothing to lose. It should not be thought, however, that they were anything but the rank and file of the extreme left. Their leaders and spokesmen were renegade monks, former secular clergy, literate lower middle-class people.

After its early days, the Bohemian revolution was not only not a peasant-based movement, but came to lose the enthusiastic support of peasant followers, whose attitude became one of passive consent, if not active opposition. The peasants were interested in the abolition of feudal exactions, the redistribution of land, and the suppression of incipient trends toward serfdom which would reach their height after Luther's Reformation. Once they had gained these objectives, the peasants lost interest in revolution and became conservatives of their own gains. Since neither Prague nor Tabor was ever able to work out effective new economic forms of production, the revolution in the cities was forced to feed upon the peasantry, and in the economic chaos was unable to make adequate return for value received. The restoration of pope and emperor meant the return to feudalism. The continuance of their new masters in power meant new exactions. The peasants remained passive.

The economy of Tabor has been called by later historians a communism of consumption, not production, but it is difficult to see how, over so long a period, the two could have been kept separate. There are recent studies of the degree of socialization of production in Tabor but they are as yet all in Czech. Tabor controlled some of the principal gold mines of the day in Europe and their production seems to have been on a completely communist basis. When the community was set up and when daughter communes were established elsewhere, large tanks were placed in the center of the town, the people sold all their property and put the money and their jewels, if any, in the tank, and from then on put their wages there too, which they earned apparently by working at their old jobs or trades in their previous fashion. The wealth so accumulated was then distributed equally to all the citizens of the commune. As the Hussite wars went on, this was augmented by loot, and loot rather than conversion was the reason for the first raids in German territory. It is difficult to see how this could have worked. As presented by later historians opposed to communism it bears a great resemblance to what is called "brigand communism" of the type that grew up in the heretical Muslim communities of the Near East. The general evidence, on the other hand, would indicate that life in Tabor, Oreb, and the other communes settled down to a fairly normal, productive communism, and that, considering the difficulties, it was by no means parasitic, or certainly no more than the decadent feudalism it replaced. Those who believed in a purely parasitic communism were expelled from the city.

Such were the famous Adamites whose life is supposed to be portrayed in Hieronymus Bosch's painting *The Earthly Paradise*. They have been celebrated in our own day by Henry Miller's *Big Sur and the Oranges of Hieronymus Bosch;* and all over America misguided young people crowd the highways, hitchhiking to an Adamite promised land called Big Sur, which they discover consists of a range of mountain cliffs above the sea, thinly populated by hostile natives who seem to know only two words of English: "Move on."

The majority of the Taborites and the Brotherhood at Oreb and their allies in Prague's New Town reached a general consensus early in the revolution. They accepted the Bible in a combination of Wycliffite, Waldensian, and Free Spirit doctrines. The Bible was the sole

authority for both faith and practice; the creeds and
translations of the Church were only corruptions, as
were its rites and ceremonies, the sacrifice of the Mass,
indulgences and prayers for the dead, prayers to the
saints, auricular confession, extreme unction, baptism
of infants, and its accessories of chrism and blessings
and holy water, Mass vestments, images, saint's days,
and the traditional chants for Mass and prayer offices.
All were denials of the life of the apostolic Church.
These people believed with the Waldenses that the
ministrations and authority of a sinful priest were invalid. Not only that, but if necessary any layman could
celebrate the Eucharist or hear confessions.

They were extreme millenarians, the most militant so
far in the history of dissent. They believed that Christ's
Second Coming (disguised as a brigand) and the universal destruction of the evil world would occur almost
immediately, at first in 1420; and when that date
passed, it was never postponed more than a few years. In
preparation for the coming of the kingdom it was the
duty of the brotherhood of the saints to drench their
swords in the blood of evildoers, indeed to wash their
hands in it. After wholesale destruction, like that of
Sodom and Gomorrah, Christ would appear on a mountain top and celebrate the coming of the kingdom with a
great messianic banquet of all the faithful.

Meanwhile the Taborites anticipated this communion of the saints by holding great gatherings on nearby
hills and mountaintops in which the Eucharist became
a mass *agapē* or love feast presided over by the military
and religious leaders as did the priestly and kingly messiahs of Qumran. In the kingdom all sacraments and
rites would be done away with and replaced by the actual presence of Christ and the Holy Spirit and all laws
would be abolished, the elect would never die, and

women would bear children painlessly and without prior sexual intercourse. In 1420 the Taborites broke all connection with the Catholic Church by the lay election and ordination of a bishop and priests. The majority of the Taborites were extreme puritans in their personal conduct, but a minority, influenced by the Free Spirit doctrines of the Pikarti, believed that the millennium had already arrived. They were the kingdom of the elect, and for them all laws had been abolished. Four hundred were expelled from Tabor in 1421 and wandered through the woods naked, singing and dancing, claiming to be in the state of innocence of Adam and Eve before the fall. Acting on Christ's remark about harlots and publicans, they considered chastity a sin and seem to have spent their time in a continuous sexual orgy.

Jan Zizka, who had already withdrawn from the Brotherhood of Tabor itself and gone over to the somewhat less extreme community of Oreb, spent the rest of the year hunting them down. Several hundred escaped and fortified an island in a river in southern Bohemia, from which they raided all the surrounding neighborhood, burning churches and slaughtering priests and all others who resisted them. After a brief siege Zizka overran the island and exterminated all but one prisoner who, after he had written a complete confession of their doctrine, was burned and his ashes thrown in the river.

So ended the ecstatic, orgiastic commune of the Adamites. Accusations of sexual irregularities and outrageous ceremonies, as well as murder and robbery, are common in the long history of heresy and are usually presumed to be fantasies of the neurotic minds of celibate inquisitors. But the story of the Adamites does not come from inquisitors, but from men who are them-

selves revolutionary heretics and who had known the
Adamites intimately and who had no reason to accuse
them falsely. Their beliefs and conduct differ from what
we know of various Free Spirit groups in the rest of
Europe only in the comparative freedom of action
briefly afforded the Adamites in a revolutionary situation.

Besides the secessions from Tabor by Zizka to the
right, and the Adamites to the left, those who objected
to the preaching of unrestrained violence withdrew
under the leadership of Peter Chelšický to rural
Bohemia and founded a community of pacifists who rejected all use of force. For Chelšický political power and
the State existed only as a necessary evil, the result of
original sin, to keep order in the world outside the
community of true Christians, where all relationships
should be ruled by peace and love. The community he
founded had no outward organization; the only bond
was love and the following of the life of Christ and his
apostles. These extreme pacifists survived all the revolutions and counter-revolutions of the Bohemian reformation to become the Unitas Fratrum, the Czech
Brethren.

Life in Tabor must have had a special glory, that of a
transfigured society, where life was lived at a pitch of
exaltation near to madness. Communion was held daily
with thousands of people singing in the open fields, and
there were other vast religious gatherings on mountain
tops, and armies returning from battle, triumph-laden
with loot and bearing trophies like the luxurious tent
furnishings of cardinals and kings, through crowds
dancing in the streets, a hundred thousand enemies
fleeing over breaking ice, armies marching to the singing of hymns in unison, and the roar of iron wagons and
wheeled cannon, a golden chalice, instead of a flag, on

a pole at their head. Tabor was the mountain where Barak and Deborah had gathered the hosts that annihilated Sisera, immortalized in one of the greatest poems in the Bible; but the Taborites believed that Mount Tabor was also the mountain of Christ's transfiguration, the Mount of Olives where he had preached his apocalyptic sermon in Mark 12 before he began his march to his crucifixion; and finally it was the mountain from which he ascended into heaven. All were symbols of the nature of life as lived in Tabor.

Plato, St. Thomas More, Campanella, Harrington, Bacon, all tried to imagine societies in which the opportunity for what the Church called original sin would be severely inhibited, and it would be practically impossible for men to pursue a lesser immediate instead of an ultimate greater good. Tabor in its first years solved the problem of utopia by denying it. The Taborites were the first to attempt to found society on the principle that liberty is the mother, not the daughter of order. They succeeded because of their continuous warfare. They became in fact a military theocracy without noticing it.

If socialism in one country is doomed to become deformed and crippled, communism in one city is impossible for any length of time. Sooner or later the garrison society will weaken, but the outside world does not. It is always there waiting, strongest perhaps in times of peace. Tabor was never able to balance its popular communism of consumption with an organized and planned communism of production, nor the exchange of goods between city communes and peasant communes. At the time it was widely preached and believed that the Czechs, when they settled Bohemia, had been communists and that the Taborites were only restoring the original Slavic community. This was probably true. Functioning agricultural communes which were revivals of the primitive Slavic peasant communities, like the Russian mir which dated back to the neolithic villages, must have existed. When the Counter-Reformation crushed the long degenerated Bohemian Utraquist Church, it was the peasant communism of the Hutterites and Brethren which survived. Serfdom was fastened on Bohemia in 1487 and reached its most extreme form after the Peasants' Revolt in Germany and Luther's Reformation.

7
The Radical Reformation, Thomas Münzer

The Reformation of Luther, Zwingli, and Calvin, when it came, was certainly a revolution, but it was a revolution within society, within the dominant culture, and within the general process of history of Western civilization. The Reformation dissolved the hierarchical nature of feudalism and shattered its web of interlocking rights and duties. It released the frozen assets tied up in ecclesiastical property —over one-half of the agricultural land of Western Europe and probably a greater proportion of its portable wealth. It abolished all the legal sanctions and the customs which kept the economy static. It sanctioned usury and permitted the lender to take any interest he could get. It did away with the guilds' suppression or control of competition amongst their members. In the Middle Ages the peasantry had clearly defined rights and duties, sanctioned by immemorial custom and by law—but so had the lord of the manor, and he in turn had his responsibilities and privileges in relation to his overlord, and so on up the ladder to emperor and pope. With the Reformation the peasant, who at first expected to gain a vague but wonderful freedom from the new social morality preached by the young Luther, found himself being reduced to the status of a serf, with no rights and, instead of duties, the naked compulsion to hard labor.

By the end of the Middle Ages society had become top-heavy with charitable organizations of all kinds which cared for the redundant unemployed, or at least kept them off the labor market. With the seizure of wealth of the Church, only a tiny fraction of these institutions were revived under private or State auspices and the absorption of the labor surplus necessary to a static economy ceased. From then on until the present day legislators would fulminate against "sturdy rogues" and "welfare chiselers." The Poor Laws of post-Reformation Europe, where they exist, all have one assumption in common—poverty is the fault of the poor and indigence is a vice. Theoretically the old fealties of the Middle Ages were replaced by a structure of contracts between individuals, man and man, or "legal persons," juridical individuals; but since the bulk of the population did not in fact enter into contracts of any kind, what resulted was progressive atomization. Medieval man was saved as a member of the body of Christ, the Church, which literally incorporated its members. Luther's Christian was saved alone, by an individual act of faith, and so his relationship to the deity was one of an utterly contingent atomic instant devoid of self-sufficiency upon God's absolute omnipotence and self-sufficiency.

Calvinism introduced only a change of emphasis. If God had predestined an elect to salvation, and all other men to damnation from the beginning of time and regardless of their merits, this elect did not form a community, because its membership was unknown and unknowable. One would think that this would have led to complete antinomianism, the abandonment of all morality. Quite the contrary, all that man could do was behave as though he belonged to the elect and hope for the best. Calvin's extreme asceticism so circumscribed man's behavior that he could do little else but work hard, save money, and invest it. Luther's was a religion of free enterprise, Calvin's of capital accumulation. In such a system as the Calvinist theocracies of Geneva, Huguenot France, Scotland, or New England, the poor were convicted *prima-facie* by their situation. Every member of the elite might not be a member of the elect, but the poor, and especially the indigent poor, obviously were not. The incompetent, the wastrel, the drunkard, and all those who lived only for pleasure rather than profit were self-evidently damned.

Although the three great reformers were to make much of an appeal to the Bible—"only by faith, only by the Bible," said Luther—to the apostolic age, and to the fathers of the Church, their theology was in fact derived directly from St. Augustine and the medieval scholastics. Their insistence on salvation by faith and predestination represents only slight changes of emphasis, if that, from the teachings of the most orthodox scholastics. It was not until the beginning of the seventeenth century in England in the Anglican Church that there begins a serious attempt to construct a theology based on the Fathers and the testimony of the united Church of the ecumenical councils. For the reformers the Church was coterminous with the State, just as it was for the

Catholic theologians, and Church and State played only slightly different roles in the exercise of power. The difference was that the Church no longer had final authority—as personified in the pope. At first the ultimate appeal was to Luther himself. The other leaders of the German Reformation deferred always to his final decision—as in the case of Zwingli's doctrine of the Eucharist; and in the question of relations with the Utraquist church of Bohemia and the surviving Taborites, and with the first Swiss Brethren; and regarding disciplinary problems such as those raised at the beginning of the career of Thomas Münzer; and finally, of course, in the matter of Luther's notorious condemnation of the Peasants' Revolt.

In practice most religious problems were met by the secular State, the town councils, the local lords, and ultimately the princes and dukes of the conglomeration of petty states and small kingdoms that made up the German empire, an overarching political community which was beginning to collapse under the blows of the universal conflict engendered by the Reformation. Once the principle was established of *cujus regio, ejus religio,* "as the ruler, so the religion," without which Middle Europe would have broken down in a war of each against all, spiritual authority was in fact vested no longer in the emperor or in an abstract secular power, but in the chance circumstances of the petty courts of Germany.

The religion of the Anabaptists and the radical Reformation was the exact opposite in almost every case of Luther's. Thomas Münzer at Mühlhausen and Frankenhausen and the apocalyptic Anabaptist commune at Münster were attempts to establish the millenial kingdom as a secular imperium, but for all their notoriety they were atypical and involved relatively few previous members of Anabaptist groups. Recent Mennonite and

American Baptist historians have stressed the ancient roots of Anabaptism and the continuity of the sixteenth-century radical reformers with similar sects throughout the Middle and Dark Ages back to the time of the apostles. They are essentially right.

The Reformation with its seeming, but quite transient, advocacy of freedom of speech, released and made public radical dissent, which had been there all the time, and briefly permitted widespread proselytizing by preachers whose doctrines were subversive of the Reformation itself, even more than they were subversive of Roman Catholicism. The record would indicate that until the Reformation the Roman Church had probably ignored most of the strange cults that flourished in the Middle Ages, unless they gave scandal or insisted on giving notice, much as it had dealt with the concubinage of the clergy. In later years the extreme sectarians and the Roman Catholics were often to form a united front against a Protestant church and state, as witness the close friendship between William Penn and James II.

Radical sectarians did not just appeal to the traditions of the Church before it was coopted by Constantine; they strove to reinstate it totally in faith and practice, as a saving remnant within a doomed world. They were indifferent to the conflict of power of emperor and pope, Luther and prince, because they did not believe in wordly power as such. They were indifferent to laws regulating competition and the taking of interest because they did not believe in what would later be called "political economy" at all. They strove to achieve the self-sufficient economy of a closed subculture, a communism of both production and consumption. In most cases circumstances did not permit this, but they always advocated an apostolic community of goods, the shared responsibility for the physical welfare of all members; and in the early days they often practiced a communism of consumption while earning their bread at jobs in the world. Deeply influenced by Eckhart, Tauler, and Suso, whom most of their theologians read, they looked on the process of salvation as the progressive deification of man in community rather than the forensic "justification" of the individual before the judgment seat of God by faith in the sacrifice of Christ—they believed in at-one-ment rather than atonement, the Christ life rather than his sacrifice, in communion rather than Mass. So they were Anabaptists (twice-baptizers) opposed to the baptism of unconscious infants or immature children. For them baptism was a divine sealing of the awakened soul into the community of the elect, a conscious act by which the individual turned from the world and embarked on the spiritual pilgrimage toward divinization in company with the beloved community.

Although practically all Anabaptists were millenarians in the sense that they looked forward to the coming of the kingdom in the indefinite future, they thought of themselves not as the army of the apocalypse to whom it had been given to usher in the last days, but as waiters on the advent of the Lord. The two most famous episodes in the early history of Anabaptism did not arise out of the main body of the movement but were generated independently.

Thomas Münzer was not an Anabaptist at all, or at least the questions of when and why to baptize were of no importance to him; and he gave contradictory answers at various times in his career. Nor until his last days at Mühlhausen did he preach community of goods, and his only definite statement on the subject was made in his final confession after torture and before execution.

Münzer was born in Stolberg of a well-to-do family in

the Harz Mountains and educated at Leipzig and Frankfurt. He seems to have visited Luther sometime around 1519 and to have spent his school years in earnest study and seeking, profoundly troubled by the apostasy of the established Church. That same year he became father confessor to a nunnery at Beuditz and with the security and leisure that his position gave him spent over a year of intensive study reading Josephus, the church history of Eusebius, St. Augustine, the acts of the general councils and those of Constance and Basel, and the mystical writings of Suso and Tauler. He began to correspond with the leading reformers, most of whom were five to ten years older than he. The next year he was recommended as a preacher to St. Mary's Church at Zwickau to replace temporarily the pastor, John Egranus. At first he appeared to be just another of the young apostles of Luther who were springing up all over Germany and immediately got himself in a violent controversy with the local Franciscans.

Zwickau in those days was one of the largest cities in Germany, three times the size of Dresden. It had been a prosperous textile center but with the development of silver mines in the nearby mountains, the weaving trade had declined and many weavers were unemployed. The city had taken on a boom-town character with the severe local price inflation typical of mining towns, the radical polarization of classes with great wealth at the top and poverty and mass unemployment at the bottom. Zwickau was just over the border from Bohemia and had been a center of Taborite agitation in the previous century; and small clandestine groups of Picards had survived to be gathered up and organized into an open movement known as the Zwickau Prophets by Nicholas Storch, the descendant of a once wealthy and powerful family forced into bankruptcy by the mine owners. When Münzer arrived Storch had made himself the leader of an extreme pentecostal, chiliastic sect of religious revolutionaries, often unemployed weavers like himself. The violence of Münzer's sermons against the Franciscans got him into trouble with the city council and the congregation of St. Mary's and with, when he returned, John Egranus, and he was forced more and more into the arms of Storch. Eventually he left the upper-class St. Mary's and became the pastor of St. Katherine's, with a large congregation of miners, poor weavers, and unemployed. At St. Katherine's Münzer became quite consciously a pastor of the poor. He ceased to be an orthodox Lutheran and became an apocalypticist like Storch and spent more and more of his time addressing the conventicles of the Prophets. The city council grew increasingly antagonistic. In the spring of 1521 Münzer was asked to leave Zwickau. Luther in the meantime had withdrawn his support.

Münzer went to Prague, where he was welcomed enthusiastically as one of the new Lutherans and invited to preach in the churches. His sermons were not Lutheran; he had not only become a full-fledged chiliast, but his language had grown extraordinarily violent, abusive, and gross, and his claim to be appointed by God to gather in the elect for the final armed struggle before the millennium was presented in terms outrageous even for those days. The sophisticated citizens of Prague had heard all this one hundred years before and were not impressed.

Münzer left, disillusioned with the Bohemians. Before he left, in imitation of Luther, he nailed a manifesto to the doors of the principal churches. It summarizes his leading ideas which were to guide him for the rest of his life, but the violence and incoherence of the language are its most notable features. During 1522 he wandered about with no regular employment. He visited Luther in Wittenberg, whom he seems to have annoyed, but who may have used his influence to get Münzer a position as pastor of St. John's Church in the small town of Alstedt in Saxony. There he gave his first sermon on Easter Day 1523. The sixteen months or so that Münzer spent in Alstedt were the quietest and most productive of his brief career. He married a former nun, Ottilie von Gersen. The next Easter day she presented him with a son. He began, quietly enough for him, as a spokesman for the orthodox Reformation, albeit an emotional and eccentric one. He had apparently decided to move cautiously and with a certain amount of duplicity, but his tempestuous sermons soon made him the most popular preacher in the entire district. People came from all around to hear him. He wrote and celebrated the first Eucharist in the German language and later published a complete prayer book with liturgies for communion, baptism, marriage, communion of the sick and funerals, and the public confession of sin before communion. His prayer book promised to be widely adopted, but after his involvement in the Peasants' Revolt it was condemned by Luther who, however, did not scruple to imitate it three years later. The most impressive thing about Münzer's liturgies is their total lack of his usual coarseness and violence. On the contrary they show an exceptional poetic and devotional sensibility.

As time went on Münzer revealed more and more of his apocalyptic message and presented himself openly as the chosen man of God. At the same time he began the secret organization of a revolutionary army. The League of the Elect started out by raiding, looting, and burning convents and monasteries in the neighboring countryside. Within a short time he was recruiting for his league in an ever-widening circle of communities in Thuringia. As they became noised abroad his activities began to worry Frederick, the elector of Saxony, and his brother Duke John, who were supporters of the Reformation, and Luther, with whom his correspondence became more and more eccentric and incoherent. Münzer also got in a violent quarrel with the local lord, the Count of Mansfeld. Meanwhile he was issuing a steady stream of pamphlets, each one more radical than the last. Frederick decided to investigate and sent Duke John, his son John Frederick, his chancellor, and various other officials to Alstedt. They invited Münzer to preach before them at the castle and on July 13 he delivered what has been called the most extraordinary public utterance of the Reformation era.

Basing his sermon on the apocalyptic visions of the Book of Daniel, Münzer announced the immediate oncoming of the war between the forces of the Devil and the League of the Elect which would usher in the millennium, and appealed to the visiting princes to join him as leaders of the army of the saints. He envisaged a new reformation with its capital in the little town of Alstedt, being spread by the word, first through Saxony, then all Germany, then throughout the world. It would be a kingdom of the elect held in unanimity, obtained by the simple method of killing everybody else. He ended by threatening his noble listeners with extermination if they did not join him. Nothing shows the intellectual turmoil of the age better than Münzer's confidence that Duke John would accept his ideas.

The sermon was printed and circulated. Duke John returned to confer with Elector Frederick, who at first was prepared to tolerate Münzer's fanaticism as long as it did not pass over into overt action. Münzer persisted in baiting both Luther and the rulers. He was called to Weimar and examined, where his claims to be leader of the last age and his bloodthirsty language became even more extreme. He returned to Alstedt, still confident that he had won over the Saxon court. Frederick, Duke John, and Luther began to exert pressure on the town council of Alstedt to expel him from the city. Suddenly, on the night of August 7, 1524, he left Alstedt, leaving behind his wife and children and all his possessions. Münzer spent the autumn and winter in travel, first to Mühlhausen, where the militant Anabaptist Henry Pfeiffer had organized his own League of the Elect and was attempting to take over the city. Münzer immediately took over the leadership from Pfeiffer, superimposed his own apocalyptic program, raised a demonstration, and attempted to drive the mayor and council from the city. The nobles and a company of mercenary soldiers dispersed the crowd and expelled Münzer and Pfeiffer.

Münzer went on to Nuremberg to visit his friend John Hut, who published Münzer's most violent, incoherent, and abusive pamphlet against Luther, an utterance of almost continuous hysterical anger. The Nuremberg authorities confiscated and destroyed all but a very few copies, arrested the printer, and expelled Münzer and Pfeiffer. Münzer went to Switzerland seeking allies amongst the Swiss Brethren, and even visited John Oecolampadius, the orthodox Zwinglian reformer. He also visited Balthasar Hübmaier in the Waldshut over the border in Germany, an Anabaptist leader only slightly less militant than Münzer, everywhere seeking allies and attempting to rouse the people for his revolution. Neither leaders nor people were impressed, and the pacifist Swiss Brethren were profoundly shocked. Münzer returned to Mühlhausen. Pfeiffer had already come back and the radicals had gained control of the city. Münzer revitalized and armed his league, expelled its opponents, and placed in office a new council to which both he and Pfeiffer declined to belong. Meanwhile the Peasants' Revolt had reached Thuringia and

Münzer was ready, not just to join but, he imagined, to take it over.

It should be understood that although Münzer is often called the hero of the Peasants' Revolt, he in fact had nothing to do with it. The revolt in Mühlhausen was an entirely separate action with quite different objectives. As the Reformation proceeded in the destruction of the social and economic relationships of feudalism, the peasants of Germany had taken Luther's professions of freedom at face value and had looked forward to a society of independent yeoman farmers and free laborers, with a money economy. The old social relationships had no sooner been done away with—from the top—than the nobles and magnates began a forcible enserfment of the peasantry, a quite different status from that of the medieval peasant who had both rights and duties. Post-Reformation serfdom was much like the Russian version, a servile status close to slavery.

As the upper classes began to close them in, peasantry all over south Germany began to rebel. From the beginning of the sixteenth century sporadic revolts broke out every year somewhere, usually under the leadership of a former soldier, Joss Fritz, and with a widespread secret organization called at first the *Bundschuh* after the peasant's clog, and later Poor Konrad. These were not small riots, but battles involving as many as five thousand armed peasants. By 1525 local actions and riots had coalesced to full-scale war in the Tyrol, Austria, and southwest Germany.

By this time Luther, who had originally been neutral and blamed both peasants and rulers, was denouncing the peasants and urging the nobility on to the kill, in language at least as unbridled as ever was Thomas Münzer's. "The only way to make Mr. Everyman do what he ought," said Luther, "is to constrain him by

law and the sword to a semblance of piety, as one holds
wild beasts by chains and cages . . . better the death of
all the peasants than the princes . . . strangle the rebels
as you would mad dogs." And when rebellion had been
suppressed by wholesale massacre "all their blood be
upon me," said Luther, who then proceeded to a
theological justification of the new serfdom.

The demands of the peasants were simple, consistent, far from millenarian, scarcely religious, and certainly not communist. They demanded the abolition of
the remnants of feudalism and of the new measures
which were forcing them into serfdom, the disestab-
lishment of the Church, a drastic reduction of taxes, the
reinstatement of common rights in pastures, wood-
lands, and free hunting and fishing. There was nothing
subversive of the new social order inaugurated by the
Reformation. On the contrary, it was the return to a
semi-feudalized capitalism, with the crushing of the
Peasants' Revolt, which held back German development for three hundred years.

Thomas Münzer was not interested in the practical
problems of the peasantry and working class. In all his
writings he shows no evidence of even being aware of
them. He was interested only in the millennium, and on
his return to Mühlhausen he began feverishly to prepare to usher it in. Couriers were sent in all directions to
gather forces wherever the League of the Elect had
members, or where Münzer had formed conventicles of
his disciples. Alstedt, Zwickau, Mansfeld, were called
upon for troops. As in Tabor a century before, footloose
ecstatics and revolutionaries, when the news reached
them, headed for Mühlhausen. Nicholas Storch arrived
at the head of his own little army. At this point Münzer,
Pfeiffer, and Storch may have introduced community of
goods, though whether on principle or as a form of siege

communism, or simply communism of a besieged town, it is impossible to tell. The subject is only mentioned in passing in Münzer's final confession.

During the first week in May the peasant army, eventually to number between eight and ten thousand, had gathered at Frankenhausen, a town which had been taken over by revolutionary Mühlhausen. On the eleventh Münzer arrived at the peasant camp and began to organize the army of the apocalypse. It is significant that he brought only three hundred of his own followers from Mülhausen and that Pfeiffer remained behind, opposed to the alliance of the city of the apocalypse with the army of the peasants. Meanwhile Duke John, who had become elector on the death of his brother on the fourth of May, and other neighboring princes had raised an army under the command of Philip, Landgraf of Hesse, who immediately marched on Mühlhausen.

On the fifteenth Philip attacked with possibly five thousand troops equipped with artillery, and with two thousand cavalry, neither of which the peasants had. Philip offered peace if they would surrender Münzer; but after an impassioned speech by Münzer himself, who promised to catch the cannon balls in his cloak, and implied that those who had complete faith would be immune to the bullets, a rainbow, the symbol emblazoned on their flag, appeared in the sky, and the peasants refused. Philip's artillery opened fire while the peasant army was singing "Veni Sancte Spiritus" and drove the peasants back against the charge of the cavalry while his infantry attacked from the other two sides. Completely surrounded, the peasants were cut to pieces. Five thousand were killed on the battlefield, six hundred captured, and the rest fled into the Thuringian forest. Philip's army lost six men.

The moment the attack began Münzer ran away and hid in an attic in Frankenhausen. The soldiers discovered him lying in bed with the covers pulled over his head. He claimed to be a sick man who had nothing to do with the revolt; but he had been unwilling to abandon his papers and these betrayed him. He was brought to Philip and turned over to his enemy, Count Ernest of Mansfeld, who had him tortured most of the night. In the morning Münzer signed a confession which named all of his confederates and in which he claimed to have begun his revolutionary career in an underground group in Halle when he was a boy.

A ducal army captured Mühlhausen, which put up no resistance but begged for mercy, on May 24. On May 26 Pfeiffer, most of the members of the "eternal council," and Münzer were beheaded in the city square. Münzer recanted and received communion according to the Catholic rite but could not remember the Nicene Creed. Pfeiffer refused and died defiant. The city of Mühlhausen was fined forty thousand gulden (over half a million dollars). Its status as a free city was abolished and it never recovered its prosperity.

The battle of Frankenhausen marked the end of the Peasants' Revolt, although the next year was spent in mopping up operations, trials, executions, and minor massacres of the demoralized peasants all over south Germany and Austria. Luther published an exultant pamphlet, *A Terrible Story and Judgment of God Concerning Thomas Münzer*. Münzer's papers fell into the hands of Philip of Hesse and George of Saxony who deposited them in the archives of Marburg, Dresden, and Weimar.

Four different Thomas Münzers were to survive in history. To the orthodox Protestants he would be the typical Anabaptist who had only pushed the doctrines of radical sectarianism to their logical conclusion. But the Anabaptists had already mostly become pacifists, and their pacifism was only intensified by Münzer and the Münster commune a few years later. Thus they repudiated him as a completely aberrant fanatic with no real connection with the main body of the movement. For the Roman Catholic historians Münzer had simply worked out the inevitable consequences of Protestant individualism, and Mühlhausen was only a slightly more extreme example of the Reformation's attack upon law and order. In 1850 Friedrich Engels published *The Peasants' War in Germany* and Münzer became a revolutionary saint, a position he has never lost. Marxian historians call him the ideologist of the Peasant War, the first political cosmopolitan. Engels said that his religious philosophy touched atheism and his political program touched communism. Karl Kautsky in his *Communism in Central Europe at the Time of the Reformation* and Ernst Bloch in *Thomas Müntzer als Theologe der Revolution,* both portray Münzer as a fully developed, although primitive, idealogue of revolutionary communism. He is a popular hero in East Germany. Many books have been written about him, streets and squares named after him. Engels' version of his story is taught to school children and his face appears on postage stamps. In recent years research in sources unknown to Engels has made it possible to draw a fairly accurate picture of the real Thomas Münzer.

8

Münster

Although perhaps a majority of the early leaders of the radical Reformation opposed infant baptism, it was not until January 21, 1525, that the first re-baptism of an adult was performed in the circle of the Swiss Brethren in Zurich, when their leader, Konrad Grebel, baptized Georg Blaurock, exactly contemporary with the beginning of the revolution in Mühlhausen. In a few years everyone who took part in it would be martyred, but the Swiss Brethren remained communitarian pacifists, to survive and provide the first Mennonite immigration to America. In their early years they preached an apostolic community of goods. In practice, partly because this was a city movement of people variously employed in the world, such communalism usually took the form of voluntary poverty and a common fund. They were millenarians, but no more so than Luther, Zwingli, or Calvin. The end of the world was coming soon, but its arrival was not imminent; and so their millenarianism took the form of an eschatological ethic—"Live as though the world were going to end tomorrow in all your dealings with your fellow men," which is in fact the morality of the Sermon on the Mount.

After the debacle at Frankenhausen, the violent millenarianism of Thomas Münzer spread north and west into the Low Countries and Plattdeutsch-speaking Germany. The itinerant bookseller and printer Hans Hut escaped from the battle and spread the gospel of revolt through south Germany, but he was caught and executed almost immediately. Little conventicles of millenarian communal groups sprang up here and there in south Germany but were quickly suppressed. Many of them, like that led by Augustine Bader, rejected all rites and sacraments, possessed all things in common, lived in accordance with the guidance of the Inner Light, and awaited the end of the world. The most important leader was Melchior Hoffmann, an associate of Münzer in his early days. He made Strassburg his headquarters but the influence of his teaching, spread by something like an organized mission activity, both of himself and his disciples, was influential throughout Germany. He was primarily a millenarian, and the Melchiorites only took up the baptism of adults as a sign of sealing into the body of the elect. Although he personally did not believe in forcing the kingdom by violence, his followers became more and more revolutionary. At the same time the repressive measures of the authorities grew more severe. Hoffmann's fervent eschatologism, preached at the risk of imprisonment or death, could not fail to elicit a defiant revolutionary violence. But in 1533 on the eve of the establishment of the New Jerusalem in Münster, Hoffmann was imprisoned in Strassburg and spent the remaining ten years of his life in prison.

Münster was one of several small ecclesiastical states in northwest Germany under the rule of a prince bishop, who was in fact often a layman. An important trading city, it suffered from a chronic severe tension between the claims of the prince bishop and the town council of merchants and guildmasters. Münster had recently gone through a time of floods, plague, local famine, and the class conflict resulting from the Peasants' Revolt to the south; but though troubled, it had emerged with a considerable measure of civic democracy, and with power in the hands of the town council.

The most influential religious leader in the town was Bernt Rothmann. From 1531 to 1533 he had moved steadily leftward from evangelical Catholicism to Lutheranism, to the Zwinglian doctrine of the repudiation of the real presence of Christ in the bread and wine, to sympathy with the Melchiorites and the apostles of the Inner Light. Up to the last step he had carried the town council with him, and the city became officially Protestant with the Catholic Church confined to the cathedral, the monasteries, and the convents.

But when Rothmann and his followers refused to baptize the infants presented to them in church, the council rebelled and exiled them from the city and replaced them with orthodox Lutherans. Meanwhile, however, the city had been filling up with Melchiorite preachers from the Netherlands and wandering disciples of Thomas Münzer and other militant sectaries. Rothmann refused to leave and a month later—by January 1534—he was back in control, with the Catholics in the cathedral and the Lutherans permitted to preach in the church of St. Lambert.

The city had been visited in the previous fall by Jan Bockelson (John of Leyden), who returned to Holland with the exciting news that the kingdom of the elect was about to be established in Münster. Jan Mattys, the

Melchiorite leader in Amsterdam, had a revelation
—that Melchior Hoffmann had misunderstood his own
visions, and that Münster, not Strassburg, was destined
to be the New Jerusalem. Early in January 1534 two
apostles from Amsterdam, ordained by Mattys, arrived
in Münster and immediately re-baptized Rothmann, his
associate Henry Rol, and a number of other clergy. In
the next eight days Rothmann and others baptized fourteen hundred citizens in private ceremonies in their
homes. Shortly afterwards, Mattys himself and Bockelson arrived, preaching the most militant chiliasm and
demanding a complete reorganization of the community; they converted Rothmann and his followers, including the mayor, Bernard Knipperdolling.

The town council attempted to resist. The bishop
gathered a force of mercenaries nearby and offered to
come to its aid, which the council rejected, but the citizens in a public mass meeting forced the council to re-
treat. A new election was held and Knipperdolling, a
wealthy councilman and cloth merchant, was elected
mayor. Knipperdolling had been a disciple of Sebastian
Franck and, before the rise of Anabaptism proper, the
two had journeyed to Sweden where they had been expelled by direct orders of the king for preaching the radical Reformation. Soon Bockelson had married
Knipperdolling's daughter Klara, and he and Mattys
were in complete control of the city. From then on
Rothmann was pushed into the background and functioned primarily as a theologian and apologist of the
movement. He seems to have had a premonition of the
apocalyptic future because he warned a friend of his to
accept an appointment elsewhere than in Münster, for,
said he, "things will not go well here."

Mattys began to institute a community of goods and
called for all wealth in money, jewelry, and precious
metals to be brought in for a common fund. The council

struggled to resist and passed by a narrow majority an order expelling the radical preachers from the city. The radicals were escorted to a city gate and evicted, went around the wall, and entered by another gate, where they were met and returned to their churches by a cheering multitude; and they then proceeded to denounce the minions of Antichrist from the pulpit. Catholics, Lutherans, and neutral people who wished to avoid trouble began to flee the city. Their numbers, over half the original population, were replaced by incoming saints. Mattys had sent out preachers all over the Netherlands and Low Germany to recruit citizens for his New Jerusalem, urging them to come swiftly, unencumbered with many possessions, for there was plenty for all the chosen. The monasteries and churches had already been looted, when Mattys, to prevent further looting, requisitioned all private movable wealth and confiscated the property of those who had fled the city. Food was declared public property and all private stores confiscated and thenceforward distributed free. Houses also were declared public property, but families were allowed to continue in them as long as the doors were kept open day and night.

The prince bishop was quite short of money as a result of all this activity, for the wealth of the Church had been in the city. He had no credit. The Protestant nobility were not interested in restoring a Catholic lord and the Catholic nobility were mostly imperialists and the empire had been for years trying to take over the rule of Münster. In fact in its early days the emperor had even sent an offer of support to the Münster commune. As the social revolution proceeded, the prince bishop was able to frighten small loans out of some of the nearby rulers and nobility, hired mercenaries, and began, feebly at first, to attempt to invest the city. The comparatively long life of the Münster commune is due to the same cause as the random, scattered character of the engagements of the Peasants' Revolt. The empire was in collapse and there was no such political entity as Germany, only an immense number of quarreling jurisdictions. The old feudal levies were impossible and the princes could rely only on armies of mercenaries and cadres drawn from those nobles who felt themselves directly threatened. Religious and imperial conflict made alliances difficult to form and almost impossible to sustain. A state, even as well organized as France and Britain were then, would have been able to mobilize sufficient forces to reduce cities like Münster in short order and crush revolt elsewhere.

Although they were slow to come to the aid of Prince Bishop Franz von Waldek, the rulers were quick enough to suppress the Anabaptists in their own territories with complete ruthlessness. In Amsterdam all participants in an attempt to seize the city hall were executed, and similar revolts elsewhere were put down in the same fashion. After Bernt Rothmann's call to all Anabaptists to come to Münster, large numbers started to move on the city. They were hunted down on the roads, killed, or imprisoned. Three thousand men, women, and children who attempted to come by sea were captured and returned to the Netherlands. The indiscriminate killing had to stop for fear of depopulating the country. In spite of wholesale roundups of Anabaptists, a surprising number got through. The population of the city was completely changed. After those who refused adult baptism were expelled, the new arrivals were in the majority. Another equally significant majority was that of women, who formed possibly as much as two-thirds of the population, and who turned the streets and squares night and day into a continuous pentecostal revival, screaming, dancing, singing, and rushing about half-clothed wth flowing hair, and falling in trances on the street.

Mattys had a sudden vision at one of the ceremonial banquets which had become an essential part of the cult of Münster, and the next day led a sortie of a handful of ecstatics against the army of the prince bishop. Jan Bockelson immediately seized sole power. He dissolved the new council because it had been chosen by men rather than God acting through himself; and he appointed a cabinet, subordinated to Bockelson, of the twelve elders of the tribes of Israel. In their name he issued a new code of law which made practically every crime, misdemeanor, fault, and defect of character a capital offense, ranging from treason and adultery to complaining and answering back one's parents. Once law and the police to enforce it were established, Bockelson introduced polygamy, against the advice of even some of his cabinet. Forty-eight of the leading citizens revolted and imprisoned him, but the populace released Bockelson and the forty-eight were put to death. After a few more executions polygamy was established. Bockelson eventually acquired fifteen wives and Rothmann nine.

At this time Bockelson, with extraordinary ingenuousness, or was it ingenuity, opened negotiations with Philip of Hesse and Emperor Charles V. The latter responded by sending an emissary to meet with Rothmann. These negotiations fell through. After a drastic defeat of the besieging forces, when they attempted to invade the town at the triumphal mass banquet, Bockelson had himself crowned King of the People of God and Ruler of the New Zion. From then on he appeared always in ceremonial state, in royal robes made from the most sumptuous religious vestments, holding a golden apple pierced with two swords and surmounted by a crown which was symbolic of his rule of the world, and preceded and followed by sword-bearers. Knipperdolling suggested that he be appointed spiritual ruler while Bockelson acted as king in all worldly matters—the priestly and kingly messiahs after David and Melchizedek of apocalyptic Judaism. Bockelson did not take this suggestion very well and had Knipperdolling imprisoned, but he was unable to get along without him and soon released Knipperdolling and appointed him master of ceremonies and in fact second-in-command.

On the thirteenth of October Bockelson issued a call to the entire population to assemble in the cathedral square and march out to overwhelm the besiegers and welcome the imaginary army of Anabaptists coming from the Netherlands. When they were all assembled he announced that this was just a test of their loyalty and invited them all to a great messianic banquet. Tables were set up in the square and the whole population laughed and danced and sang while the king and queen and councillors served them, and at the end passed out sanctified bread and wine in holy communion. Bockelson then announced his abdication but Jan Dousentschuer, the limping prophet, immediately had a communication from the deity forbidding the abdication, and ceremoniously anointed and crowned Bockelson again, while the assembled people cheered.

Before he had become a religious leader, Jan Bockelson had been a writer of religious plays and pageants, and it has been said of him that he wrote and staged the Münster commune as a religious melodrama. Certainly he gave the people plenty of pageantry in the ceremonies of his court: open-air religious gatherings, communion, messianic banquets, and actual plays, still in this revolutionary situation based on the medieval mystery and miracle plays. One of his important acts was to tighten up the distribution of goods and food and, most important, to introduce a communism of production. Guild members whose work was essential to the life of the community were ordered to work without wages and contribute their products to the pool of goods from which all could take freely according to need. His entire program seems to have worked with little resistance. A few people were executed for hoarding and a few women for opposing the allurements of polygamy—he even decapitated one of his wives—but that was about all the objection to his communist measures. Many of his executions seem to have been motivated by his fondness for decapitation. He had a folkloristic conception of royalty—the king who is constantly shouting "Off with his head!" This attitude of course was shared by most of the populace. In fact the whole ideology of Münster as it emerges from the documents has a folklore quality about it, a combination of the legends of apocryphal Judaism, the peasant tales of the Grimm brothers, and the legends of the Middle Ages, underlying the theology of Anabaptism, which ceases to play an exclusive role. As the fall and winter wore on von Waldek slowly gathered money, allies, and mercenaries, and the siege grew even tighter. Emissaries were dispatched to raise help but they were all caught and executed except one, Henry Graess, who turned traitor and revealed the plan for mobilization points for relieving Anabaptist forces. Few responded. Those who did were cut down, but Graess himself who had returned to Münster was exposed and decapitated.

By spring the city was hungry. By June 1535 famine had set in. Women and children, except for Queen Divara and a few others, and the aged men, were sent out of the city. Von Waldek refused to allow them through his lines and they remained trapped between the walls and the besieging army until most of them were dead. This act of extraordinary cruelty was at the specific order of the archbishop of Cologne to whom von Waldek had appealed for advice.

It looked as if Münster might hold out through the summer when suddenly two men, Hans Eck and Henry Gresbeck, escaped from the city and betrayed one of the gates to the prince bishop. After a day-long battle of fiendish intensity the city fell and the invading army went through the town slaughtering most of the inhabitants. Bockelson, Knipperdolling, and Bernard Krechting, chief counselor of the king, were captured. Rothmann disappeared and was never found, dead or alive. For six months the three leaders were paraded about the country in cages. They were then brought back to Münster, tried, condemned, and literally tortured to death. Afterwards their bodies were placed in cages and hung from the tower of St. Lambert's church, where they remained until the end of the nineteenth century, when the tower was rebuilt and only the cages were replaced. So ended the only communist commonwealth to be established in a regular State until the Russian Revolution—in Western civilization at least.

Thomas Münzer had lasted only a few days at Mühlhausen, and it is doubtful if any of his and Pfeiffer's communizing measures had ever been made effective, nor were they at all central to his millenarian polity. The amazingly long endurance of Münzer was due to several factors. Both Burgomaster Knipperdolling and John of Leyden were remarkably skilled politicians and organizers, for all their fantastic language and ceremonies, and Rothmann was an apologist of unusual intelligence. They did not scruple to use the most extreme terror. It not only kept rebellious elements suppressed, but it unified and excited the majority of the population who consented to it.

Communism was not incidental to Bockelson's millenarianism, nor was it merely "siege communism." It was central. Mass adult baptism sealed the members into a covenant and mass communion kept them together. The sacraments were not primary. The community in which all things were held in common was. Every effort was made to intensify this sense of community. Life was melodramatized. Pageants, executions, vast messianic banquets, even the siege itself contributed to the exultation. If life in Tabor was exalted, life in Münster for most of its participants was ecstatic and entranced, a continuous *agapē*. There was little chance to pause and recollect oneself. If even the most convinced but sane Anabaptist had been able to pause and think for a few days he would have begun to suspect that he was not a citizen of the heavenly Jerusalem but someone caught in a trap. Few were ever permitted to pause. They were swept on in a tide of revolutionary fervor tremendously augmented by myth-making.

There were positive gains to be made from the Münster experience, but few of them were ever realized. Most important was precisely the demonstration of the revolutionary commune as a dramatic, ceremonial cult. This was something that future revolutionaries would seldom be prepared to admit. Only Robespierre at the height of his power and the Bolsheviks in the first years of the Revolution and Civil War consciously adopted such a concept or practice. Undoubtedly there were things to be learned from the actual political economy of Münster but we know nothing about the subject. However, a surprising number of people escaped to turn up later in pacifist communal groups elsewhere and they probably brought some practical benefits from their experience.

To this day Anabaptism has never been able to live down Münster. The earlier persecutions were greatly intensified. The discovery of an Anabaptist conventicle, no matter how small, was greeted with horror by the authorities and the members often executed out of hand. Nevertheless the movement was large enough to begin with, to judge by the large numbers who fled Münster and were turned back; and in the next few years it spread abroad and greatly increased. A political hysteria somewhat like McCarthyism in the twentieth century swept over Europe. The authorities saw Anabaptists everywhere and any unorthodox gathering not Catholic, Lutheran, or Calvinist was immediately labeled Anabaptist. English ecclesiastics swore that the whole south and east of England was swarming with Anabaptists. If so they came and went with scarcely a trace, and only a handful of emigré Germans and Dutchmen were caught and exiled or executed. As for the Anabaptist movement itself, from Münster on it became rigorously pacifist—which in fact in the majority of organized groups it always had been.

9

Anabaptists, Hutterites

For years after the fall of Münster the Anabaptists were a hunted people. They had been persecuted enough before. Now Protestants, Catholics, and almost all the states of Middle Europe united to exterminate them. This was no small task. There was a significant number of Anabaptists in Switzerland, where the movement had been born only ten years before; in the Austrian Tyrol, on the Italian side of the Alps, in Moravia, Silesia, Danzig, Poland, southwest Germany and the Lower Rhineland, the Rhone Valley, and Picardy in France; and in Belgium and the Netherlands where, until the arrival of Calvinism and the struggle for freedom from the empire, Anabaptism was the principal form taken by the Reformation.

In spite of the great numbers of people who had attempted to come to the relief of Münster from the Netherlands, militant chiliasm was not at all typical of Dutch Anabaptism. The majority were pacifists who, if they were millenarians at all, had already begun to etherealize that item of their belief. Most of them were deeply influenced by the parallel movement of the Spiritualizers, who placed little stress on baptism and holy communion, or had abandoned the sacraments altogether. In the years to come Spiritualizers, Sebastian Franck, Caspar Schwenkfeld, Hans Denk, Valentin Weigel, and the rest, down to Jakob Boehme, were the favorite reading matter of the reorganized and reformed Anabaptists—who would come to be called Mennonites. Under the blows of relentless persecution the movement divided into three parts: pacifists, who refused oaths, military service, and public office, but who rejected communism; those who were both pacifists and communists; and the surviving militant chiliasts who mostly would literally die out under persecution.

Menno Simons was born in Friesland, the son of a peasant, trained for the Roman priesthood, and was ordained in 1524. From the beginning he seems to have been a Catholic evangelical and early rejected the doctrine of transubstantiation. His brother Peter died fighting while attempting to lead a band for the relief of Münster. Menno was profoundly shocked by the violence on both sides at Münster. At the height of the subsequent persecutions he resigned his priesthood. He went underground and spent the rest of his life as a wandering preacher and organizer with a price on his head, hunted by the authorities, but always protected by the faithful. In due course he was able to turn what had been a movement of independent and often antagonistic conventicles into a church somewhat loosely organized—both communists and non-communists were included—but organized nonetheless, and disciplined by congregational excommunication—the "ban."

Menno gathered up and systematized the theology of Anabaptism and although his ideas were not universally accepted they provided from then on a normative, central nucleus. In ten years Anabaptists generally were beginning to be called Mennonites. As the century wore on the use of the ban, which had originally been a unifying principle, led to splits and schisms over the practice of "hard ban" or "soft ban," divisions which still today in America separate the various bodies of "plain people." However, these divisions did not prevent the Mennonites from presenting a united front to the world.

In 1577 as Protestantism in the Netherlands was becoming more and more Calvinist and the country was battling for freedom from the empire, William of Orange was able, as a condition of his leadership, to push through the Estates General a guarantee of religious freedom throughout the Netherlands, and there at least persecution came to an end. In the course of time Dutch Mennonites would become wealthy and accepted as part of the establishment and would finally permit their members to accept public office and, in some cases, participate in war. The original strict pacifist communitarian tradition, although not communism itself, would survive amongst the American Mennonites.

But in the years immediately after the fall of Münster it was not easy for the hunted Anabaptists to practice communism. The militants, under the leadership of John of Battenberg, one of the leaders who had escaped from Münster, went underground. They practiced no public ceremonies of baptism, communion, or the *agapē* but scrupulously attended the Catholic Church. They practiced polygamy as best they could and held their goods in common and augmented the common fund by looting churches and monasteries. Battenberg was caught and executed in 1538 but the movement survived in the Low Countries for another five years. Those who rejected polygamy, violence, robbery, and nudism were more or less united by David Joris, an artist, poet, and hymn writer. Better read than most of the surviving Münsterites, he was deeply influenced by the apocalyptic "three kingdoms" prophesies of Joachim of Fiore and the mysticism of Meister Eckhart and of the contemporary Spiritualists. The followers of Joris carried on an active propaganda in southeastern England. Their ideas had much to do with determining the character of the English radical Reformation from then on. The principal influence, however, came through the purely Spiritualist movement originating from Henry Nicholas—the Family of Love. David Joris took refuge in Basel and led his movement by correspondence and missioners. He was one of the few Anabaptists to die peacefully in bed, in 1556. After his death some of his followers accused him of keeping a harem and other gross immoralities, and his body was dug up and burned. Small communist groups survived here and there in Switzerland and the Low Countries for another generation but most emigrated to safety.

Since 1528 a communist sanctuary had been preparing in Moravia. In 1526 Jacob Hutter arrived in the colony at Nicolsburg, which was under the patronage of the twice-baptized Lord of Liechtenstein. Hutter was a violent millenarian and a violent communitarian, but he was also a "violent pacifist." He split away from the Anabaptist community, the majority of whom were followers of the more conventional Balthasar Hübmaier, who in 1528 in the course of this disputation was caught and burned to death in Vienna. Hutter went on to meet martyrdom himself, but his pacifist, communist group, under the leadership of Jacob Wiedemann and Philip Yaeger, set up their own community. After a winter-long, peaceable discussion, Lord

Liechtenstein asked them to leave. They decided to move to Austerlitz in Moravia, and in the words of the *Hutterite Chronicles:*

Therefore they sought to sell their possessions. Some did sell, but others left them standing so, and they departed with one another from thence. Whatever remained of theirs the Lords of Liechtenstein did send after them. And so from Nicolsburg, Bergen, and thereabouts there gathered about two hundred persons without [counting] the children before the town [of Nicolsburg]. Certain persons came out . . . and wept from great compassion with them, but others argued. . . . Then they got themselves up, went out, and pitched . . . in a desolate village and abode there one day and one night, taking counsel together in the Lord concerning their present necessity, and ordained [geordnet] ministers for their temporal necessities [*dienner in der Zeitlichenn Notdurfft*] . . . . At that time these men spread out a cloak before the people, and every man did lay his substance down upon it, with a willing heart and without constraint, for the sustenance of those in necessity, according to the doctrine of the prophets and apostles [Isa. 23.18; Acts 2. 4 and 5].

On that outspread robe in the spring of 1528 were laid the foundations of the longest-lived communist society the world has yet seen. Leonhardt von Liechtenstein escorted them to the borders of his principality and begged them to stay. He had threatened to defend his Anabaptist refuge with arms against Vienna, and the leaders answered him, "Since you promise to resort to the sword, even to protect us, we cannot stay." They sent couriers ahead to the von Kaunitz brothers, Lords of Austerlitz, who replied that the Hutterites were welcome, even if their numbers were a thousand. After three months on the road they were welcomed enthusiastically—there was already a colony of radical members of the Bohemian Brethren there. In a short time they had built houses and started to farm and work at their crafts. They brought with them a twelve-point program for a practical religious communism which had been developed for a group of Anabaptists in Rattenburg and this document survives in the *Hutterite Chronicles* and their first constitution. Soon refugees began to arrive from Switzerland, the Low Countries, and especially the Tyrol. The latter must have been in the majority because today the ceremonial as well as the familiar "little language" is an old Tyrolese dialect, although since then the Hutterites have been forced to wander over two hemispheres.

During the next five years the communist Anabaptists everywhere were given over to sectarian splits and expulsions too complicated to describe briefly; but in 1533 Jacob Hutter, who had been called in by various groups, including those at Austerlitz, as a mediator, brought his own followers from the Tyrol and inaugurated a movement for reunion and federation which for the next two years carried all or almost all before it. At the beginning of the persecutions which accompanied the Münster commune he and his wife were caught and repeatedly tortured. Hutter did not succumb under the most fantastic cruelties to the besetting temptation of all revolutionaries to discuss their doctrines with their captors, much less to reveal the names of his comrades, or any secrets of the movement. He remained silent in the face of the agents of the Devil. The authorities wished to behead him in secret; but Ferdinand, who was Archduke of Austria, King of Bohemia, and Holy Roman Emperor, refused, and he was publicly burned on February 25, 1536. He was caught in the town of Klausen in the Tyrol.

After Münster Ferdinand demanded that all Anabaptists be expelled from all territories subject to the Austrian throne. In many places they were expelled and they hid out in the forests and mountains until the storm of persecution had passed; but the Moravian nobles seem to have protected them, and as soon as Ferdinand's attention was distracted elsewhere, they were re-established in their former colonies. During these years under the leadership of John Ammon the Hutterites began a missionary activity to central Europe. They sent out apostles, four-fifths of whom were martyred, to Danzig, to Lithuania, to Venice, to Belgium.

One of the most active of the missionaries was Peter Riedemann, who, in and out of prison, began to develop a systematic theology and social order for the Hutterites. On the death of Ammon in 1542 he was elected leader, although he was being held in prison, very loosely it is true, by Philip of Hesse. By this time incidentally, the Hutterites had come to call their leaders bishops, although these bore little resemblance to members of the Catholic episcopacy. Leonard Lanzenstiel had been appointed by Ammon as his successor and Riedemann and Lanzenstiel shared the leadership until 1556 when Riedemann died in a new colony of Protzko in Slovakia, and his place was taken by Peter Waldpot, one of the greatest of the Hutterite leaders, who died in 1578.

Over a generation had gone by, and communist Anabaptism had become a successful polity, prosperous, seldom troubled any more by sectarian contentiousness, and with outlying colonies in Slovakia and Bohemia. The core of the movement, those directly under the administration of Waldpot, numbered as many as thirty thousand adults. From the beginning in Austerlitz they had realized that a communism of consumption was not enough and had organized work-shops, little factories of craftsmen, and work brigades and communal farms, with detailed manuals for the different trades. They established their own schools (the first nursery schools and kindergartens) with grades up through adolescence. Higher education they rejected, as they still do, as unnecessary to the welfare of the community, and as distracting from the love of God and the love of neighbors. But their elementary schools were the best in Europe in their day. Child care was socialized. The children usually lived in the schools and were visited by their parents. Each Hutterite colony had an active, careful public-health program. The villages were not only clean and neat but their hygiene and sanitation were unparalleled. Marriages seem to have been arranged by the collaboration of the elders, the community, and the individuals and were commonly very successful. Of all Anabaptist groups, or for that matter of all communists and pacifists whatever, the history of the Hutterites is singularly free from sexual scandals.

With a system of production and distribution far better organized than anything else at the time the colonies grew wealthy. Since they believed individually in living in "decent poverty" they soon accumulated considerable surpluses, particularly after the colonies were permitted to sell their products to Gentiles. These surpluses were invested in capital improvements and in the subsidizing of new colonies, a necessity, as it still is today, because of the high birth-rate, and low death-rate, in those days due to their exemplary public health. The Hutterites had discovered a dynamic, continuously expanding economy of the type that Marx would later diagnose as the essence of capitalism, but this was a communist economy and it was based on a very high level of peasant prosperity, the source of its accumulation of capital. In other words the Hutterites in their little closed society solved the contradiction in capital accumulation and circulation which in different forms bedevils both the Russians and Americans today. The golden age of the Hutterites lasted until 1622, when the Moravian nobles, who had been their patrons, were forced by the Church and empire to expel them from their estates. They scattered, finding refuge in Slovakia, Transylvania, and Hungary. Their harassment increased during the Thirty Years War when the imperialists were able to obliterate the Utraquist Church of Bohemia and drive the Czech Brethren underground. By the eighteenth century communism of production had necessarily been abandoned and community of goods was practiced only in the form of a common welfare fund, but the Hutterites still wore their traditional costume and held to their manner of worship.

In 1767 a decree was issued, upon the urging of the Jesuits, who had led in the persecution, that all Hutterite children in Hungary, including Transylvania, should be taken from their parents and raised in orphanages. The Hutterites fled to Rumania and found themselves in the midst of the Russo-Turkish War. In 1770 the Empress Catherine invited German Pietists and Anabaptists to settle in the Ukraine and there for a time we can leave them. They would develop, deteriorate, revive, and emigrate at last to the United States and finally Canada, where they would flourish as never before. We will return to them when we come to discuss modern communalism, of which they are incomparably the most successful practitioners.

During the last half of the sixteenth century there were isolated survivals and sporadic revivals of communism amongst groups of Anabaptists and Spiritualists. Community of goods endured as an apostolic ideal amongst Swiss and Czech Brethren who were no longer able to practice it, to be revived for a while when some of them migrated to America. There were communist colonies in the once-powerful Unitarian Church of Transylvania.

The only community that can be compared with those of the Hutterites was that of Rakow in Little Poland northwest of Cracow. Founded in 1569 by Gregory Paul, it attracted Anabaptist, Spiritualist, and Unitarian leaders from all over Poland, Prussia, Lithuania, Silesia, and Galicia, the whole northeast of central Europe, which in those days, before the Counter-Reformation, seemed to be turning to the radical Reformation. One of the most remarkable features of the radical Reformation in this territory was the very large number of the nobility who were converted, freed their serfs, sold their land, distributed their goods to the poor, and took part as equals in the communism of Rakow —in that order of frequency. That is, many only freed their serfs, and only a few came to Rakow, but nonetheless a good number of the most powerful nobles were sympathetic toward Anabaptism.

The Rakovians sent a delegation to the Hutterites in Moravia, proposing to affiliate with them and learn their methods. The Rakovians were impressed by Hutterite efficiency and prosperity, but they rejected their Trinitarianism and were offended by what they considered their arrogance, intolerance, and conceit. At this time, to judge from the Polish testimony, the Hutterites believed that "anyone who owns a house, land, or money, and does not bring it to the community, is not a Christian but a pagan and cannot be saved." To the Rakovians communism was not a condition of salvation but simply the counsel of a more perfect apostolic life. The Hutterites on their part objected, of course, to the Unitarianism of the Poles, but surprisingly, not very strongly. More important by far were practices that would seem to us trivial. The Hutterites baptized by pouring, the Poles by immersion. But more important still was a class difference. The Hutterites were peasants and workers whose education, though sound, was limited to the Bible and a few spiritual writers. They were offended by the Poles' aristocratic manners, their "cold hearts," their knowledge of languages, their Latinized names, and their refusal to submit outright to Hutterite authority. Peter Waldpot went so far as to demand that the Poles be rebaptized by the Hutterites. Correspondence and visits went on for two or three years but at last the Rakovians gave up hope of affiliation with the Hutterites. The overtures had all been one way and even after negotiations had been broken off the Poles still occasionally visited the Hutterite colonies. There is no record of any Hutterites visiting Rakow.

Out of the Polish radical Anabaptism was to come Faustus Socinus, one of the major theologians of the entire Reformation period, who had migrated to Poland from Italy. He elaborated a fully developed system in which Unitarianism, pacifism, community of goods, baptism by immersion, and all the major tenets of Polish Anabaptism and Spiritualism were rationally interrelated in a systematic philosophy which was at the same time consistently evangelical. When the Polish Brethren were driven out of Poland and found refuge in Holland they came to exert both in doctrine and practice considerable influence on the more radical Dutch Mennonites and through them on the development of the movement in England and America. In Poland the Counter-Refomation led by the Jesuits did its work thoroughly and the communalist Polish Brethren are extinct.

As a footnote it should be pointed out that the basic difference between the Hutterites and almost all other Christian sects, orthodox or heterodox, was that the society of the Hutterite colonies was what modern theorists would call a "shame culture," fundamentally unassimilable by the "guilt culture" of Christianity and rabbinical (as differentiated from Hasidic) Judaism.

10

Winstanley, The Diggers

Suprisingly the seventeenth century with its almost continuous wars of religion was not a good time for the radical Reformation. *Cujis regio, ejus religio*—religion had become a matter of large-scale politics. Wars fought between nations and alliances of nations divided Europe into blocks of Catholics, Lutherans, and Calvinists. Small groups of the elect were crushed out by the sheer weight of the contending monsters. Then, too, the Thirty Years War, which was fought to destroy the Holy Roman Empire as the dominant power in Europe, also crushed or profoundly distorted the culture of the various parts of the empire. Germany emerged fragmented and wasted and did not recover for generations. The radical Reformation had been a natural outgrowth of the culture of the late medieval middle of Europe and the Thirty Years War destroyed its roots. In the Netherlands, Switzerland, and amongst the Hutterites in their remote refuges, a process of fossilization had set in.

The English Civil War and commonwealth were essentially a product of class struggle, and the prolifera-
tion of sects in the latter days of the Civil War took place
almost entirely in a lower middle class and upper working class context. In spite of their name, the Levellers
were far from being unbridled democrats. They proposed to extend participation in power only to men of
substance—small, middle-class substance—like themselves. The Fifth Monarchy men were such extreme
chiliasts as to have no real social program.

The Ranters were only incidentally millenarians.
Basically they were a revival of the Brotherhood of the
Free Spirit, who believed that once divinized and absorbed into the Godhead the soul was incapable of evil.
Like the Adamites who were expelled from Tabor they
lived exalted in an amoral ecstasy. If they practiced
community of goods, nudism, speaking with tongues,
and sexual orgies it was all part of a frantic, hurried,
and hunted life lived in a state of unrelieved excite-
ment. Some Ranters were simply extreme Spiritualists,
descendants of Meister Eckhart and the Rhineland
mystics; and with the Restoration of Charles II they
were absorbed into the Quakers. They really lay completely outside the development of English Puritanism.

The agitation of the Levellers lasted only three years.
They were primarily a political party who wished to see
the promises of the Rump Parliament—the recruiting
propaganda for the second stage of the Civil War
—fulfilled. Their leader, John Lilburne, had been an
associate of Cromwell's at the beginning and the Levellers were perfectly right when they accused him of sel-
ling out. Although the final form of their *Agreement of
the Free People of England,* their political manifesto,
proposes a broader democracy than would come to England until the end of the nineteenth century, they did
not believe in universal franchise, but excluded ser-

vants, paupers, farm laborers, Roman Catholics, Episcopalians, Royalists, "heretics," and, of course, women. Essentially they were left-wing Calvinist republicans. By the end of 1649 they had been completely suppressed.

In 1653 the Nominated or "Barebones" Parliament, chosen from the leaders of the Independent Churches, sat briefly; but its attempts to inaugurate the rule of the saints were so radical and disorganized that Cromwell dissolved them and became dictator—"Protector." This led to a revolt of the more extreme millenarians, to whom Cromwell became the "Little Horn" of the Beast of the Apocalypse. They proposed to establish a ruthless despotism of the elect in preparation for the final kingdom of the millennium. The Fifth Monarchy movement, lacking both ideology and social program, sprang up through an inflamed rhetoric which consisted exclusively of the reiteration and rearrangement of the apocalyptic language of the Books of Daniel and Revelation. It was a massive hysterical outburst of rage by men who knew they had been betrayed. Unlike the Levellers, they took to armed revolt. In April 1567 a handful of men rushed about London fighting as they went and were quickly suppressed. In January 1661 another, even more frantic and desperate attempt occurred, and those who were not killed in the streets were executed, and the sect came to an end.

Movements like the old Family of Love, the Seekers, and the Quakers grew in the interstices of the English Reformation, at first so clandestinely that from Henry VIII to the emergence of the Quakers we know surprisingly little about them. Various groups were accused of practicing community of goods; but although the movement was widespread, at least in the imagination of its persecutors, each individual group seems to have been a tiny conventicle, with members meeting in one anothers' homes and sharing their resources. Theologically the older Anabaptism died out in England and was replaced by Spiritualism. The modern Baptist sect which arose in those days was an independent development which owed practically nothing to continental Anabaptism but was rather a special form of Calvinism. In the writing and preaching of George Fox and the earliest Quakers there were no special social or economic concerns, and it was only after the Restoration with the consolidation of modern Quakerism in the days of William Penn that the Quakers became anti-political.

A little group of unemployed laborers and landless peasants gathered at St. George's Hill near Walton-on-Thames in Surrey on April 1, 1649, and began to dig up the common land and prepare for sowing vegetables. Their leaders were William Everard and Gerrard Winstanley. At first their activities aroused curiosity and a certain amount of sympathy but as time went on the local lords of the manor, the gentry, aroused the populace and the mob shut the Diggers up in the church at Walton until they were released by a justice of the peace. Again they were captured by a mob and locked up in the nearby town of Kingston and again released. On April 16 a complaint was laid before the Council of State, who sent two groups of cavalry to investigate.

The captain, Gladman, reported that the incident was trivial and sent Everard and Winstanley to London to explain themselves to Thomas Fairfax. They explained that since the Norman Conquest England had been under a tyranny which was now abolished, but that now God would relieve the poor and restore their freedom to enjoy the fruits of the earth. The two men explained that they did not intend to interfere with private property, but only to plant and harvest on the many wastelands of England, and to live together holding all things in common. They were certain that their example would be followed by the poor and dispossessed all over England, and in the course of time all men would give up their possessions and join them in community.

A month later Lord Fairfax stopped by on his way to London, to see for himself what was happening, and decided it was a matter for the local authorities. In June another mob, including some soldiers, assaulted the Diggers and trampled their crops. Winstanley complained to Fairfax and the soldiers were apparently ordered to leave the Diggers alone. In June the Diggers announced that they intended to cut and sell the wood on the common, and at this point the landlords sued for damages and trespass. The court awarded damages of ten pounds and costs, and took the cows Winstanley was pasturing on the common, but released them because they were not his property.

Perhaps because of the judgment, and because their crops had all been destroyed, the Diggers moved in the autumn to the common of Cobham Manor, built four houses, and started a crop of winter grain. By this time there were over fifty Diggers. When they refused to disperse, Fairfax finally sent troops who, with the mob, destroyed two of the houses and again trampled the fields. The Diggers persisted and by spring they had eleven acres of growing grain and six or seven houses and similar movements had sprung up in Northamptonshire and Kent. The landlord, a clergyman, John Platt, turned his cattle into the young grain and led a mob in destroying houses and driving out the Diggers and their women and children.

On April 1, 1649, Winstanley and fourteen others (Everard, who seems to have been demented, vanishes early in the story) were indicted for disorderly conduct,

unlawful assembly, and trespass. There is no record of
the disposal of the indictment, but this was the end of
the little communist society at Cobham.

This is all there was to the Digger movement, a trivial
episode which was a ninety-day wonder in the news
sheets when it first started, and which was almost
without influence at the time, and easily could have
been lost to history—except for the writings of Gerrard
Winstanley. All during the course of the experiment he
issued a series of pamphlets which, as his ideas rapidly
evolved, came to constitute the first systematic exposition of libertarian communism in English.

All the tendencies of the radical Reformation seem to
flow together in Winstanley, to be blended and secularized, and become an ideology rather than a theology. Spiritualism, radical Unitarianism, apostolic
communism, evangelical rationalism—one could easily
believe that he was well read in the entire literature of
the radical Reformation. Yet we know nothing of his
intellectual background, reading, or influences. He
never quotes a secular authority, only the Bible, in all
his writings, and we know nothing about his education,
and little enough about his life. He says again and
again that his ideas owe nothing to any other man or to
any book, only to the Inner Light and to its "openings"
in visionary experiences. Perhaps that is true.

Gerrard Winstanley was born in the village of Wigan
in 1609, in a family of small gentry and merchants that
had long been prominent in England. His father Edward was registered as a mercer and the son was raised
in the cloth trade. Somewhere he must have received a
fairly good education for a provincial middle-class boy
because, although he never uses, as did everybody else
in his day, a classical quotation, this very avoidance
would indicate not only that he was well educated but

quite sophisticated, and the prose style in his later pamphlets is that of a highly literate man. At the age of twenty he was in London, apprenticed to Sarah Gater, widow of William Gater of the Merchant Taylor's company, and at twenty-eight he became a freeman and went into business for himself. Three years later he married Susan King. In the depression which began in 1643 he went bankrupt, and he was still being sued by one of his creditors in 1660. After his bankruptcy, he left London to stay with friends in the neighborhood of Cobham and Walton-on-Thames in Surrey where, to judge from his troubles over the cows, he made a living pasturing other people's cattle on the common.

At some time before his first publication Winstanley joined the Baptists and may have been a preacher for them, but before 1648 he had come to believe that baptism was only an unimportant form and had ceased to attend Baptist conventicles. Rather he met with those little groups of Seekers who gathered in one another's homes and waited for the Inner Light, and spoke only *ex tempore*. At this time he went through a period of temptation, guilt, fear of death and damnation, of devils and ghosts, and a sense of loss and abandonment, a time of spiritual crisis universal in the lives of the great mystics. Finally, he came to an abiding consciousness of God within himself, the assurance of universal salvation, and the peace which comes with direct experience of mystical illumination. His first two publications are really devoted to assimilating this experience. They move from a highly spiritualized chiliasm, developing a well-reasoned doctrine of universal salvation, to a highly spiritualized philosophy of history rather than a theology.

Even in these early pamphlets Winstanley has original insights. His chiliasm does not take the form of the salvation of a handful of the elect but of the divinization of man. In his teachings on sin and salvation the original sin of Adam was not lust but covetousness— selfishness and the desire for power—in which Winstanley shows himself an incomparably more astute moralist than the Puritans. Ultimately, the God who operates in history, in all things, and consciously in the soul of man, is called "Reason." It would be a mistake to decide from this, as some modern writers have done, that Winstanley was a precursor of eighteenth-century rationalism. His reason is the ineffable God of Plotinus and Meister Eckhart apprehended in the mystical experience, though not separated from man as the Omnipotent Creator, but as the ultimately realizable in all things. So for him the narrative of Old Testament and the life and passion of Christ cease to be historical documents about something that happened in the past and become symbolic archetypes of the cosmic drama of the struggle of good and evil that takes place in the soul of man.

When the Digger tracts began with the adventure at St. George's Hill, Winstanley's basic appeal was not to the practice of the apostles or to an eschatological ethic in preparation for apocalypse. His communism begins with an "opening," an actual vision, and the appeal is always to his transcendent and imminent Reason—to a spiritualized natural law, not unlike the Tao of Chuang Tsu.

Likewise I heard these words: 'Worke together. Eat bread together. Declare all this abroad.' Likewise I heard these words: 'Whosoever it is that labours in the earth or any person or persons that lifts up themselves as Lords and Rulers over others and that doth not look upon themselves equal to others in the creation, the Hand of the Lord shall be upon the labourer. I the Lord have spoke it and I will do it. Declare all this abroad.' [*The New Law of Righteousness*, 1648]

This vision came not as a command from on high, but as a voice opening out of the experience of nature itself, for, says Winstanley, the doctrine of an anthropomorphic deity, set over against and independent of nature,

is the doctrine of a sickly and weak spirit who hath lost his understanding in the knowledge of the Creation and of the temper of his own Heart and Nature and so runs into fancies. [*The Law of Freedom in a Platform or True Magistracy Restored*, 1652]

To know the secrets of nature, is to know the works of God; and to know the works of God within the creation, is to know God himself, for God dwells in every visible work or body. And indeed if you would know spiritual things, it is to know how the Spirit or Power of Wisdom and Life, causing motion or growth, dwells within and governs both the several bodies of the stars and planets in the heavens above and the several bodies of the earth below as grass, plants, fishes, beasts, birds and mankinde. [*Ibid.*]

Belief in an outward heaven or hell is a "strange conceit," a fraud by which men are delivered over into the power of their oppressors,

. . . a fancy which your false teachers put into your heads to please you with, while they pick your purses and betray your Christ into the hands of flesh, and hold Jacob under to be a servant still to Lord Esau. [*The New Law of Righteousness*]

True religion and undefiled is this, to make restitution of the Earth which hath been taken and held from the common people by the power of Conquests formerly and so set the oppressed free. [*A New Yeers Gift for the Parliament and the Armie*, 1650]

The earth with all her fruits of Corn, Cattle and such like was made to be a common Store-House of Livelihood, to all mankinde, friend and foe, without exception. [*A Declaration from the Poor Oppressed People of England*, 1649]

And this particular propriety [property] of mine and thine that brought in all misery upon people. For first it hath occasioned people to steal from one another. Secondly it hath made laws to hang those that did steal. It tempts people to do an evil action and then kills them for doing it. [*The New Law of Righteousness*]

Now, this same power in man that causes divisions and war is called by some men the state of nature which every man brings into the world with him. . . . But this law of darknesse is not the State of Nature. [*Fire in the Bush*, 1650]

. . . the power of Life (called the Law of Nature within the creatures) which does move both man and beast in their actions; or that causes grass, trees, corn and all plants to grow in their several seasons; and whatsoever any body does, he does it as he is moved by this inward Law. And this Law of Nature moves twofold viz. unrationally or rationally. [*The Law of Freedom in a Platform or True Magistracy Restored*]

In the beginning of time the great creator Reason made the earth to be a common treasury . . . not one word was spoken in the beginning that one branch of mankind should rule over another. [*The True Levellers Standard Advanced*, 1649]

. . . the power of inclosing Land and owning Propriety was brought into the Creation by your ancestors by the Sword which first did murther their fellow-creatures men and after plunder or steal away their land. [*A Declaration from the Poor Oppressed People of England*]

They have by their subtle imagination and covetous wit got the plain-hearted poor or younger brethren to work for them for small wages and by their work have got a great increase. [*The True Levellers Standard Advanced*]

By large pay, much Free-Quarter and other Booties which they call their own they get much Monies and with this they buy Land. [*Ibid.*]

No man can be rich, but he must be rich, either by his own labors, or the labors of other men helping him: If a man have no help from his neighbor, he shall never gather an Estate of hundreds and thousands a year: If other men help him to work, then are those Riches his Neighbors, as well as his own, For they be the fruit of other mens labors as well as his own. But all rich men live at ease, feeding and clothing themselves by the labor of other men and not by their own; which is their shame and not their Nobility: for it is a more blessed thing to give than to receive. But rich men receive all they have from the laborers hand, and what they give, they give way other mens labors not their own. [*The Law of Freedom in a Platform or True Magistracy Restored*]

. . . if once landlords, then they rise to be Justices, Rulers and State Governours as experience shewes. [*The True Levellers Standard Advanced*]

. . . the power of the murdering and theeving sword fomerly as well as now of late years hath set up a government and maintains that government; for what are prisons and putting others to death, but the power of the Sword to enforce people to that Government which was got by Conquest and sword and cannot stand of itself but by the same murdering power. [*A Declaration from the Poor Oppressed People of England.*]

. . . the Kingly power sets up a Law and Rule of Government to walk by; and here Justice is pretended but the full strength of the Law is to uphold the conquering Sword and to preserve his son Propriety. . . . For though they say the Law doth punish yet indeed the Law is but the strength, life and marrow of the Kingly power upholding the Conquest still, hedging some into the Earth, hedging out others; giving the Earth to some and denying the Earth to others, which is contrary to the Law of Righteousnesse who made the Earth at first as free for one as for another. . . . Truly most Laws are but to enslave the Poor to the Rich and so they uphold the Conquest and are Laws of the great Red Dragons. [*A New Yeers Gift for the Parliament and the Armie.*]

Winstanley borrowed from the Levellers the idea that, in Anglo-Saxon England there had been an equitable sharing of land; and that at the Norman Conquest great estates had been created, and the old population dispossessed or driven into serfdom; and that this unequal division of the basic wealth of the land had been perpetuated ever since solely by the power of the sword; and that law and established religion were just devices to uphold the sword; and finally, that the overthrow of the king, the heir of the Norman power, had resulted in no important change. The old laws still stood. A new Church, first of the Presbyterians and then of the Independents, was established, and the grandees of the new commonwealth were enriching themselves like William the Conqueror's knights, while the common people sank deeper into poverty. Winstanley's interpretation of English history has been considered naïve, but there is much to be said for it. Anglo-Saxon England was in fact a frontier country, and all through the Dark Ages, following the catastrophic depopulation that began in the fifth century, there was much free land all over Europe and even more in the British Isles.

He says of caterpillar lawyers that "they love money as dearly as a poor man's dog do his breakfast in a cold morning and they are such neat workmen, that they can turn a cause which way those that have the biggest purse have them."

O you Parliament-men of England, cast those whorish laws out of doors, that are so common, that pretend love to everyone, and is faithful to none. For truly, he that goes to law, as the proverb is, shall die a beggar. So that old whores, and old laws, picks men's pockets and undoes them . . . burn all your law books in Cheapside, and set up your government upon you own foundations. Do not put new wine into old bottles; but as you government must be new so let the laws be new, or else you will run farther into the mud, where you stick already, as though you were fast in an Irish bog. [A New Yeers Gift for the Parliament and the Armie.]

As for the church:

> And do we not yet see that if the Clergie can get Tithes or Money they will turn as the Ruling power turns, any way . . . to Papacy, to Protestantisme; for a King, against a King; for monarchy, for Some Government; they cry who bids most wages, they will be on the strongest side for an earthly maintenance . . . There is a confederacie between the Clergy and the great red Dragon. The sheep of Christ shall never fare well so long as the wolf or red Dragon payes the Shepherd their wages. [*Ibid.*]

For Winstanley private property, but especially the property in land as the source of all wealth, "is the cause of all wars, bloodshed, theft and enslaving laws that hold the people under miserie." Private property divides man from man and nation from nation and leads to a state of continuous war on which the state power flourishes.

Winstanley was the first to discover that axiom made famous by Randolph Bourne—"War is the health of the State." He also had the curious and original idea that only in time of war does the power structure encourage scientific invention. "Otherwise the Kingly Bondage is the cause of the spreading of ignorance in the earth for fear of want and care to pay rent to taskmasters hath hindered many rare inventions and the secrets of creation have been locked up under the traditional parrot-like speaking from the Universities and Colleges for Scholars." War, says Winstanley, makes the rich richer and the poor poorer and tightens the bonds of power.

Winstanley was a devout pacifist all during the Digger experiment; and one reason for the violent abuse of the Diggers, the destruction of their shanties, and the injury and killing of their livestock, was due to the fact that they put up no resistance. They believed that their example, if only they were permitted to cultivate the

commons and wastelands, would be so infectious that
soon it would be followed by all the poor of England;
and that when they had established a community of
love, interpenetrating all of English society, their success would lead even the rich and powerful to join
them, and eventually all Europe would turn communist
persuaded only by example.

Socialists, modern Communists, anarchists, all claim
Winstanley as an ancestor. In fact his ideas bear most
resemblance to those of the left-wing followers of Henry
George's Single Tax. For him the source of all wealth
was in land and its development in the application of
labor to the resources of the earth. If these resources
were held in common, and all men were permitted to
develop them freely, and men labored in common, then
the resulting wealth, even of crafts and manufactures,
would naturally become communalized. Modern contemporary Marxists have called this economics naïve,
but it was held at the beginning of the twentieth century by an economist who was anything but naïve,
Henry George, who attracted many thousand intelligent followers, and it is after all the fundamental assumption of Marx himself. But it was not his economics
that was most important to Winstanley. What he sought
was a spiritual condition in mankind which would be in
harmony with the working of Reason in nature—the return of man, who had fallen into covetousness, to the
universal harmony. Winstanley's communism was not
an economic doctrine, but mutual aid followed from his
organic philosophy as a logical consequence.

After the suppression of the little commune of Diggers Winstanley was quiet for a while. Then in 1652 he
published, with a preface submitting it to Cromwell, his
plan for a new commonwealth—*The Law of Freedom in
a Platform or True Magistracy Restored.* The Digger
pamphlets present no plan for administrative or gov-

ernmental policy. Winstanley seems to have assumed that the example of small anarchist-communist groups working in occupied land in brotherhood would sweep all before it and convert England and eventually the world. The problems of self-defense and internal disruption are met by total pacifism before which power must simply dissolve. The violent suppression of the Diggers by both mob and authority forced Winstanley to consider the question of power anew.

The Law of Freedom, after a general introduction, is concerned largely with administrative plans, and the introduction is an appeal to Cromwell to use his power to introduce the new commonwealth. If you do not, says Winstanley, abolish the old power of conquest of the king and nobles, but only turn it over to other men, "you will either lose yourself or lay the foundation of greater slavery to posterity than you ever knew," a chilling forecast of the dark Satanic mills of early British capitalism.

In the preamble he outlines the principal popular grievances, lack of religious toleration, survival of the old priesthood, the burden of tithes—a tenth of all income for an established Church, arbitrary administration of justice, the old laws are still enforced, the old feudal dues and obligations are still used to oppress the people, while the upper classes ignore their feudal obligations and enclose or abuse the common lands. These are the same grievances we are familiar with from the Hussite Wars and the Peasants' Revolt in Germany.

Winstanley points out that true freedom does not consist in free trade, freedom of religion, or community of women, but freedom in the use of the earth, the natural treasure of society, and that the first duty of the new commonwealth should be to open the land to all people and to take over the former holdings of the king, the

Church, and the nobility. To do this properly, and to use the land fruitfully for the good of all, society needs true government, administrative officers who will be devoted to freedom and the commonweal.

The original root of magistracy was in the family, and the first magistrate is the father, as the finally responsible member of a group in which all are mutually responsible. Officers of the society should be chosen by complete manhood suffrage for all over twenty, and at first only representatives of the old order need to be barred, although notorious evil livers are not fit to be chosen. They should be above forty years of age and hold office for one year only so that responsibility can be rotated throughout the community. First are the overseers, the peace officers who form a local council in each community. They preserve public order and suppress crime and quarrelling and disputes over household property and other chattels which remain in private possession. Others plan the distribution of labor and assign the young to apprenticeships. Others oversee the production of the craftsmen and farmers. Winstanley envisages manufactures as being carried on largely in people's homes with a few public workshops. Apprenticeships normally take place within the family; only boys who do not wish to follow their fathers' trade are assigned to the public workshops. Others organize the distribution of goods and food which go to warehouses and shops, both wholesale and retail, from which both craftsmen and consumers are free to choose what they wish.

In each community there is a "soldier," what we would call a policeman, whose duty is to enforce the decisions of the peacemaker, a taskmaster to whom is given the rule of those convicted of crimes against the community and who assigns them to common labor. There is also an executioner who administers corporal or capital punishment to the hopelessly recalcitrant. Winstanley's system of penalties may seem excessively severe to us, especially in a utopian society, but in their day, when people were hung for petty theft, they were relatively mild. In the county or shire the peacemakers of the towns, the overseers, and the soldiers, presided over by a judge, form the county senate and court of first appeal. Over all is parliament, which Winstanley seems to have thought of as primarily a court of final appeal, and he is very strongly opposed to its indulging in promiscuous legislation. Laws should be as few and simple as possible. What Winstanley had in mind was a polity like the Israelites in the Book of Judges—in fact the neolithic village with spontaneous justice administered by the elders sitting under a tree. Curiously he says nothing about juries or any other form of democratization of justice. Society defends itself by a militia and Winstanley has a most perceptive section on the evils of standing armies, militarism, and war.

Education in the new commonwealth is free, general, compulsory, and continues through life. Everyone is to be taught a trade or a craft at which he is to work part-time, whatever else he comes to do. No caste of intellectuals or academicians set apart from the people by booklearning is to be permitted to arise, although after the age of forty men "shall be freed from all labor and work unless they will themselves." The death penalty is decreed for those who attempt to make a living by law or religion. In each community there shall be a "postmaster" who corresponds with all the others in the country directly and through a central postmaster in the chief city. They exchange news, especially news of progress in science, invention, and technology. Sunday is a day of rest. The people gather to listen to a reading of the laws, the news of the postmaster, and what we would call papers on learning and science. Religious services are not mentioned. The people are apparently at liberty to attend them if they wish. Marriage and divorce are civil, exclusively at the will of parties, and take place by simple declaration before the community with the overseers as witnesses.

Winstanley's utopia has been criticized as being excessively simple and himself as naïve; and even more naïve, his idea that Cromwell would put in force such a policy, or probably even bother to read his pamphlet. Ideological discussion with his sectarian opponents was, whenever he had time, an indoor sport with Cromwell, but he never allowed it to influence him. We must not forget he lived in a time of revolutionary hope. In those days, as in the beginning of the Reformation on the continent, it seemed quite possible to intelligent men that an entirely new social order might be established. Everyone was something of a millenarian and believed that a new historical epoch was beginning. They could not foresee the rise of industrialism, capitalism, the secular State. To us, their future is the past and seems to have been inevitable. There was nothing inevitable about it to them. Perhaps if Cromwell, or even Luther, had foreseen the horrors of the early industrial age in the nineteenth century, or the genocide and wars of extermination of the twentieth, they might have chosen the commonwealth of Winstanley or the community life of the Hutterites. In each great crisis of Western European civilization, the Reformation, the French Revolution, the revolutions of 1848, the First World War, the Bolshevik Revolution, the Spanish Civil War, the Second World War, it has seemed quite possible to change the world. It is only after the fact that the historical process appears to be the only way in which events could have worked out.

Was Winstanley's utopia a workable polity? Within limits, yes. Whether he knew it or not, it is remarkably similar to that of the Taborites, the Moravian Brethren, the Hutterites, and the most successful and enduring communalist settlements in nineteenth-century America. His plans went into the common stock of ideas of later English communists and directly or indirectly influenced John Bellers, Robert Owen, Josiah Warren, William Morris, Belford Bax, Édouard Bernstein, David Petegorsky. Other socialists, Communists, and anarchists wrote extensively about him in the first half of the twentieth century and after the Second World War he became extremely popular. Revolutionary communalist groups in England, America, Germany, and France would even call themselves Diggers.

Although the Quakers are by far the best known and largest, and a still surviving community descended from the Spiritualist Anabaptists, and hence ultimately from the underground apostolic community of the Middle Ages, they did not practice community of goods. Rather each Seventh-Day Meeting, as they called their conventicles, had a common fund for the relief of members in need. As a majority of Quakers became prosperous—due to their strict honesty in trade and crafts and, prior to 1760 when they refused to pay tithes and so gave up farming, their advanced agricultural methods—these common funds became quite large and many poor people joined the Society of Friends to obtain welfare funds vastly superior to contemporary poor relief. At first this caused problems but within a generation members who had joined for these reasons had been absorbed into the general economy of Quaker mutual aid and poor Quakers were less than a third of the proportion of poor in the general population, while well-to-do members were proportionately three times as many. Quaker welfare funds came to be used more and more for the general relief of the poor in systematic ways which would foster self-help. Quakers were the principal, almost the sole, financiers, besides himself, of Robert Owen's model factory town of New Lanark, and they have continued to invest in communal and cooperative movements of which they approve to this day.

In his youth at Manchester College Owen's closest friends were the Quaker John Dalton and another young Friend named Winstanley, quite possibly a descendant of the great Digger.

Far more than Robert Owen, the most systematic theorist of a cooperative labor colony was the Quaker John Bellers, who greatly impressed Marx. Owen always denied that he was influenced by Bellers and claimed that he had never heard of him until Francis Place showed him a unique copy of his forgotten pamphlet in 1817. Owen immediately had a thousand copies printed and distributed them to those he thought would be interested, and so Bellers survived.

Bellers was born in 1654, a birthright Quaker. He became a friend of William Penn and other leading men of the time. In 1695 during the long economic depression in the last years of the century, he published *Proposals for Raising a College of Industry of All Useful Trades and Husbandry*. He called it a college rather than a work house or community because the first was identified with the servile institutions of state poor relief and the second implied that all things should be held in common. For a capital investment of fifteen thousand pounds—worth considerably more than ten times as much today—Bellers envisaged a self-sustaining colony of three hundred adults with shops, commissary, crafts, farm land, barns, dairies, pottery. The community was to be self-sufficient even in fuel and iron. All members, from common laborers to the overseers and managers, were to be paid in kind. The dwelling house would have four wings—one for married couples, one for single men and young boys, one for single women and girls, and one an infirmary. Meals were to be in common. Bellers, like Winstanley before him, placed great emphasis upon education in the humanities, in the arts, and in crafts and trade combined. Bellers thought that the creative life of the community and the advanced educational methods would attract many who would wish to come as visitors or even permanent boarders; and even more would wish to enroll their children in school, and for these privileges they would be expected to pay well. He worked out in considerable detail the projected bookkeeping of his community and demonstrated that the original investors would gain a considerable profit, while at the same time the standard of living of the members would be far higher than that of the contemporary working class. The first edition of the pamphlet was dedicated to the Society of Friends, the second to Parliament, but no one came forward to invest in such a colony. During his remaining years Bellers issued a series of pamphlets, some of them devoted to a careful economic analysis of a semi-socialist economy, others proposing a league of nations, an ecumenical council of all Christian religions, a national health service, a reform of Parliament and the electoral process, a total reform of prisons, and a reform of the Poor Laws.

Although Robert Owen had worked out his own system before he read Bellers' pamphlet and although Fourier, Saint-Simon, and Cabet had certainly never heard of him, he anticipated most of their more practicable ideas and in far more practicable form. Although all his writings soon became excessively rare, he should be considered the founder of modern, socially responsible Quakerism of the Service Committee variety. Furthermore the various measures he proposed in his reformist practice have almost all been incorporated in the modern welfare state. Although Marx called him "a veritable phenomenon in the history of political economy," amazingly there has never been an edition of his collected works nor, with all the immense flood of scholarly research and Ph.D. theses, has anyone written a book about him. He is not even mentioned in Beer's *History of British Socialism.* Most information about him is to be found in the final chapter of Édouard Bernstein's *Cromwell and Communism.*

II

The Near East
and Russia

 In the Near East, where it first appeared, the communal life of the neolithic village has endured, been warped and crippled by the invasions of the State and an external economy, to the present day. Until the Second World War or until the discovery of oil in the vicinity, life in an isolated village in the Middle East went on very much as it had for eight thousand years. So it is not surprising that communalist movements have come and gone in the very birthplace of the centralized State, nor that they have failed, since the larger economy based on irrigation, regional granaries, and national planning of agriculture demanded a centralized administrative apparatus.

The official Persian religion, Zoroastrianism, could be considered a reflex of the centralized State of the Near East, with its palace system and its absolute monarch. The *yasnas* of the *Zend Avesta* contain many maxims directed against communism, disrespect for

155

nobles, pacifism, and the nomadic freebooting community, yet communalist tendencies were there, working underground, to emerge in the religion of Mazdak in the latter years of the Sassanian dynasty.

Mazdak was born toward the end of the fifth century and his preachers spread his doctrine so rapidly over Persia that they soon converted large numbers of important people and eventually King Kawaz himself.

For Mazdak the source of all evil was due to the malevolent action of the devils, Envy, Wrath, and Greed, who had destroyed the primitive equality and community of man. Mazdak's disciples held all things in common including, according to their enemies, women. Like most heretics they were accused of indulging in sexual orgies. On the other hand they were also accused of extreme asceticism, vegetarianism, and the refusal to take life under any circumstances. Communism was not incidental to Mazdaism, but central. The greatest of mortal sins were those of possessiveness and violence, and the greatest virtues were those of the community of love.

We have inadequate information as to what happened following the conversion of the king, but the social effects must have been drastic and supposedly led to his temporary deposition by his brother Jamasp. On his restoration his son, later Khusraw I (Chosroes I), tricked Mazdak into coming to court with all his disciples to receive Khusraw's formal submission and public profession of the new religion. As the Mazdaites entered one of the royal gardens to partake of a great banquet, each group was seized and buried head downward in the earth with their feet protruding. Khusraw then led Mazdak through the garden and said, "See the crop which your evil doctrine has brought forth," and had him buried, head downward, in the midst of his followers.

The massacre, which took place in A.D. 528, did not exterminate the sect. On Khusraw's accession three years later a new persecution broke out and the Mazdaites were hunted throughout Persia. However, a remnant seems to have continued underground, to pass on their doctrines and practices to the strange sects which broke forth from the Ismailians and Assassins, themselves schismatics from the main body of Islam. For his efforts in defending orthodox Zoroastrianism Khusraw was given the title *Nushirwan-Anushak-Ruban* —"of immortal spirit"—and is still venerated by the Persians as a saintly hero.

It is unfortunate that we know practically nothing of the details of what after all was a major historical episode. Zoroastrian, Muslim, and Christian sources, though some of them are by eye-witnesses, substitute abuse for economics and sociology. We know even less of the communism attributed to the inner circle of the earlier Manichaeans whom their opponents called Zandiqs, who corresponded to the Cathari amongst the later European Albigenses descended from the Manichaeans. Amongst the Zandiqs communism seems to have been practiced by an elect minority who chose to follow counsels of perfection similar to the Christian monks. Far more than Mazdaism, which flourished only within the limits of the Sassanian empire, Manichaeanism, and later Gnosticism, profoundly influenced the development of Islamic heresy. Since, most especially in its early days, Islam partook of the character of an immense band of nomads led by caravan merchants, raiding the settled societies on its ever-expanding perimeter—a war of the steppe against the sown—there was always an element of piratical communalism in its social ethic and to a lesser degree in its practice. Although Mohammed was a merchant and spoke for the mercantile communities of Mecca and

Medina, the distinction between raiding Bedouins and trading merchants was hazy. The latter had evolved from the former and remained dependent upon them. The difference, an essential one, was between loot and profit. The nomad band shared loot; the merchant kept his profit for himself. So those communities of Islamic heretics who practiced communism were usually pirates of the desert and the steppe, or, like the Assassins, a secret society of extortionists.

Yet the source of most Islamic heresy lies not in the main body of Mohammedanism, Sunnism, the religion of most Arabs and of the lands they conquered and held, but in the Shia, the religion of Persia. The Shiites reject the notion of an elected caliph and of a clergy that functions as a kind of rabbinate with a body of law always subject to discussion—like the Talmud—in favor of an hereditary caliphate descending from the prophet through Ali, the son-in-law of Mohammed, through a line of divinely ordained successors, the seven (or the twelve, depending on the sect) Imams who come to acquire the character of direct emanations of the deity. In Persia the line also descends from the last of the Sassanian kings through the daughter of Yazdigird, Harar, the gazelle, the wife of the martyr Husayn, and the mother of Ali Asghar. Thus combined in one hereditary line are the mystic divine incarnation of the Persian King of Kings, the Hellenistic *Basileus ó Soter,* the incarnation of Ahura Mazda, and the divinely sanctioned caliphate, all together as an emanation of the deity. The final Imam is hidden, only to appear at the end of the world, and is represented before the world—a saviour or Mahdi, himself usually inaccessible and represented before the people by *dais,* missioners—who carry on their propaganda clandestinely. Sometimes the Mahdi and Imam are identified, or in the Fatimid dynasty in Egypt, function as actually ruling caliphs. Amongst the

Ismailians the final vanished Imam is the Seventh, Ismail, on whose reappearance, like the Second Coming of Christ, the world will come to an end. In most Ismaili sects he is the final emanation of the series of seven, not to be confused with the Seven Imams who are all spiritually identical, but of a Gnostic, metaphysical character, similar to the Aions of Gnostic Valentinian or of the Sephiroth of the Jewish Kabbala. We are dealing here with an emanationism, a soteriology, and an apocalypticism which goes back to the dawn of recorded religion in the Near East—for instance, to the Egyptian "Memphite theology," and finds analogues in Mahayana Buddhism. The resemblance to the prevailing form of Zoroastrianism, a religion which has varied widely under the Sassanids immediately before the Muslim conquest, and even more to its heretical expressions, is pronounced. Shiism has been called the revolt of Persia against Arabic Sunnism, although Shiism flourished for a time in Egypt, and even as far away as Spain and Indonesia. It is the present religion of Persia, and of the Ismailis in India, whose Mahdi is the Aga Khan.

Both in structure and in doctrine most advanced forms of Shiism are like Chinese boxes, a hierarchical government becoming ever more inaccessible, and an occult religion, an inclusive series of mysteries whose final secret is that there is no mystery. The appeal of such a religion and secret society is immense, especially when it is coupled with actual worldly power.

Contemporaneously with the establishment of the Fatimid dynasty at the end of the ninth century in Tripoli and the conquest of Egypt in 972 A.D. the closely related sect of the Carmathians developed in the lower end of the Mesopotamian valley and along the northwestern shores of the Persian Gulf. The orthodox Sunnite Abbasid Caliphate in Baghdad was preoccupied

with a great revolt of Negro slaves, the Zanj insurrection. The Carmathians attempted an alliance with the
Zanj leaders. This proved to be impossible, but they
were able to pursue a parallel opposition and after the
suppression of the Zanj revolt the Carmathians not only
were in secret control of the northern shores of the Persian Gulf, but had organized subversion in Yemen,
Syria, and even Baghdad itself. In 900 A.D. the troops of
the caliphate were defeated at Basra and from then on
the Carmathians controlled Bahrayn, sometimes
Basra, and many other towns between Mesopotamia
and Arabia, cutting the pilgrim routes to Mecca, and
usually the sea connections of Baghdad. Here they established what was probably the only communist society to control a large territory, and to endure for more
than a generation, before the twentieth century.

The Carmathians also raided the pilgrim caravans to
Mecca, often killing thousands of people, and laid siege
to cities as far away as Damascus, where they seem to
have had a considerable body of secret followers. Finally they attacked Mecca itself and carried away the
sacred Black Stone, the holiest object in Islam, as well
as immense loot (928 A.D.). Within Bahrayn itself there
was a complete absolutist communism. The citizens
paid no tribute or tax; their welfare was guaranteed
from birth to death, in sickness or health. All hard, menial, or unpleasant work was performed by Negro
slaves, who seem at first to have been the defeated remnants of the Zanj revolt who fled to their quasi-allies
and voluntarily chose slavery with the Carmathians
rather than extermination with the Sunnites. The orthodox accused the Carmathians of community of wom-
en and all manner of orgies. As a matter of fact they
were strictly monogamous, a military caste something
like Plato's guardians or the Teutonic Knights, who led

a pure, severely regulated life. The use of wine and all minor vices were strictly forbidden. Women were unveiled and circulated freely in public and enjoyed considerable influence. The specific ordinances of Islam, however, were not enforced, not even the Friday meeting, the daily prayers, or the eating of food that was taboo. The esoteric practices of Mohammedanism were replaced by a cult of Light, a contemplative mysticism related to Sufism, and very like that of the greatest Sufi theologian, Ibn el Arabi. Like the Sufis the Carmathians dressed exclusively in white and placed great emphasis on moral and physical purity. We are still in the world of the Essenes, the Therapeutae, and the Light by Light emanationism of Philo Judaeus. If any of the accusations of their persecutors or any of the secret traditions of the occultists are true of the Knights Templar, this is their source.

In 1084 A.D. Bahrayn was overthrown, but another branch of the Ismailians, a new brotherhood of mystery and adventure, the Assassins, arose, far to the north in Syria and on the Caspian Sea. Based on a series of fortress communities in remote desert and mountain areas, of which Alamut was the most famous and the longest lived, the Assassins functioned all through the period of the Crusades as a secret brotherhood of extortionists—and assassins—who terrorized the entire Near East. They were able to extract loot, exert political influence, and exact obedience from Christians and Muslims alike. The authoritarian communism of the Carmathians gave way to a pure authoritarianism in which the rank and file were supposedly controlled by a kind of mass hypnosis induced by the excessive use of hashish, hence their name, Hashishim. Their fortresses were destroyed and they were exterminated almost to a man by the Mongols under Hulagu, who seems to have specially hated them. After the Grand Master of Alamut was captured, sent to Hulagu, but escaped, they survived as the followers of the Aga Khan.

The Carmathians and the Assassins are the first clear examples of a communal mutual-benefit society living on the plunder of other communities. Such a body can only be interstitial and function in the gaps between classes in a highly organized State, or on the marches of two antagonistic States, or on the borders over against less highly organized societies. This is the communism of the urban gang or the roving band of robbers in times of social disorganization—like the band immortalized in the Chinese novel, *The Water Margin (All Men Are Brothers)*, and, of course, in the tales of Robin Hood. The Carmathians flourished in the march between the fundamentally antagonistic Arab and Persian civilizations. The Assassins were the most famous of several similar esoteric religious communities who lived by plundering their neighbors along the northern borders of Persia, in the Caucasus, along the Caspian, and across the Oxus, and in what is now Afghanistan.

Before the Crusades, Islamic civilization was incomparably higher and wealthier than that of Western Europe. The Crusades themselves were a species of religious brigandage, just as Islam had been, when the Bedouins and traders of Arabia looted the Byzantine Empire. So it is not extraordinary that the type of organization invented by the Carmathians and Assassins should pass to the Crusaders. The Knights Templar and the other military orders were at the beginning similar, authoritarian, communist societies, of religious bandits distinguished only by their vows of celibacy.

If we are to accept anything of the charges made against the Templars when they were suppressed by Philip the Fair in 1307, they had copied not only the organizational structure of the Assassins but also their

THE NEAR EAST AND RUSSIA · | · 163

graded esotericism, leading to skeptical deism and accompanied by rites and practices the orthodox considered blasphemous and obscene. The Templars were accused of spitting on the cross upon initiation, institutionalized pederasty, and nocturnal orgies, but they were suppressed because they had become the wealthiest organization in Europe and a state within a state, independent of both kings and papacy, as well as an immense corporation of "international bankers."

On the shores of the Baltic and into the interior, the Teutonic Knights were organized similarly to the crusading military orders except that they were fixed to specific territory. As the Templars had succeeded to the Assassins and Carmathians, so the Teutonic Knights were successors to the pagan Varangian communities that dotted the waterways from the Baltic to the Black Sea, fortified communities of Scandinavian trader-warriors amongst the more barbaric populations of Finns, Letts, and Slavs. They seem to have practiced the economy of robber bands, sharing the wealth, but with the biggest share going to their chiefs. They were not celibate like the Teutonic Knights. Their women were slave concubines taken from surrounding peoples, and in some instances seem to have been immolated on the death of their chief and master. One of their principal commodities of trade with the Byzantine and Persian Empires were blonde slaves. The Varangian colonies of greater Russia never managed to unite to form a single Scandinavian state, although they laid the foundations for the Kievan monarchy, and even the Romanovs pretended to be descended from them. However, for a while, in the Viking period, the Jomsvikings from their fortress city of Jomsburg somewhere on the southwestern shore of the Baltic (the site has never been certainly identified) functioned as a state on equal terms with Norway, Sweden, and Denmark.

The Mongols' conquest destroyed the Scandinavian power in Russia and the settlements on the Baltic withered. As the Mongols overwhelmed the interior and destroyed Slavic and Varangian domains alike at the beginning of the thirteenth century, the Teutonic Knights shifted their activities from the Holy Land to pagan Prussia where they subjected the Finnish and Slavic population in genocidal war, and eventually came to control the entire southern shore of the Baltic.

This type of predatory, parasitic, mutual-benefit association would drop its communist, and to a certain degree its religious, characterstics and emerge at the beginning of the capitalist epoch in the great Oriental trading companies, the Dutch and English East India Companies and similar joint stock, chartered bodies of combined military brigands and traders.

In such society juridical or implicit contractual relations, which prevail between the members and are scarcely felt, are exchanged for the warm fraternity of men united by constant danger and the hope of wealth without hard labor. Obedience, loyalty to the death, devotion of self to the cause, sacrificial help to brethren in distress, flourish far more in a society of bandits than amongst the refined citizens of a stable community. Such a body grew in antagonism to the values of the societies outside itself, whether more civilized or more barbaric. It gained strength by presenting a mysterious face to all outsiders, and developing onerous rites of initiation and grades of advance. In the highest circles, which deliberately trained and manipulated the lower ranks, complete skepticism usually prevailed and when one was admitted to the governing, final council, the last secret was revealed to be that there was no secret. Another characteristic of such a society was the merciless purge of all members from bottom to top who could not adapt to sudden changes of rule or policy. Community depended upon absolute obedience and in the most perfected form authority continuously narrowed until it vanished in a pinnacle, the metaphysical principle of authority itself. Such societies, whether Templars, Jesuits, or Bolsheviks, have always filled the surrounding greater societies with terror, been the subject of horrifying legends, and subjected to ruthless persecution.

Scientific historians dedicated to unemotional weighing of evidence, and usually committed to a social gospel of liberalism, have almost always dismissed the charges of outrageous and obscene conduct brought against secret societies, heretical groups, and occult movements as products of the diseased minds of their accusers. Partly this is due to prior commitment to the doctrine of the inherent goodness of man. Many pages have been devoted to proving that the Carthaginians did not sacrifice babies to Moloch, that pederasty has never been known on Mount Athos, or that the witches were just crazy old women. One can reject the evidence if one wishes, but there is certainly a mass of it to the contrary. The witches of Europe and New England may have confessed under torture to things that they did not do, but all over the world in Asia, Africa, and primitive America witches and shamans still do precisely those things.

•

The social relations that prevailed in the neolithic village community in the fertile agricultural regions bordering the great Eurasian steppe from the plains of the Danube basin across the Ukraine and into Siberia—what American ecologists would call the long grass prairie climax—endured for millenniums, in a sense down to the twentieth century. The environment was such as to permit an exceedingly stable mixed farming, with a basis of small grains, and the sedentary domestication of animals for meat and milk. Such communities were subject to continuous raiding from the nomadic pastoralists who ranged over the great sea of the steppe beyond them. Most centralized states were imposed on this peasant community by the nomads, and came and went in a few generations, as other nomads pushed them aside.

A way of life endured in a typical Ukrainian or Great Russian village from as far back as there are archaeological traces, until the imposition of serfdom in the modern epoch, and proved singularly resistant to the special Slavic form of feudalism and its later serfdom. The Slavic peasant community survived even the abolition of serfdom and the only partially successful attempts of the State and the new upper classes to "free the serfs" and establish a wage-labor and sharecropping agriculture—which would permit the primitive accumulation necessary to capitalist development. Even the long struggle of the Bolsheviks to industrialize agriculture, abolish the small communities, and substitute agricultural towns on vast collective and State farms has never been completely successful. The collectivized agriculture of modern Russia, however highly rationalized and communalist it may be in theory, lags far behind the productivity per capita and per acre of Western European, much less American, large-scale agriculture, and so far has proved to be less productive than the old time, two-hundred acre, mixed farming of the American Middle West. This is true although the Slavic lands, but most especially the Ukraine, include some of the most fertile soils in the world.

Thousands of years ago, when man first entered these regions, he developed a way of life, and with it a kind of community, almost perfectly adjusted to this special environment, and all attempts to change it have only brought about disorder, inefficiency, and demoralization. For fifty years every Soviet or Party congress has had to face a permanent agricultural crisis, however the facts may have been disguised with oratory. Russian literature and revolutionary theory, except for Marxism, is full of a mysticism of the Russian peasant community. Typically the Socialist Revolutionaries, the majority Party of the Russian Revolution, hoped to reorganize Russian society in forms developed from the peasant community, the mir, or even the upper-class community administrative unit, the zemstvo—in other words they envisaged a kind of peasantization of the entire industrial and civic structure. This is in fact what the early Soviets really were, and they had grown up spontaneously in the 1905 revolution amongst workers, citizens, soldiers, and sailors, a majority of whom had come, in one or two generations or less, from peasant villages.

Certainly the peasant community was highly idealized by the entire revolutionary populist movement, from *Narodnaya Volya*—"the People's Will" of the nineteenth century—to the Socialist Revolutionaries. Thousands of educated young men and women "went to the people" in the belief that if only the peasant were educated he would spontaneously produce a special Slavic communism which would redeem industrial society—eventually all over the world. The brutal facts of peasant life are well enough shown in the stories of Chekhov, and it is probable that the leftist Social Revolutionaries would have found it as difficult to introduce a neolithic village ethic into modern factories and banks as the Bolsheviks have found it to industrialize agriculture. Still the fact remains that communal forms whose origins were lost in the most remote antiquity appeared quite naturally, though briefly, in the 1905 Revolution, and in the 1917 Revolution until the Soviets and farm communes were suppressed by the Bolsheviks in the two years after their seizure of power.

In modern times, of course, the Slavic village community was not communist. It was very far from sharing all things in common. Poverty and grinding exploitation made the peasant desperately rapacious. However, Russian dissent is characterized by an over-all drift to communism. Russian Anabaptism appears in history about the same time that it does in the West —during the sixteenth century—but, as in the West, there are indications that it led a clandestine occult existence dating back to the first centuries of Christianity in Russia. The two leading Baptist sects, the Doukhobors and Molokani, have continuously budded off communalist groups which were usually ruthlessly suppressed, however harmless and insignificant. This process has continued in the immigrant communities in Canada, South America, and the United States, but none of the schismatic movements has endured very long. There are a number of extreme sects which somewhat resemble the Gnostics and Manichaeans, and may be related to the Paulican-Bogomile-Cathari-Albigensian movement that spread in the Middle Ages from Asia Minor to the south of France. Other groups like the Khlisti and Skoptsi, ecstatic orgiastic cults, who nevertheless are celibate to the point of emasculating themselves, bear more resemblance to the Mandeans of the Mesopotamian marshes, or to some of the more extreme cults which have developed out of Shiite Islam, than they do to Christianity. The peasant background and the savage persecution they have suffered has often created an enforced communism amongst them, but they never established permanent communities where all things were held in common.

After the Hutterites and Mennonites were settled in Russia they had a certain influence on the peasant society about them. There still exist Russian-speaking Anabaptists who are essentially Mennonites, although if there were ever purely Russian communities which followed the strict Hutterite communist way of life they are unknown. In the first years after the Bolsheviks took power they had hoped to use the inherent communalism of Russian dissent in the development of a program of communal farms, as distinguished from collective farms, and for a while such farms, both secular and Dissenter in leadership, flourished in spite of bureaucratic meddling. With Stalin's drive for the collectivization of agriculture, the first Five-Year Plan, and the suppression of all political dissent as "Trotskyism," both communal farms and Dissenters were suppressed, and the former were liquidated. During the great purges probably fifty per cent of all Russian Dissenters were exterminated, and most especially those whose way of life could be interpreted as political heresy.

Of all those who idealized both the Slavic peasant community and the inherent communalism of the Russian Dissenter by far the most influential, more influential as a single person than any populist party, was Leo Tolstoi. Under his inspiration many little communities of intellectuals dedicated to communism, pacifism, vegetarianism, and a secularized mystical religion sprang up here and there in Russia in the late nineteenth and early twentieth centuries. Often, like the Polish Anabaptists, landowners turned their estates into communes, invited their bohemian friends from the city, and urged "their" peasants to share in the building of nuclei of a new society in the womb of the old. As might be expected, few of these lasted more than a couple of years and their tragi-comic stories

make pensive reading today. Although there were
many such communities and a few of them were successful, there is no history of them in any Western
European language, unless Czech is classed as such.
Both the Yugoslavs and the Czechs during their brief
period of intellectual freedom have shown great interest in all aspects of the history, religious and secular,
peasant and industrial, of communist groups and
movements.

A special Russian development of the late nineteenth
and early twentieth centuries was the establishment
by wealthy industrialists, who were also great landowners, of heavily subsidized communities of artists.
These, of course, however strong their community life,
were far from being economic communist groups. They
included some of the leading artists of pre-revolutionary
Russia and they had a profound influence on Russian
art and indirectly at first through the *ballets russes,*
and then, through their emigrated former members,
upon modern painting in the West. The famous
Bauhaus, almost all of whose leaders were free communists and many of whom had been in Russia in the
first, exciting, pre-revolutionary years, was for its short
life under the Weimar Republic an attempt to realize
the disappointed hopes of the Russian Constructivists,
Comfuturists, and other modernists for a community of
artists which would by its work and teaching revolutionize the mind of capitalist society. Alas, Hitler
destroyed the Bauhaus and dispersed the artists, most
of whom became very capitalist industrial designers
and architects in the United States.

12

Early Communes in America

A seldom mentioned, but very important, chapter in the growth of religious communalism was the degeneration and decline of Roman Catholic monasticism and the consequent disappearance of many social services. There were more hospital beds, for instance, in many European cities at the beginning of the thirteenth century than there would be again until well into the twentieth, and what we now call "social work" was entirely a function of the medieval sisterhoods. With the Counter-Reformation a new kind of monasticism was established, dominated by militant, highly disciplined orders of clerics regular, like the Jesuits, who were outside the organic community in a way that the monks and friars had never been. They operated on it, rather than from within it, and there was no significant role, much less a determinative one, left for lay brothers or women.

This development was more or less conscious or deliberate. The papacy and the papal theologians had learned ever since the fourteenth century to distrust the great popular movements of lay monasticism and communal mysticism which had grown up especially in the Rhineland and the Lowlands and all too easily lapsed into heresy. To this day the Béghards and Béguines, the Brethren of the Common Life, Meister Eckhart, Jan Ruysbroeck, Henry Suso, Nicholas of Cusa, Thomas à Kempis, and Angelus Silesius are frowned on by the strictly orthodox; and though some have acquired the title of blessed, none has been declared a saint, and all of them have had at least some "theses" of their teachings condemned.

Almost all the pre-Reformation advocates of the return to the apostolic life, such as the Anabaptists and the Pietists, believed at least in the ideal of the devotional community—contemplative communism—at least for those of their members who felt a special calling, a religious vocation, to what was in reality a new and reformed monasticism. Since these groups led a harried life in the interstices of the cities, or for short periods under the defiant protection of some nobleman or noblewoman on an isolated country estate, and were subject to furious persecution by both Catholics and Protestants alike, it was exceedingly difficult for them to sustain community life for any length of time, even in those areas of Europe, like the lower Rhine, where they found most popular sympathy.

The earliest colonization of America offered even less opportunity for the establishment of community than did Europe. The Spanish and Portuguese colonies were subject to their own local Inquisition and even unfortunate Indians were occasionally burned alive for heresies of which they had never heard and could not possibly conceive. Persecution was not so violent in New France. Due to the ignorance of the ordinary colonists and the corrupt cynicism of the upper classes, dissent scarcely came into existence and dissenters deported from France seem to have vanished. The English colonies were no better than the Spanish. Virginia was strictly Anglican. Massachusetts was strictly Independent or Puritan and did not stop persecuting Quakers and divergent Protestants until well into the eighteenth century. Things were different in what are now the Middle Atlantic states, New Jersey, Delaware, Maryland, and Pennsylvania, in the beginning settled by the Swedish and the more liberal Dutch, which had been explored by prospectors for the Quakers and similar sects. When Pennsylvania was given to William Penn in 1682 and opened for colonization with guarantees of absolute religious liberty, a strain of hope ran through all Pietist and Apostolic Europe. Penn travelled on the continent recruiting settlers and the largest immigration so far to what is now the United States began. The Quakers predominated. Eventually the majority of English Quakers migrated, but the Mennonites and Moravian Brethren came too, and a great variety of German Anabaptist sects, most of whom united in the New World as the German Baptist Brethren.

The first Communist colony was established by the followers of Jean de Labadie more or less independent of Penn's settlement of Pennsylvania but under his influence and at exactly the same time. This was Bohemia Manor.

Labadie was born in 1610 at Bourg near Bordeaux and ordained a Jesuit priest; but his pastorate was in Switzerland, the Low Countries, London, where for a while his influence on the Separatist churches was quite extensive. His doctrines included community of goods, mystical marriage, millenarianism, celebration of the seventh-day Sabbath, and the setting aside of a celibate elite. Descartes was familiar with his ideas and if there is anything to the mysterious signature René Descartes R.† C., Labadie may have incorporated some of the ideas of the Rosicrucian Brotherhood assuming—which has been disputed—that such a group then existed. Persecuted by the authorities, Protestant, Roman Catholic, and Anglican, the sect moved its headquarters several times to Herford, Bremen, Altona, West Friesland where they survived with communities scattered through the Lowlands until well into the late eighteenth century. They first sent a colony to Surinam whose governor was a patron and possibly a member. He was murdered in 1688 and the colony removed to Bohemia Manor on the Chesapeake where the first of their settlers had already proceeded.

Bohemia Manor had been patronized by Augustin Herrman, a sympathetic landholder from Bohemia (whose son was a member) but who later repudiated the sect without being able to reclaim his property. The leader of the colony from 1683 was Peter Sluyter, who seems to have been a religious confidence man of the type that would bedevil religious communalism throughout its history in America. Sluyter died rich and dissolute in 1722. The colonists, over one hundred people, on the other hand, lived lives of the strictest poverty, chastity, and obedience. Men and women were separated for meals and worship. The day and much of the night was spent in hard labor, silent or chanted prayer, and meditation. Diet, clothing, all living conditions, were as ascetic as could be borne and all proceeds sent into a common fund controlled by Sluyter. Before his death the land was distributed and private property permitted, but all profits still went to the common fund and the community life remained just as onerous. Between 1727 and 1730 the colony broke up and during the next ten years the churches in Europe returned to the Dutch Reformed Church—and not, interestingly, to the Mennonites—where they engendered a widespread spiritual revival.

On trips through the Rhineland and the Lowlands, Penn invited all German Quakers, Mennonites, Anabaptists, and other Pietists to migrate to his new land. The first to go was a large contingent of German associates of the Society of Friends led by Francis Daniel Pastorius in 1683 to settle around what is now Germantown. They were shortly followed by a Mennonite and Schwenkfeldian immigration which included the apocalyptic, millenarian disciples of Johann Jakob Zimmermann, who died on the day his followers were to sail. Leadership was assumed by his first lieutenant Johannus Kelpius, an extraordinarily learned man, deeply read in philosophy, mysticism, and theology, both orthodox and occult, and an acknowledged Rosicrucian. Kelpius proved his powers by stilling the waves in a violent storm. The colonists debarked at Bohemia Landing and went on to the neighborhood of Germantown on June 24, 1694. According to Zimmermann the apocalypse was only three months away.

The colonists celebrated midsummer night with rites that were a strange mixture of occultism, paganism, and Pietist Christianity and soon set out about building the Tabernacle of the Woman in the Wilderness crowned by the rosy cross, to the astonishment of their simpler or more conventional neighbors.

The mystical number of forty colonists settled down in their forty-foot-square building to watch and pray and await the coming of the rebirth of the world. Kelpius set himself up as an anchorite in a nearby cave. The community of both men and women was strictly celibate and life was at least as ascetic as amongst the followers of de Labadie. They differed primarily in their much greater learning, even sophistication. In fact, it would be well into the nineteenth century before any

religious communist colonies would recruit such cultivated people. They have been called superstitious, but
indeed they were anything but. There is a vast difference between the superstitions of the illiterate and the
occultism of the over-educated.

The tiny colony endured until 1748 and before that
period its cultural influence on Pennsylvania was out of
all proportion to its numbers. They produced the first
book of hymns to be published in America, and many
other examples of the earliest printing, including
a study, with vocabulary, of the Lenni Lenape Indians—whom they believed to be one of the lost tribes
of Israel—the first book of its kind to be done in English
America. They taught school and were in great demand
as skilled craftsmen and builders, even architects.
Time was spent in hard labor, choral and solitary
prayer, meditation, and, unlike other such groups, in
the study of the classics of mysticism and occultism
from Hermes Trismegistus to Meister Eckhart, Jacob
Boehme, and the Kabbala. Curiously enough their interest in astrology and alchemy led them to chemical
and physical experiments and to watching all night
long through their telescopes for the signs of the Second
Coming. A direct line stretches from them to the scientific activities of latter-day Philadelphia, made famous
by the experiments of Benjamin Franklin.

The great weakness of the Woman in the Wilderness
(their own name for themselves was "the Contented of
the God Loving Soul") was the shortfall of their
prophesies beginning with Zimmermann himself who
said that the millennium would come at the autumn
equinox of 1694. The date passed and the Second Coming had not come. Also they believed they would never
die. But Zimmermann died before they set out. The pre-
cociously brilliant Kelpius died at thirty-five in 1708
and the last leader, Conrad Matthaei, in 1748. By 1750

the community had been absorbed into the general society of Quakerism and German Pietism, on which it left traces which endure to this day.

In 1720 Conrad Beisel and three companions left Europe intending to join the Woman in the Wilderness. When they reached the colony they discovered that Kelpius was dead. Most of the members had left and those who remained were lost in contemplation while the Tabernacle fell into ruins around them. On the way to Ephrata the four men had stopped in Conestoga where Beisel was baptized by the German Baptist Brethren and soon rose to become assistant leader of their colony. Beisel was a Seventh-Day Baptist. After long discussion the Dunkards decided to continue celebrating Sunday so Beisel left with his followers to found, in 1735 on the Cocalico River, the colony of Ephrata, one of the most successful and longest lived intentional communities in the world.

At first the Ephratans were the most ascetic of the groups so far founded in America. Men and women lived together as celibates. They dressed in an adaptation of the Franciscan habit, alike for both men and women. The women's hair was cut short and the men were tonsured but wore full beards, which they tugged vigorously in greeting one another. Food was extremely meagre, mostly dry bread or porridge. They used no iron whatever and as little metal as possible; buildings and furniture were pegged, dowelled, and mortized. Eating utensils were of wood and many cooking utensils of pottery. Like the Benedictines before them, they rose at midnight to sing matins, and again at five for a second service. Meals were held in silence while a lector read from the Bible. Communion was proceeded by washing each others' feet. They each made a written confession of sins weekly which was read in choir by Beisel. Every clear night they took turns watching the heavens through their telescopes for signs of the Second Coming. At first they did not use horses but pulled their own ploughs and carts, carried their own freight, and walked wherever they went.

In spite of this vigorous asceticism they lived lives of considerable creativity, learning, and aesthetic satisfaction. Beisel wrote poetry and composed hymns of a singular beauty, as did some of the others. The musical idiom of the Ephratan hymns (which are still sung) is unmistakable. They produced many books in their peculiar scholarship, most of them printed by Christopher Sauer, including Sauer's Bible, the first in German in America.

Almost immediately the colony began to prosper. Penn offered them an additional five thousand acres but they refused because such riches would distort their spiritual life. For a while after the arrival of the three Eckerlin brothers the colony added a number of industrial enterprises, milling and small manufacturing, which became so successful that the members revolted and expelled the Eckerlins. In the course of time branches of Ephrata were established around the British colonies. The monastic community dwindled and most of the members incorporated themselves into a regular church, the German Seventh-Day Baptists, which still exists. A small number of Ephratans have continued to practice a limited communism, and specially devoted members take care of the various buildings which have become historic monuments and teach others the choral art of Ephrata. In recent years there have been attempts on the part of the new communalists to revive the ancient Ephratan community but so far without much success.

Ironically the Harmonists or Rappites are remembered mostly as the predecessors of Robert Owen's colony at New Harmony. The Owenites lasted in their pure form scarcely any time at all. New Harmony managed to commit most of the mistakes possible to an intentional community and ended in a series of financial disasters. The Rappites flourished, became exceedingly prosperous, and, although they are no longer communists, their descendants can still be found in or near the old communities.

George Rapp was born in Württemberg, son of a small vineyardist, probably in 1757. At the age of thirty he became a Separatist-Pietist preacher, and gradually accumulated around himself a small sect which was persecuted by Lutherans and Calvinists alike. In 1803 he went to Baltimore seeking refuge from persecution for his people and bought five thousand acres of still wild country in the Conoquenessing Valley north of Pittsburgh. In the following year over seventeen hundred men, women, and children were settled on the land and had organized the Harmony Society, at first as a cooperative, but almost immediately as a communist community. The men were mostly hard-working, practical farmers with considerable skills as builders and mechanics. In an extraordinarily short time, a little over two years, they had produced a flourishing, almost self-sufficient community. Each family was housed in its own home; there was a church, a school, a grist mill, a large community barn, carpenter and blacksmith shops, a saw mill, a cannery, a woolen mill, a distillery and wine cellar, and five hundred and fifty acres planted in wheat, rye, tobacco, hemp, flax, vineyards, and poppies for sweet oil. Grazing in the uncleared land were cattle, milch cows, pigs, horses, and the first merino sheep in America. Most of their whiskey and brandy they sold, but they drank light wine at each meal.

After ten years, when the colony had become rich and flourishing, they decided to move because the land was not suitable for the production of satisfactory wine and in addition lacked water communication with the outside world. They had already in 1807 adopted celibacy as a general rule although husbands, wives, and children continued to live together in separate family houses with so little strain that they have amazed everyone who has ever written of them. In later years they often adopted children.

In 1814 they bought thirty thousand acres in the Wabash Valley in Indiana and sold the first settlement for one hundred thousand dollars, a vast sum of money for those days, but probably no more than the value of the improvements on the land. By 1815 they had all moved to Indiana and a greatly improved village was rising around them. This was Harmony, later to become famous as Robert Owen's colony. Once again they flourished. But in another ten years they decided that the site was malarial and the farmers around them were antagonistic. In 1824 they sold the town and twenty thousand acres to Robert Owen for a hundred and fifty thousand dollars and moved back to near Pittsburgh on the Ohio River and established a final settlement, the village of Economy, which endured until the beginning of the twentieth century.

In less than twenty-five years they had built three well-equipped towns and cleared many thousands of acres, a unique record not only for an intentional community but for any kind of settlement. The Rappites owed their success to the kind of people they were, skilled German, mostly Swabian, farmers, vineyardists, and mechanics, who were satisfied with what would have seemed to the intellectuals, as we would call them today, of the Woman in the Wilderness, a very low-pressure utopia. It needed only hard, skilled work for them to establish and preserve a community which satisfied them.

Father Rapp was a man of great charismatic power but he was also gifted with common sense. Belief in the imminence of the apocalypse and the Second Coming and the millenarian kingdom may seem cranky, even ignorant and vulgar, to most people today. But there was nothing very eccentric about such beliefs in the first half of the nineteenth century. It was quite possible to hold them and yet be considered intellectually respectable. And of course they were demonstrably the beliefs of the first generations of Christians and probably of Jesus himself. Furthermore, as Albert Schweitzer has demonstrated in our own day, an "eschatological ethic" is a remarkably effective rule of life—"live as though the world is going to come to an end in the next twenty-four hours."

George Rapp provided the spiritual and moral leadership—the "father image"—and his adopted son, Frederick Rapp, was at least as effective as an organizer, administrator, and businessman before the Rappites ever left the Wabash. The younger Rapp had established outlets for the products of the community throughout the settled Mississippi drainage and had agents as far away as New Orleans. After George and Frederick Rapp had both died the colony was equally lucky in the trustees and administrators it chose.

As the numbers dwindled the Rappites closed down many of their small shops and invested largely in railroads and when the community finally dissolved it was still rich. Their efficiency is well shown by the success they made of silk and wine. In those days sericulture and viticulture bankrupted many an American farmer. For years the Rappites planted their steeper hillsides with mulberry trees, raised silk worms, and spun and wove and tailored their own garments of silk. They are certainly the only communists who habitually went clad in silk. When eventually sericulture became completely unprofitable and time-consuming they had the good sense to abandon it.

Only once was the even tenor of their ways disturbed. A manifest rogue, Bernard Müller, who called himself Count Leon, wrote from Germany that he and his followers had been converted and wished to join the colony. When he arrived he turned out to be a military man and a wastrel who immediately tried to seize control of the finances. It took the non-violent ascetic Rappites a little over a year to get rid of him and his followers whom they bought off with more than one hundred thousand dollars. One-third of the colony left with Müller and established a settlement ten miles away and in less than a year lost all their money; whereupon they attacked Economy with arms, but were driven off by a posse raised among the neighboring communities. Bernard Müller and a few of his people left for northern Louisiana, where he died of cholera.

The Count Leon episode was a godsend to Economy because it served to purge those who were not sincerely committed to the Rappite way of life. From then on to the end of the century no other serious factional disputes arose. To this day the descendants of the community still get together for anniversaries. Many of them still live in the neighborhood of Economy, and others near the industrial colony Economy founded at Beaver Falls. The church in Economy still stands and the Evangelical Lutheran congregation numbers several descendants of the Rappites. But it primarily enshrines the memory of Robert Owens' unsuccessful community rather than Father Rapp's eminently successful one which built most of the surviving buildings.

The group of Separatists from Württemberg who settled the village of Zoar in northeastern Ohio between thirty and forty miles south of Canton in 1817 were closely related to Rapp's community. They were, however, more radical in their rejection of the dominant society. They did not vote. During the Civil War they remained pacifists. Although they permitted marriage within the group and lived in families, they were much more ascetic in life style. They were also possibly less well educated, and Joseph Bäumeler was much more of a spellbinder than George Rapp.

When they arrived in America the Separatists were not definitely committed to a communal way of life, but adopted it as the most efficient way of dealing with the wilderness. As long as they were communists they prospered with a woolen factory, two large flour mills, a saw mill, planing mills, machine shop, cannery, dyehouse, their own common store and general store for the surrounding farmers, a popular summer resort hotel, a wagon factory, a blacksmith's, carpenter's, tailor's, dressmaker's, and shoemaker's shop, a cider mill, a brewery, and looms for weaving linen, as well as seven thousand acres of prime farm land in Ohio and a settlement in Iowa. Eventually their industries were to employ a considerable number of outsiders and some of their farms were let to sharecroppers. In 1874 there were three hundred members with property worth considerably more than a million dollars. The town of Zoar was noticeably rougher, cruder than any of the previous settlements with poor dwellings and plain community buildings and church. Bäumeler died in 1853 and the colony slowly declined. In 1898 they abandoned communism completely and almost immediately thereafter failed economically in all their enterprises. Little is left of Zoar today.

Although "Doctor" Keil had migrated to America from Prussia in 1835, Bethel and its daughter colony Aurora were the first intentional communities to be gathered in America. In Germany Keil had been a milliner with ambitions for the stage. He was self-educated

in occult and mystical literature, Boehme, Paracel-
sus, and Cagliostro. In New York and Pittsburgh he
flourished as a hypnotist, faith healer, and purveyor of
mysterious elixirs and potions whose recipes he said he
found in an ancient book written in human blood. He
was converted to Methodism, made a melodramatic
penance for his years as a charlatan and *Hexendokter*,
and publicly burned his bloody pharmacopeia.

But Keil soon left Methodism and founded his own
sect which disdained to call itself by any name, but
which opposed all churches and denominations which
had departed from the communal, apostolic life of the
"true Christ," the Central Sun. Keil remained a melodramatic actor to the end of his life, and the congregational worship of his group was far more hysterical than
even the most extreme of his predecessors. Daily life in
the commune was simple and unadorned, but Keil provided his congregation with many holidays and festivals, celebrated with food, drink, and dancing, to which
all the surrounding settlers were welcome.

Keil's first colony was founded in 1844 in Bethel,
Shelby County, Missouri, then on the wild frontier, and
included the remnants of Count Leon's followers. In a
fairly short time they had a well-equipped town and
were farming four square miles of land. In 1855 Keil
decided Missouri was filling up, and the colony moved
to Willapa in what is now the state of Washington. The
heavy rainfall and dense forest were too much for them,
and they soon moved to the Willamette Valley in
Oregon, where they deliberately avoided the more fertile plain and settled in the forest, so that they would
have plenty of lumber to build their town. As the colony,
called Aurora, prospered they were able to buy out the
farmers on the plain. Bethel and Aurora repeated the
history of the other communities as long as Keil was
alive and they shared all things in common. They pros-

pered and in fact became rich. After he died they divided the property and assets amongst themselves and soon disintegrated.

Aurora and Bethel represented another step down, except for their many festivals, in richness of life satisfaction. The communities were simply not well educated enough and were too self-satisfied to produce another leader like Keil. "Professor" Christopher Wolff was the leader of the second contingent to travel, in 1863, from Bethel to Aurora. He seems to have been a bookish man familiar with Cabet, Baboeuf, Fourier, Proudhon, Wettling, and Marx. As such he only bewildered the rest of the colonists and never seems to have played an important role in Aurora. However, he is notable as the first person to appear in the history of religious communalism familiar with theoreticians of secular communism. It is curious to speculate on what his life must have been like, isolated amongst semi-literate peasants on the most remote frontier.

If the previous leaders of religious communalism in America were increasingly charismatic personalities, the founder of Bishop's Hill, Eric Janson, was personally apocalyptic. He did not believe in the Second Coming of Christ. He believed himself to be Christ come again. The sect began quietly enough in Sweden under the leadership of Jonas Olson, who was a disciple of the first Methodist missionaries from Great Britain, as an association of Pietists who met in one anothers' homes for preaching and devotions and Bible study, and who eventually came to call themelves Devotionalists. They were almost entirely confined to the province of Helsingland and were mostly peasants and self-employed mechanics and artisans. They went along quietly enough for seventeen years as a Pietist movement within the Church of Sweden.

In 1843 Jonas Olson gave lodgings for the weekend to

a traveling dealer in flour. This was Eric Janson, who was thirty-four years old and who from the age of twenty-six had experienced a series of trances, illuminations, and messages, and who had already broken with the Lutheran Church. He seems to have been a man of violent personality and intense charisma. Outside observers in later years thought that he acted like a madman. His effect on Olson was revolutionary. He became the spiritual leader of the group, although Olson remained the practical manager, and he moved them steadily toward the most extreme form of Wesleyanism, a far more "pentecostal" religion than it is today. The established Church responded with relentless persecution and the Devotionalists were driven to becoming a separatist sect. Their conventicles were broken up and they were excommunicated and eventually arrested again and again. In retaliation they burned the theological and devotional works of orthodox Lutheranism in a great bonfire. Janson was arrested and released only due to the influence of the king. After his second book-burning he was arrested again; and after six arrests, a fugitive with a price on his head, he was forcibly freed by his followers and smuggled through the mountains to Norway, from whence he went to Copenhagen and finally New York. In July 1846 he arrived in Victoria, Knox County, Illinois, where he had already sent Olaf Olson to find a suitable location for the community.

By this time Janson had come to believe himself the Christ of the Second Coming, sent to redeem the true Church which had been in captivity since the Emperor Constantine, and to build the New Jerusalem in America's green and pleasant land, from whence the millennial kingdom would spread throughout the earth. The sect in the meantime had become far more a movement of poor peasants and proletarians, at the best only semi-literate. Remarkably enough Janson nevertheless retained the loyalty of most of the original members who, one would have thought, were too well educated to accept his increasingly extravagant claims.

Olaf Olson and Janson bought a tract in Henry County, Illinois, about forty miles southeast of Rock Island, and named it Bishop's Hill after Biskopskulla. Eleven hundred Jansonists gathered in Swedish ports to leave for America. One boat load was lost at sea, another wrecked off Newfoundland. Of the first boatload of immigrants to arrive in October 1846, many walked from New York to Illinois and all except the weaker women and children tramped one hundred miles from Chicago to Victoria in the beginning of winter. They continued to leave Sweden, which they believed an angry God was about to destroy once their saving remnant had left, until four hundred were settled in the first year at Bishop's Hill.

The land was ideal. Some of it was cultivated and the rest extended in unbroken prairie and a little woodland, but the accommodations were appalling—two long houses, four tents, a sod house, and twelve dugouts. The dugouts were used as dormitories, terribly overcrowded and with no proper sanitation. The mortality was frightful. In the first year they had very little food. One hundred and fourteen people died of cholera in a single fortnight. Yet they persisted in spite of the nightmare conditions. Colonists continued to arrive and slowly new buildings were built and more land was bought and cultivated.

At the end of the second year there were eight hundred settlers. They had their own grist mill and saw mill and were busy manufacturing adobe bricks. Eventually they would have a brick kiln and a pottery. They erected a four-story brick house, one hundred by forty-five feet, extended it another hundred feet, and then a large frame church. The first summer they harvested with scythes, the next year with cradles, the third year with reapers. All their methods improved at a similar rate. Already in 1847 they grew flax and manufactured over twelve thousand yards of linen and carpet matting. Sometimes the looms, worked by women and helped by children, were running night and day. When they closed out the linen business, except for home consumption, due to commercial competition, they had sold over one hundred and fifty thousand yards of material. Again and again they were attacked by cholera. No other colony of the time seems to have suffered so severely, and this is a good indication of the chronic lack of proper sanitation and general cleanliness. In these first years Jonas Olson seems to have played a less active role and Janson was both spiritual and economic leader. Everything was done under his direct supervision, and he represented the community in the markets of Chicago and St. Louis. At the same time he became more and more extreme in his prophetic, pentecostal behavior.

In 1848 the colony was visited by an adventurer, John Root, a Swede, recently discharged from the army of the Mexican War. A less likely person for such a colony is hard to imagine but he was welcomed by Janson and soon assumed the position of leadership, and married one of Janson's cousins with the written agreement that if he ever left the colony she could remain if she wished. He spent his time hunting and roistering in the nearby town and was suspected of the murder of a Jewish peddler. Later he disappeared for several months while his wife gave birth to a child. When he returned, Root attempted to take his wife away against her will. Eventually he kidnapped her, but was caught by a mounted posse of Jansonists. He went to court and was given possession of his wife and took her to his sister in Chicago who notified the colony. Again a mounted posse set out and stationed some of their number in relays along the road to Chicago. Again she was rescued. With Root and his cronies in pursuit, she was rushed back one hundred and fifty miles to Bishop's Hill, without a stop except to change horses. Root twice organized a mob who besieged the village and attempted to burn the buildings, but were driven off by an armed posse of settlers and neighboring farmers. Janson was brought to trial for kidnapping and keeping a wife from her husband in Cambridge, the county seat. As he left for court he had a premonition that he would never return. The day before he had preached his most powerful sermon, and in the evening distributed the Lord's Supper. During the noon recess of the court Janson was standing by a courtroom window when Root appeared in the doorway, called his name, and shot him dead. It was the thirteenth day of May, 1850. The colony was less than four years old. Usually when so powerful a leader died the communist colonies, whether religious or secular, disintegrated or passed to individual ownership. The contrary was the case with Bishop's Hill.

At the time of the murder, Jonas Olson was on his way to California, sent by Janson to dig for gold. He returned immediately to Bishop's Hill, with the consent of the community, setting aside Janson's son and heir, his guardian and his wife, and assumed leadership. Under the new charter the commune was administered by seven trustees under the leadership of Olson. For a while the community thrived. The village was cleaned up, the land more efficiently farmed, several small industries started, and contacts made with the Oneida Perfectionists, the Rappites, and the Shakers. Janson's widow left and became a Shaker. In 1854 under their influence Olson decided the community would become celibate but continue to live in families, a move that

led to resignations, expulsions, frustration, and factionalism among those who remained. As the country
became more densely settled and penetrated by railroads and canals the society became fairly wealthy and
one of the trustees—Olaf Johnson—took over its financial operations. By 1860 his speculations had brought it
to the brink of bankruptcy. In 1861 the property was
divided and the communist Bishop's Hill ceased to
exist. By 1879 the Johnsonites and anti-Johnsonites
had sued one another into poverty and only three
hundred inhabitants lingered on in the decaying village
to the end of the century. A remarkable thing about the
Bishop's Hill community is that, although it did everything wrong from the very beginning, it survived and
prospered until corrupted by free enterprise, which
proved far more deadly for its existence as a community
than ever did cholera.

13

Amana, The Shakers, St. Nazianz

With the exception of the Hutterites, by far the most successful of the religious intentional communities has been Amana, the Community of True-Inspiration. Its roots go back as a distinct group to the seventeenth century. But its sources are to be found in the late medieval monasticism of the Rhineland and the Low Countries, the Béghards and Béguines. The Amana society was comprised of pentecostalists in the strict meaning of the word. They believed and still believe that the prophetic and apostolic inspiration of the Spirit of God continues to possess selected men and women and to inspire them with his word and will to act as messengers of divine teaching to the world.

The first Inspirationist groups came out of the Pietist movement in Lutheranism toward the end of the seventeenth century under the leadership of a noblewoman, Rosemunde Juliane of Asseberg, the first Inspired Instrument (*Werkseuge*), followed by Johann Wilhelm Peterson, a professor at Lüneberg, whose hymns and prophetic utterances are still used. The movement had died down for a few years and then was revived by Eberhard Ludwig Grüber and Johann Friedrich Rock who separated themselves from the Lutheran Church in 1714 and established, in the face of violent persecution, Inspirationist conventicles throughout the Rhineland, Switzerland, and the Low Countries. After their deaths no new *Werkseug* appeared for over fifty years.

In 1817 M. Kraussert of Strassburg was inspired but could not persist in the face of persecution and was succeeded by Barbara Heinemann, an illiterate peasant girl, and Christian Metz, a carpenter. Barbara Heinemann was expelled for having "too friendly an eye upon the young men," returned, married, lost her inspiration for twenty-six years—regained it, and accompanied Christian Metz to America. After his death she was to be sole oracle until 1883 when she died at nearly the age of ninety. There has been no generally accepted Inspired Instrument since, but the divine utterances of all the Amana prophets have been recorded, beginning with Rosemunde Juliane, and are read in church and consulted as equal to the Bible for direction in every imaginable contingency.

Christian Metz gave the True Inspiration societies a strong, practical organization in congregations governed by elders, and established cooperative colonies which, although not fully communist, shared the profits of their small enterprises through a mutual fund from which anyone could borrow without interest. The colonies thrived, but they were continuously harassed because they refused to send their children to the public schools, to bear arms, to take oaths, or in any way cooperate with the wordly State. In 1842 they sent a committee to America which bought five thousand acres of the Seneca Indian reservation to which they added later another four thousand. In the next three years some eight hundred people came over, cleared the land, and built four villages, each with a store, church, school, and community enterprises, to which they later added two more villages in Canada.

They called all their villages Ebenezer—Upper, Middle, Low, and so forth—and themselves the Ebenezer Society—"Hitherto hath the Lord helped us" (I Samuel 7. 12). They had not originally planned anything more extreme than a cooperative economy, but they found absolute communism the most efficient way of coping with the wilderness. Although the Indians had sold the land for ten dollars an acre, a high price in those days, they refused to evacuate it and caused the colonists considerable annoyance. Also the city of Buffalo was growing so rapidly that its outskirts were beginning to approach the colony. (The site is now well within the city of Buffalo.)

So in 1854 they decided to move out to what was then the frontier, where they could live untroubled in their own way. After considerable prospecting they bought what eventually became twenty-six thousand acres of land, twenty miles from Iowa City in one of the most beautiful and fertile sites along the banks of the Iowa River. Here they eventually established six villages which they named Amana (Glaub Treu, Believe Faithfully) and incorporated themselves as the Amana Society. All the details of this immigration were done under the direct inspiration of Christian Metz. Inspiration dictated the paragraphs of their charter, as it had dictated to Grüber their rule of life, and recorded inspiration took care of all the details of settlement, government, and economy. What eventually emerged was a community living under what they considered divinely revealed law, something like a combination of the Torah, the law books of the Old Testament, and the Rule of St. Benedict with all its commentaries.

Amana had an ideally charismatic leadership—the Instruments were, when possessed, literally anointed by the Spirit of God and spoke with a divine authority surpassing that of *hadith* or Talmud, the sacred traditions of Muslims and Jews. From these oracular utterances there was no appeal. When not possessed, the Instruments sank back into their human role as practical administrators. Metz at least seems to have been as gifted an administrator as Father Rapp. Amana was so well organized, and eventually the charisma was so well distributed throughout the community, partly of course due to frequent consultation of the mass of written tradition, that it was able to survive the death of Metz, and then of Heinemann and the passing of Inspiration altogether.

Communism of both production and consumption was complete, although it soon became necessary to hire outside labor at peak seasons. Very early Amana developed a large variety of industries and crafts, so that the colony became almost self-sustaining. In addition, it produced a number of specialties, at first mostly textiles, for export with the return of a capital surplus—a very favorable "balance of trade." With all of its industrial activities Amana remained solidly founded on agriculture, exporting large agricultural surpluses. The community functioned like a small capitalist nation, with a complete circulation of capital, profitable export, and a rising, rather than a falling, rate of profit.

Families lived separately in their own homes, but neighborhoods dined together in local dining halls and "kitchen houses." The children were educated in community schools in both English and German. School lasted all day and all year, although the time was divided into periods of study of secular subjects and religion, trade apprentice work, and organized play. Women wore black bonnets, gray dresses, and a kerchief folded across shoulders and breasts. Men wore work clothes except for church.

Of all the successful colonies the Amana villages seem to have been least concerned with aesthetics: the houses were unpainted, the streets unpaved, and the villages had a generally dishevelled air. The women compensated for all this by growing flower gardens. However, in the mid-century visitors remarked that the flowers were interspersed with vegetables. Commitment was reinforced by public confession and daily private examination of conscience. Jobs were commonly rotated and there were a considerable number of collective tasks involving the entire village from harvests to various working bees. Artistic expression except for the singing of hymns was discouraged and forbidden. Amana produced no famous bands, like Father Rapp's colonists or semi-pagan festivals like William Keil's, or the Mormons' music, or architecture or "socials"; much less the ecstatic, emotional rituals of the Shakers.

Amana was a stolid, low-pressure utopia. Although the True Inspirationists had started off with a number of intellectuals and minor aristocrats in their ranks, by the time they had reached Iowa they had become a community dominated by simple, unimaginative German peasants and workers who found sufficient satisfaction in farming, working, and worshipping. Persisting in a life of as-simple-as-possible satisfactions, they grew rich. In 1933, a hundred years after coming to America, and almost two hundred and fifty years after the first beginnings of the movement in Germany, they returned to private enterprise, and set themselves up as a church and a business corporation. Forty years later Amana was one of the leading manufacturers of domestic utilities in the United States.

•

The Shakers, who called themselves the United Society of Believers in Christ's Second Appearing, or The Millennial Church, are usually considered the most successful of all the American religious communalists sects. They could as easily be described as a lay monastic movement, more akin to similar unorthodox groups known from the late Middle Ages but with roots that go back to the heretical cults of the beginning of the Christian era, not only in their rule of life but in their theology, both of which featured millenarianism, a divine avatar, convulsive group ecstasies, echolalia, and speaking with tongues. At least at first, with no knowledge of the ancient heterodox traditions, they managed to unite and revive most of them, and in addition they introduced what had hitherto been a non-Christian, in fact a non-Western, belief in possession by the dead. They anticipated modern spiritualism by several decades and their foundress was a shamaness of a primitive, Oriental type. Their compulsive ecstasies, which gave them their popular name, and their ritualized dancing and whirling can be traced back through a definite continuity to at least the fourteenth century. Strangely enough, and hardly remarked, these were common practices amongst both American Indians and Negro slaves. Robert Manning of Brunne in his *Handlyng Sinne* tells in "The Tale of the Kolbeck Dancers" the story of a classic episode in one of the dance manias of the later Middle Ages that swept like pandemics over Western Europe. Our popular term for chorea, St. Vitus's Dance, survives from those times. Modern commentators have tended to attribute these medieval phenomena to ergotism—St. Anthony's Fire—due to eating moldy rye, but their organized character would indicate a heretical religious base like the various flagellant movements. Although ergotism may have been a contributing factor, convulsionary ecstasies were common but unorganized amongst small heretical groups, ancestors of the Quakers, in England and the Low Countries in the sixteenth century, who were also reputed to practice community of goods and either celibacy or sexual orgies. Holy Jumpers and Rollers were found amongst the first conventicles of the Methodist revival, especially in Wales. Similar practices swept over France in the eighteenth century, both within and without the Roman Catholic Church, with their focus in Flanders and Brittany where the dancing manias of the Middle Ages had so often originated.

Early in the eighteenth century a group of Quakers in Manchester, led by James and Jane Wardley, were converted to the doctrines of the French Prophets or Camisards of Dauphine and Vivarais, who more or less systematized an inchoate movement. The Wardleys in turn converted Ann Lee, the twenty-two-year-old daughter of a Manchester blacksmith, who soon became the leader of the group. She was frequently imprisoned for jumping, shouting, dancing, disrobing, and blasphemy, and while in prison had a revelation that the millennium had in fact arrived, and that the time had come to gather the saved remnant out of the doomed world. It followed that the Second Coming too had already arrived and around 1770 her followers began to refer to her as "Ann the Word," the incarnate Woman Christ, the female half of the eternal syzygy. (In Shaker theology, as it developed, all spiritual entities were male and female united in mystical union —the ancient Valentinian Gnostic doctrine.)

Ann Lee was married against her will to Abraham

Standerin, whom the Shakers called "Stanley," and bore him four children, all of whom died in infancy. She began to dictate extensive revelations and was finally "ordered" to take a select group of her followers to America—eight or ten people, mostly relatives, but including a moderately wealthy man, John Hocknell. For two years they supported themselves by common labor in and around New York.

In 1776 Hocknell bought a large tract of undeveloped land at Niskayuna in the township of Watervliet near Albany and the Shakers settled into their first colony. Watervliet and nearby New Lebanon were to remain the motherhouses of the society until its dissolution in the twentieth century. During the Revolutionary War they were subjected to mild persecution as pacifists and refusers of oaths, but were soon let alone by the authorities and neighbors. Considering their extraordinary behavior it is remarkable how little persecution the Shakers ever suffered. Unlike many pentecostal and millenarian sects, the Shakers were a peaceable people and had carried over from Quakerism the gift of the soft answer that turneth away wrath.

During the Revolutionary War other communities were established in New York, Massachusetts, and Connecticut; and in 1784, when Mother Ann died, her little church was flourishing and gaining recruits at every revival. For three years they were led by James Whittaker. On his death he was succeeded by Joseph Meecham who was at least as richly endowed with the gift of revelation as Mother Ann; and by Lucy Wright, who shared the leadership and after Meecham's death ruled alone for twenty-five years. Its rule, or rather its revelations, gave Shakerism its final form and its extraordinarily detailed regulation of community life.

Mother Ann's husband seems to have been an unregenerate rascal and in New York City he took to drink and ran off with another woman. Her children had died in early infancy after painful births. Thus the essence of Mother Ann's revelation was her detestation of sexual intercourse, for which she substituted a cosmogony of spiritually united male and female beings, which she also described as bisexual with, as it were, male and female polarities. From the early days of the movement her followers were called to practice celibacy if unmarried, or the strictest chastity if they came into the sect already married. Mother Lee was the female incarnation of an eternal Christ of which the historic Jesus was the male, not the incarnate deity or the Second Person of the Holy Trinity but a primary emanation. Both celibacy and these semi-divine couples are common to many religions, Christian and pre-Christian, Persian, Manichaean, Gnostic, and Tantric, but celibacy was usually a privilege of the elect, the pure. Mother Ann made it mandatory for all her followers.

The necessities of colonization on the edge of the wilderness had led to the practice of cooperative enterprises verging on communism. Under the leadership of Meecham and Wright the strictest communism was introduced; and progressive revelations were embodied in laws which governed every detail of life, even as to which foot should get out of bed first. Men and women lived in the same large, dormitory-like buildings of a characteristically severe architecture, many of which still survive, but they were strictly separated with different staircases and entrances. They were forbidden to speak to one another except under the most pressing necessity or with the rare permission of the elders and eldresses. Each residential building constituted a "family." There was complete equality of men and women in both administration and worship. Some Shaker villages contained four or five such families, self-governing and rather widely separated. Eventually Shaker villages were scattered from the Atlantic coast to Ohio and Kentucky and south to Florida.

Although the surviving documentation of the Shakers is far greater than that of any other communal sect it is difficult to discover exactly how the entire body was governed from the mother foundation in New Lebanon. After the middle of the nineteenth century certain differences began to develop. The villages in Maine, for instance, emphasized faith-healing. In others possession by the spirits of the dead, which originally took place in almost every evening service, had declined sharply and was beginning to be accompanied by a certain skepticism.

The early Shaker leaders possessed a remarkable instinct for rules and devices which would intensify commitment to the community and diffuse particular attachments. The neophyte made a detailed confession of every sin and fault before being accepted by the society and periodic confession was enjoined for even the most minor transgressions. Since life was so carefully ordered, many elderly Shakers at the end of the century told interviewers that they had been able to live for many years without sin.

Both men and women wore uniforms—the men wearing a broad hat and long blue coat, with hair cut off in front and long behind. The women wore voluminous dresses of dull colors with a kerchief across the breast and back, a light cap indoors, and a deep sunbonnet outdoors, and underneath hair cut short. In some families there was a strictly limited visitation. Small groups of men and women seated on opposite sides of the room under the governance of an elder and eldress were permitted a recreation of brief chatting which was carefully controlled to avoid all significant content. In some families men and women were paired, and the women functioned as a kind of *soror mystica,* to give each other spiritual guidance. Men and women worked at separate tasks, usually at separate buildings, and ate at separate tables in silence. Daily life was carried on with a minimum of speech, almost as great as in the strictest monastic orders. And like the Trappists, Shakers often communicated by simple sign language.

The Shaker buildings were famous for their extreme cleanliness and the stark simplicity of their furnishings, this at a time when ordinary furniture was more ornate than ever before or since. There were no carpets and only a few small rugs, and every morning the ladder-back chairs and little rag rugs were hung on pegs; and all the floors were cleaned and polished and the beds which had been stripped and the bedding aired by each person on arising were made up by a cleaning crew. In spite of this emphasis on outward sanitation several villages made no provision for baths whatever and some were struck by small epidemics of typhus, due of course to body lice.

No pictures or musical instruments were permitted until late in the decline of the society, no poetry from outside, no novels, not even history, which would bring in the long story of the evils of the world—the small libraries contained books of the strictest practicality, and only religious works which were closely akin to Shakerism, and the society's own literature, which grew ever more extensive. Some families and many members of all families were vegetarians—pork, alcohol, even light wines, smoking tobacco (hopeless addicts were permitted to chew a little), and usually tea and coffee were all prohibited.

The days were spent in strict asceticism. After supper the evening worship was certainly the greatest ritualized collective discharge of libido of any American communalist sect, with parallels to be found only in the trial testimony of medieval heretics in the anti-heretical polemics of the orthodox, and in (probably imaginary) secret pagan religion, which modern occultists attribute to the witchcraft cult.

After hymns and brief sermons by one of the elders or eldresses, men and women lined up on opposite sides of the room and began a peculiar shuffling dance, accompanied with motions of the bent arms something like using a rolling pin (Parkinsonism), meanwhile chanting hymns, often in "strange tongues," some of them traditional, others spontaneous. In some families and at some times the ranks of men and women would pass each other and everyone would embrace and kiss. Descriptions of these contacts by the participants always speak of them as accompanied by the most intense waves of love conceivable. Interestingly, no one, even in exposés by former Shakers, speaks of these embraces and presumably orgasms as having anything specific about them. The embracing couples focus the love of the community. As the evening wore on dancing in rank gave way to lines and ring dances and then to paired and single gyrations of the kind a later day would call jitterbugging.

Finally the spirits would possess one, two or three young women and speak through them. These spirits were commonly those of great historical figures —Napoleon, or Julius Caesar, or the heroes of the republic, like George Washington and Benjamin Franklin, or most especially famous Indians. Often a whole tribe of Indian spirits would visit a Shaker meeting. As time went on the Shakers undertook regular missions amongst the dead, sending out their spirit converts to preach the Shaker gospel to all sorts of bygone people but especially to the American Indians, who if they had enjoyed few of the advantages of Christianity in their lifetimes, at least when dead were converted by the thousands and established their own Shaker communities in the spirit world. Spirit visitations of this sort always amazed flesh-and-blood visitors because the entire Shaker meeting seemed possessed with a collective hallucination and went through elaborate psychodramas, dancing and conversing with their guests, giving them imaginary food and drink, and listening to their inaudible music. Psychodrama is the only word we have for such activity because it is impossible to accept them as genuine hallucinations; and Shaker leaders often admitted to outsiders that they were really make-believe. Entertaining whole tribes of Indians was only a small part of it.

Shaker communities had annual rites and drank imaginary nectar from imaginary fountains and feasted on imaginary ambrosia while dressed in imaginary garments of blinding splendor. The resemblance of all this to Haitian *vaudon* (voodoo), the juju cults that survived on some slave plantations in the United States, and to the original religions of West Africa is certainly remarkable. No one has ever demonstrated any contact although fairly large numbers of freed Negroes were converted to Shakerism. On the other hand there are also resemblances to the cult practices of the Iroquois, neighbors of many early Shaker communities. Modern Spiritualism arose in the same neighborhood and it is disputed whether the first "spiritualistic" phenomena occurred amongst the Shakers or the self-professed spiritualists.

Since these performances occurred with greater or less intensity every night in most communities and culminated in periodic great festivals, it is not difficult to see the advantage they gave the Shakers over every other communalist movement. Twenty hours were spent in the strictest discipline, even sleep was governed by rules; but every evening each individual libido was poured out into the community. Then if ever a collective unconscious was made manifest. Love was dissolved in community. George Washington dancing with the sisters, quaffing ambrosia while Squanto played the fiddle—this may strike us as ridiculous, but such were the materials for orgiastic myth available to the Shakers. They made as much of them as the Greeks of Bacchus and Orpheus.

Like the Greeks before them the Shakers tamed the irrational and harnessed it to the rational community. Away from the meeting, life was lived with mathematical order. Although they renounced all art and decoration, their strictly functional architecture and furniture are amongst the most beautiful of their kind. They found it necessary to restrain the success of many of their industrial enterprises. They were the first in America to practice intensive agriculture. Eventually many Shaker communities raised only high-quality seeds and breeding stock for the market.

It is rather difficult on the surviving evidence to determine how the society was so efficiently governed. All officials, administrators, business representatives, and religious leaders were appointed from the top. They were subject to a minimum of control by community meetings, more perhaps by "revelations," although revelation never played the consistent, determining role that it did at Amana. So autocratic a system of government, especially over small communities scattered from New Hampshire to Kentucky when much of the country was still wilderness, would be expected to result in factionalism and schism; yet in the case of the Shakers it did not. In both secular and religious governance the Society led an unusually untroubled life.

All through the middle years of the nineteenth century, under the leadership of Frederick W. Evans, who before his conversion had been a secular reformer and communalist, the society flourished, reaching at one time to more than six thousand members in twenty villages. Celibacy, which had been a most important factor in their strength, eventually proved their undoing. Their doctrines were too barbarous to be etherealized by a more literate and sophisticated generation or to draw converts from the class of people otherwise attracted to Shakerism; and so they could not replenish themselves. Married converts brought their children into the society with them and every Shaker village was amongst other things a free orphanage which raised unwanted children at no expense to the State. The children were raised as Shakers but most of them left as soon as they were employable elsewhere. By the middle of the twentieth century the society, which for many years had consisted of less than a hundred aged people, was to all intents and purposes extinct. The great revival of communalism which began after the Second World War focused new interest on the Shakers and there recently have been attempts to revive the society.

•

With the example of medieval religious orders, of monks, nuns, and associated lay people living in community before them, one would expect that at the height of the communalist movement in the first half of the nineteenth century there would have appeared Roman Catholic communist villages both in Europe and the United States; but there are very few examples, and indeed it is difficult to find out anything about them. Primarily this is due to the extremely reactionary character of the Church in the nineteenth century. Anything suggesting the preaching of community of goods was condemned as heresy, one which was an even graver threat to the wealth and power of the Church than it was to theological orthodoxy. A widespread movement for return to the apostolic life might have had devastating effects on the Church of the nineteenth century. In America the Church was more orthodox than the popes, and after the Irish Potato Famine and the troubles in south Germany the American church was founded on largely illiterate or semi-literate congregations of recent immigrants. Since most of the early historians of the communist societies in America were millenarian Protestants or secular socialists, they were anticlerical on principle, and therefore often ignored the existence of the one Catholic communalist settlement in the country.

In 1854 Ambrosius Oschwald, a Catholic priest, led a band of colonists from the hills of Baden and the Black Forest to Manitowoc County, Wisconsin, some hundred miles north of Milwaukee. They purchased some thirty-eight hundred acres of dense wilderness at three dollars and a half an acre and set about clearing the land and building two convents for celibate men and women and a village of family dwellings for married people. They called themselves the St. Nazianz Colony after St. Gregory of Nazianzus, the fourth-century theologian who led the return of the Eastern Church from Arianism to strict orthodoxy, and who was the founder of the so-called Cappadocian school of theologian-philosophers who are responsible for the lingering influence of the apostolic life and the mystical doctrine of the divination of man in Eastern Orthodoxy. St. Gregory held an archbishopric for only a short time and retired early from the conflicts of ecclesiastical politics to his own extensive estate where he established a mixed community of monks, nuns, and lay people about which we know little. The historians of communalism give no evidence of knowing who the patron saint of the colony was, or why he was chosen, but it is of the greatest significance that he was the favorite father of the Church of many of the great mystics of the Rhineland and south Germany. For such were the spiritual ancestors of the pre-Reformation Pietist movements out of which came, however indirectly, almost all the religious communist sects of America—as well as, for instance, the Tolstoyan movement.

The St. Nazianz Colony flourished as long as Father Oschwald was alive. The land was fruitful and produced surpluses for the market. The members manufactured almost all their own necessities: food, clothing, tools, furniture, again with an exportable surplus. The celibate members lived under a rule similar to the Third Order Regular of St. Francis, the married members as fully dedicated Third Order Seculars. All took part in the daily liturgy of the Church. The community was essentially governed by the sacraments. Confession and penance were sufficient to insure order and holy communion to preserve commitment. Not unlike the Shakers they were held together by cult, by ritual that had its sources in practices that went back before the time of civilization and sprang from the deepest layers of the human mind. Father Oschwald and an ephorate of twelve members saw to the administration of the material affairs and moral welfare of the community and their decisions were subject to review by meetings of the whole. The community seems to have functioned with singularly little friction.

On the death of Father Oschwald, it was discovered that the property, which had all been held in his name, could not be left by his will to the colony because it was not a corporation. Thus the members incorporated as a Roman Catholic religious society and each member sued the estate for his share due to past services and then returned it to the new corporation. They continued for another generation under a board of trustees, wearing the simple peasant dress of the eighteenth-century

Black Forest, their lives governed by the sacraments, the liturgy, the rites of passage, and the rites of the year, but toward the end of the century they began to die out. Like the Shakers, they had adopted orphan children but few of these remained with the community after they grew up. The village of St. Nazianz still exists, but of all the successful religious colonies in the United States it is by far the least known.

There was another, apparently very similar group near Milwaukee, called Nojashing, led by Fathers Anthony Keppler and Matthias Steiger, who came from Bavaria in 1847. They both died four years later, but the colony endured to the end of the century. At this time it became an order of sisters. Some significance should probably be attached to the fact that these two ventures found their homes in Wisconsin, where the Roman Catholic Church—and the Anglican as well—were far more radical than elsewhere in the United States and where schismatic groups like the Polish National Church, the Old Catholics, and others found a home. The very "advanced" Anglo-Catholic Bishop Griswold of Fond du Lac often spoke wistfully of his hope that the revival of the mixed order of St. Gilbert of Sempringham would take place in his diocese, but it never did. Thus the colony of St. Nazianz remained the only successful attempt to transport to America the kind of communist society made famous by the Jesuit communes in Paraguay.

14

Oneida

Millenarianism, chiliasm, pentecostalism—we are inclined to think of these terms as applying to movements in a religious underworld of theological proletarians, of semi-literate people—in fact, much like the early Christians. John Humphrey Noyes, born in 1811 in Brattleboro, Vermont, the founder of the Oneida Community, and a sect known as the Perfectionists, was a graduate of Dartmouth who turned first to the study of law and then to theology at Andover and later at Yale. Under the influence of the revivalist movement he underwent an experience of spiritual conversion and came to believe that it was possible for men not only to be saved but to become perfect—or perfected—in this life. Intensive Bible study accompanied with much meditation and prayer convinced him that this end could be achieved best by a literal following of the apostolic life.

In 1834 Noyes returned to Putney, Vermont, where

his father was a banker, married the granddaughter of a congressman, and slowly gathered about himself a group of persons, at first mostly his close family, who followed him not only in belief but in undergoing the same experiences and convictions, and in spending their time in Bible study and prayer. In the course of ten years the little group of perfectionists worked out the main body of their doctrines, and gained a few converts and correspondents throughout New England and New York. In 1846 they began to live together holding all things in common. At this point they aroused the wrath of the citizens of Putney and were driven out of town.

In 1848 the Perfectionists purchased forty acres and a poor house near Oneida in northern New York, and in the next couple of years established branches in Brooklyn and Wallingford, Connecticut. At Oneida the land was poor, the buildings were tumbling down. At first there were fewer than a hundred people, who were able to bring comparatively little money to the founding of the community. However, they soon got the land under production, added more acreage, and were able to feed themselves, whereupon they embarked upon a carefully planned program of small-scale diversified industrial development. They sold farm crop and cattle, put up fruits, vegetables, jellies, and jams, made furniture, raised and wove silk and wool, made traveling bags and matchboxes, and ran a saw mill and blacksmith shop. In the latter they began to make, at first by hand, traps of their own invention and this eventually became the most profitable of their manufacturing enterprises, before they took up the silversmithing which as a private corporation still continues.

In 1874 the full members at Oneida and Wallingford (Brooklyn had been moved to Oneida) numbered two hundred and nineteen adults, about twenty per cent more women than men, sixty-four children, and about two hundred and seventy hired farm laborers, fruit-pickers, and workers in the shops, including thirty-five women and girls in the silk mill at Wallingford; and in addition to this they employed a considerable number of domestic servants. In 1873 they had sold over three hundred thousand dollars worth of produce and manufactures. In other words, in twenty-five years the Oneida colonists had become modestly rich, were able to employ help on a ratio of more than one employee to one adult colonist, and to live lives with a higher level of satisfaction both materially, culturally, and spiritually than any other religious colony. Oneida seems to have been a thoroughly enjoyable place to live. This remarkable success was probably due to the high quality of the colonists themselves and especially to their leader, a man of truly exceptional intelligence and will, the product of the best education of his time, who believed in not asking anyone to do anything he could not do himself and so worked as farmer, blacksmith, administrator, cattle-breeder, and, at one time or another, in all the other enterprises of the community.

Viewed from the perspective of late twentieth-century secular culture, thoroughly skeptical of science as well as religion, John Humphrey Noyes may seem to be a crank. Of course, anyone who belonged to a communalist group by definition was something of a crank. But it should be remembered that in the first half of the nineteenth century the foundation of education and learning and life philosophy was still for most people, however cultivated, the Bible, especially in America. The founding fathers may have been radical intellectuals, and amongst them there may have been a few rationalists and deists, but the majority of educated Americans, particularly after the reaction against the French Revolution, were devout Christians. Noyes was a devout Christian, but he was also a radical and

212 · | · COMMUNALISM

rationalist Christian who, in his little study group in Vermont, set about trying to discover exactly what the word of God meant. If the New Testament was approached in this way, with a mind consciously shorn of preconception, it seemed obvious that apostolic Christianity was millenarian, chiliastic, pentecostal—and communalist.

Oneida was in many ways a mirror image of the Shaker communities, with methods of building group commitment which might seem to have been direct contraries to Shaker practices. Most famous was Oneida's special form of group marriage. Everyone was available to everyone else, but the actual pairing of couples was under the guidance of the community, ultimately it would seem of Noyes himself, and the unions were usually relatively short-lived. Coupled with this group sex ("complex marriage") was Noyes's special discovery of "male continence." Men were expected to control themselves in sexual intercourse until the woman had one or more orgasms and then withdraw, apparently without ejaculation. This sounds like a nerve-wracking custom but in fact, as has been demonstrated by various erotic yogic practices, it is quite possible for a man to train himself to separate orgasm from ejaculation. The functions are controlled by two different sets of nerves. Also in some of Noyes's writing on the subject he seems to be talking in a very occult manner about oral sex. The significant thing is that the entire community practiced birth control by withdrawal and was committed to the sexual pleasure of women—most extraordinary notions for the mid-nineteenth century. Noyes continuously stresses his, one is tempted to say, "startling discovery" that the sexual act has two functions, procreation and pleasure—the greatest pleasure in life. Sometimes behind his rather cryptic language he seems to have stumbled on a kind of Tantrism, the erotic mysticism of the sexual trance.

As the colony matured Noyes, who as we have seen was a successful cattle-breeder, introduced the idea of controlled eugenic breeding, which he called stirpiculture. Only those people who were judged to be the best breeding stock with physical and mental qualities which, if developed genetically through the generations would produce a superior race, were allowed to have children. Noyes and a special committee, after long observation in the community, picked them out and instructed them to mate, whatever their previous unions may have been. Today such practices have become identified with extreme reaction, but perhaps the future will decide that one of the greatest evils of Nazism was discrediting eugenics. Once, after it was popularized by Noyes, eugenic reform was a common belief and hope of almost all social radicals.

Noyes was a food mystic too, and most of the people in the community were vegetarians. Only two meals a day were served. They drank tea and coffee, but no alcohol, and used no tobacco. They believed that disease was a kind of sin and treated it with a combination of self and group criticism and faith healing—ideas which resemble Samuel Butler's and George Bernard Shaw's, whom Noyes probably influenced. They seem to have been about as successful as the orthodox medicine of their day. Instead of private confession before admission to the community, and after any serious sin later, as practiced by the Shakers, Oneida used a form of group criticism which went on as the occasion offered throughout life. There is a certain resemblance to the group criticism practiced by present-day Synanon with the vast difference that in Oneida this was done with gentleness, consideration, and respect for the individual.

The change in the public temper of the United States

214 · | · COMMUNALISM

is well indicated by the dominant society's reaction to
Oneida. The strongest objections were not to communalism or political radicalism but to the colony's
strange customs—complex marriage, stirpiculture, the
equality of women, and, not least, the manner of dress.
Men were attired plainly but conventionally. Women
wore short hair, skirts to the knee, long trousers, and a
good deal less underwear than was common in those
days of corsets, corset covers, many petticoats, ruffled
pantaloons, and bustles. Visitors found what seems to
us extremely modest dress most exciting. But the
Oneidans were also amongst the most advanced political radicals of their time. There exists a letter to William Lloyd Garrison from Noyes which he called his
Declaration of Independence from the United States
and its collective responsibility for slavery. Insofar as
the community paid attention to worldly politics it
uniformly took what we would consider the most radical
position on every issue of the day.

Throughout the daily life of the community in every
department, in every activity, the member encountered
built-in checks, controls, and short-circuits designed to
prevent, abort, or cure every vestige of acquisitiveness
and selfishness. After weaning, the children were raised
in nurseries by specialists, both male and female, and
early played at work or worked alongside their elders as
children do in primitive societies. They were usually
permitted some time each day with their parents. All
toys were held in common and from then on, all but
articles of the most personal use, including "clothing to
wear outside," was drawn from and returned to a common wardrobe.

Government was by a vast array of interlocking
committees, which were permitted considerable initiative, subject always to the meeting of the whole com-

munity; and if a division did occur, the decision, as with the Quakers, was postponed until unanimity could be reached. Oneida shared with the Society of Friends two ideas that seem rather commonplace but which are really quite startling and are held by hardly any other Christian, or for that matter, secular group. First was that it is indeed possible and not really terribly difficult to be good (their official name was the Perfectionists). Second, they believed there can exist scarcely any social emergencies where consensus need be sacrificed to decisiveness. Agreement was more important than disagreement.

Noyes's specifically theological ideas were not too unusual for a time of religious eccentricity. He believed in the authority of the Bible, but beyond it, in the ultimate authority of the Spirit of Truth, which, like the Quakers and their Inner Light, could be turned to by every man. He believed that God was dual, male and female. The Second Coming of Christ had already occurred at the time of the fall of the temple. We are now living after the apocalypse but before the imminent spiritual transformation of the world that would usher in the open rule of the kingdom of heaven. Complex marriage was not just a social technique for a communalist society—it was the method by which the spiritual union of the sexes which had been broken by the fall of Adam and Eve would be restored and mankind would once again be a divinized syzygy reflecting the Godhead. Death would be overcome and man would return to eternity.

As we read Noyes today it is easy to see through his dated, biblical language to the working of a powerful mind. He was the only religious communalist leader who was a radical intellectual, and he continuously stressed Oneida's as it were apostolic succession from

Brook Farm, certainly the most far-out intellectual highbrow activity of its day, which dissolved the month Oneida was founded.

As Noyes grew old and the new generation of colonists grew up, as usual there was more and more objection to details of the colonists' life. In 1879, worn out by attacks from both within and without, Noyes wrote a letter proposing the abandonment of complex marriage, and the general meeting approved the proposal with only one negative vote. From then on, bit by bit, practice by practice, the colony rapidly disintegrated, and the miscellaneous property was distributed. In 1881 Oneida became a joint-stock company engaged primarily in the manufacture of silverware and so continues to this day. The former colonist stockholders, if they kept their stock, grew rich, but the business became a capitalist enterprise, and very far from being a workers' democracy.

15

Robert Owen

Before the nineteenth century, communalism was practically confined to millenarian religious bodies. The first attempt of any significance to form a purely secular community was Robert Owen's New Harmony. Owen was born in 1771, the son of a small saddler and ironmonger. He left school at the age of nine, and by nineteen had become the manager of a cotton mill in Manchester employing five hundred people, which he made one of the best in England, not only in the quality of his product, the first thread of long staple sea-island cotton spun in England, but also in the efficiency of his production and the welfare of his workers.

This was a period of tremendous expansion and great profits in the textile industry in Great Britain. Within a few years Owen's business, run on strictly rationalist lines, had become so profitable that he was able to persuade his partners to buy the largest cotton mill in Britain, at New Lanark on the banks of the Clyde in Scotland. The total labor force was around fifteen hundred, about two-thirds of whom were women, and five hundred of whom were children, paupers, and orphans from the poorhouses and orphanages of Edinburgh and Glasgow, many of them only five or six years old.

Owen immediately improved the living conditions of the workers, raised the minimum age to ten, and progressively reduced the hours of labor from thirteen or fourteen to twelve, with ten-and-a-half hours of actual labor. He opened a general store which sold goods and food of the best quality at cost plus a part of the overhead expense, and he began gradually to inhibit the sale and consumption of liquor. Owen likewise established a school for the children which not only was the most progressive in Britain, but which originated a number of ideas that were not to be accepted elsewhere for almost a century.

New Lanark was in no sense a utopian venture. Its enlightened patriarchalism operated on the strictest business principles, and it showed remarkable profit even in years of depression. It was an industrial village of a type that would become common later in the century, especially in the businesses of Quaker industrialists. A good example in America is the town of Hershey, Pennsylvania, founded by the Mennonite chocolate-processing family. Contemporary with Owen, Jebediah Strutt in Derbyshire was operating a quite similar patriarchal mill town.

Owen looked upon New Lanark as something more than a model factory colony. He was a deist, an environmentalist, and a moderate necessitarian. He believed that human beings were morally the product of their environment, and especially of their early training, and could not be held responsible for their faulty behavior in later life. The school at New Lanark was far

more important to Owen than anything else, for he
hoped by his educational methods to produce an entirely new kind of working man.

The limited measures of community organization
which Owen was able to introduce made a surprisingly
rapid change in the character of his workers. When he
took it over, New Lanark was ridden with poverty, disease, prostitution, promiscuity, and alcoholism. The
strict discipline resulted in clean, vermin-free homes,
cooperative enterprises, lectures and dances in the
evening, social security, and eventual prohibition of
drink; and of course the schools worked an amazing
transformation in a comparatively short time. Soon
large numbers of visitors, some even from the continent
of America, were touring the works. Since Owen was
able to show that his methods were eminently profitable, New Lanark began to exercise a definite effect on
factory reform, long before the passing of the Factory
Acts. "An idle, dirty, dissolute, and drunken population," said Owen, "was transformed by the application
of proper means into one of order, neatness, and regu-
larity."

From the point of view of Owen's evolving theories of
community, New Lanark had faults, or at least limita-
tions. It was far from self-sufficient. There were various
mechanics attached to the factory, and a few small
craftsmen like shoemakers and tailors in the village,
but the community did not provide itself with most of its
goods and services. Furthermore, it lacked an agricultural base, although there were garden allotments for
any of the workers who wanted them. There were also
community dining rooms and laundries, but the women
seemed to have resented them. The majority of the employees were women and children, so that many of the
men had to find work outside the community. There
were only about twenty managers, clerks, and teachers.

All the rest were proletarians of the strictest definition, illiterate or semi-literate, with nothing to sell but their labor power.

The schools were a different matter. Here Owen had a free hand to do much as he wanted, limited only by the difficulty in the early years of the nineteenth-century of finding teachers able or willing to carry out his ideas. Owen believed that children should not be annoyed with books, but taught by sensible signs and familiar conversation. The natural interest of childhood formed the basis of his educational method. Children learned through playing, dancing, singing, and participating in "military exercises" (what we would call calisthenics). Owen was a passionate believer in dancing, and visitors were fascinated by the children dancing in their kilts, and the neighboring Scottish Presbyterians were outraged that he permitted little boys to dance "without trousers" with little girls. The evening dances for adults were a very important part of Owen's social discipline and therapy, and seem to have been enthusiastically welcomed by the workers, and no doubt more than were the lectures on rationalist, utilitarian, and radical subjects.

Although New Lanark made money, often when other mills were losing it, Owen twice found it necessary to reorganize the business and change his partners. They objected on moral (or more properly immoral) grounds to his methods, and especially to his deism, in those days verging on Gnosticism, and his disdain for all organized religion—attitudes which he insisted on inculcating in his workers and in the children in the schools. These principles were to cause him trouble throughout his career, although interestingly enough the objections grew, rather than declined, as the Enlightenment died out in England, to be replaced by what would come to be called Victorianism. In the final reorganization, he was able to secure the support of a number of English radicals, including Jeremy Bentham.

As the fame of New Lanark grew, Robert Owen became a very important person and in 1817 he was invited to submit a report to the House of Commons embodying his suggestions for reform and the "cure of pauperism." By this time Owen had given much thought to the problem and had evolved a definite system. He shared with Ricardo and anticipated Marx in the elementary working-out of a labor theory of value. He rejected Malthus's theory of the growing pressure of population and, consequently, impoverishment, and charged on the contrary that capitalist production resulted in under-consumption. He accepted the steady increase of the use of machinery but proposed to limit and diffuse industrialization and keep it secondary in agriculturally based small communities. He also proposed that about twelve hundred people should be settled on collective farms of about an acre per person. All would live in one large building in the form of a square with a public dining hall. Each family would have its own room and the care of children until the age of three, after which they should be brought up by the community, although their parents might have access to them. All work should be cooperative and its proceeds communally shared. There should be small shops with the best machinery available and enough craftsmen to make each community largely self-sufficient, although certain communities also would turn out specialized products for trade.

Coupled with this rational analysis and plan was a definite strain of millenarianism. Owen was already beginning to believe that society as then constituted was doomed to disaster and that the capitalist's methods of what Marx would call "the period of primi-

tive accumulation" were profoundly evil. He shared
William Blake's judgment of the dark Satanic mills and
was coming to think of himself as a messiah called to
lead man into a New Moral World.

It is extraordinary how well received his proposals
were. Leading capitalists, politicians, nobility, even the
Duke of Kent, the father of Queen Victoria, became enthusiastic supporters. Unfortunately, Owen's belief
that men were shaped almost entirely by environment
and could be changed by changing their environment
was closely linked to his rationalistic deism and his hos-
tility to all forms of institutional religion. Thus at a
great meeting in London he was carried away and
launched into an anti-religious diatribe and immediately lost a large share of his support, although it is
remarkable—considering the storm such a speech
would raise in the next generation, at the height of Vic-
torian reaction—how many people, even important figures in the establishment, continued to support him,
and how much this support cut across class and political lines. His followers were by no manner of means all
radical Whigs. In fact, Owen, with his profound sense
of the responsibility of wealth, power, birth, and education, and his rejection of "free enterprise," can actually
be considered one of the founders of radical Toryism.

Although Owen found plenty of verbal support and
sympathetic interest, he did not find the decisive action
from the State or the establishment which naïvely he
seems to have expected. Owenite clubs were formed.
He gained articulate disciples who promulgated his
ideas, and in the course of time a movement grew up
which would last until the third quarter of the century.
Eventually a number of communities embodying the
principles of either his projected communal settlements
or of New Lanark, or something of both, were established. Most of them failed within a year, but for over a

generation Owenite communities continued to be formed in Great Britain. The longest lived were Queenwood and Blues Spring in England, Orbiston in Scotland, and Ralahine in Ireland. Essential to the life of all these communities were their schools, where the malleable young would be formed into citizens of the New Moral World.

The Owenite communities lead directly to the cooperative garden villages of a later generation, but their greatest influence was probably upon education. Owen's special combination of his own ideas and those of the Swiss educational reformer Pestalozzi established the progressive model of British education. As we have seen, one amusing aspect was Owen's enthusiasm for dancing. Here Owen seems to have instinctively discovered one of the most important forces for commitment and community—the orgy. Dancing was almost as important to him as it was to the Shakers, in whom he had early been interested, and from whom he learned more than he may have acknowledged.

However much of a following Owen may have obtained in Great Britain, he became increasingly aware of widespread resistance and of the iron crust of custom. There was freedom in America, unlimited land in the New World. It would be possible to build the New Moral World, and in an open, flexible society it would be quite possible to convert, by successful example, the entire country in a relatively short time. Owen decided to found his major colony on or near the American frontier. He began to withdraw from the government of New Lanark in 1828 after a long period of friction with his partners, resigned all connections, and in 1825 went shopping in America for a site.

In March he began the negotiation to buy Harmony for one hundred and twenty-five thousand dollars—the entire colony, village, shops, and land—from the Rappites; and in May they moved out to their new colony in Pennsylvania, which became even more successful than Harmony had been. Characteristically, Owen did not bother to investigate sufficiently to find whether rumors of malaria being endemic at the Harmony site on the banks of the lower Wabash were true.

Owen and his first colonists took possession in April—thirty thousand acres of land, a complete village with one hundred and sixty houses, churches, dormitories, flour mills, textile factory, distilleries, breweries, a tannery, various craftsmen's shops, over two thousand acres under cultivation with eighteen acres of vineyards and orchards, as well as additional pastureland and woods.

From the beginning the man who had been so canny, businesslike, and careful at New Lanark seems to have proceeded with a truly exceptional lack of good sense. He began by touring the eastern United States, addressed Congress and met the President, and exhibited a large model of his future colony building, which greatly resembled the later planned, but never built, Fourierists' phalansteries. He was listened to with the most serious attention because, of course, in the early years of the last century there was a widespread hope that it might be possible to make a radical turn in the development of society away from the industrial capitalism which so obviously was destroying both men and values and purposefully steer society into a new moral order of collective cooperative life. Capitalism, as a social system, had yet to develop an ideology and propaganda of its own, and least of all a "consensus." Many of Owen's ideas and special terminology derive, in fact, from radical Freemasonry.

In April 1825 Owen made an impassioned speech at New Harmony inaugurating a New Order of the Ages, and affirmed that in a very short time the example of New Harmony would convert the civilized world. In May a constitution was adopted and the Preliminary Society of New Harmony was formed, with Owen in charge of the community for three probationary years, during which time all property would remain in his possession. Meanwhile, he had advertised in the papers inviting all men of good will to come and take part in the founding of the new civilization! They came—in a few months more than nine hundred of them. Some were convinced Owenites. A few were skilled mechanics, very few were experienced farmers, most of the serious people were intellectuals and what we would call white-collar workers. There were no people to operate many of the enterprises left by the Rappites and no serious effort was later made to recruit such workers. Although colonists came in the hundreds, in fact, Owen unbelievably left to make more speeches.

During the succeeding year, over ten Owenite colonies were founded. Those in New York, Pennsylvania, Ohio, and Nashoba, Tennessee, were of historical importance, but within a year most had failed. The Mormon leaders may have learned from Owen. They systematically recruited by ordering their missionaries to speak out and convert exactly those trades and professions needed for a well-rounded, self-sustaining community, with a base of farmers and agricultural workers. They even sent orders to their missionaries for the conversion of specifically needed craftsmen. Owen did quite the opposite as a matter of policy. He welcomed anyone who came. New Harmony was what today would be called an "open-gate commune." Soon there was an ever increasing proportion of crackpots, loafers, and rascals. From his travels he wrote back to his son in New Jersey to get to work on the immense communal building, for which there were neither workers nor stone, and gave instructions for other equally visionary and impractical schemes. His son replied with desperate requests for experienced mechanics and farmers.

Owen obliged by returning in January 1826 with the famous "Boatload of Knowledge," a whole bevy of intellectuals, some of them of very considerable importance, who would have been a credit to any European university, though they were not the people needed to build utopia on the American frontier. The most important was William McClure, the president of the Philadelphia Academy of Natural Sciences, the "Father of American Geology," and the most active American advocate of the Pestalozzian system of education. There were other scientists—Thomas Say, Gerard Troost, the famous explorer Lesueur, the educator D'Arusmont, Madame Fretageot, and Frances Wright, one of the leading feminists and radicals of her time. There was also Josiah Warren, who had organized an orchestra and was to become one of the founders of Mutualist Anarchism, and who had already anticipated many of the theories later to be identified with Proudhon.

McClure, D'Arusmont, and Madame Fretageot immediately organized a school. Within a short time some of the colonists split off to form a nearby settlement called McCluria, concerned almost exclusively with education, and ignoring economic problems, agriculture, and industry. On January 25 they adopted a new constitution. Owen withdrew as "dictator." The colony was reorganized on the basis of complete communism, with the general assembly of all members as the authority embodied in an executive committee of six. Work was no longer to be rewarded for its worth to the community, but rather all goods were free to all members alike. Owen set up a sort of public cash box, not unlike that long ago set up at Münster, from which any member could draw at will, but this was soon abandoned as the unscrupulous emptied it daily. Within two weeks New Harmony obviously was breaking down, and the assembly by majority vote begged Owen to resume authority. The worst rascals and idlers withdrew under pressure and an effort was made at production in the fields and shops. Within a month another group split off. They were mostly farmers who came with Owen from Great Britain, who objected to his prohibition of alcoholic drink. They named their colony FeibaPeveli, in accord with a system invented by an English eccentric, Whitwell, in which a cipher represented the latitude and longitude of any given place. New York was OtkeNotive, and London LafaVovutu.

The fragmentation of the settlement continued with a new constitution in April, and three more during the summer. Each schism was settled somewhere on the estate. Whenever the daily rhythm of crises reached a peak, Owen's solution was to make a speech and adopt a new constitution. On the Fourth of July 1826 he persuaded the community to adopt a "Declaration of Mental Independence" which forthrightly denounced religion, marriage, and private property—all of which led to further and more serious schisms. By the end of the year Owen's euphoria was beginning to wane, and early in 1827 a large part of the town was split up into houses and lots for sale, and into private small businesses and establishments including gin houses. In March eighty people left to start a community near Cincinnati. The communal life had broken down. The community kitchens and dining rooms, recreation centers, meeting house, warehouses, and granaries were abandoned. The school, however, continued and in one form or another would survive, and there the remnant of the colonists took their meals and carried on what community life they could. Leaving his son Robert Dale in charge, Owen went off on a speaking tour urging, with the greatest optimism, the development of more Owenite communities. But when he reached New York he took ship for England and never came back. The first secular communist community was dead and Owen had lost about a quarter of a million dollars, although most of the property was still administered by his sons. A few other colonies were formed, one as far away as Wisconsin, then a wilderness, but by 1830 all had ceased to exist. Owen went on to become a leader of British radicalism, a founding father of modern trade-unionism and the cooperative movement, and a strong influence on the development of British cooperative villages—"garden cities." In his old age he became a Spiritualist.

This bare account of the brief life of New Harmony as a communist colony makes it difficult to understand its influence and historical importance. Owen did practically everything wrong. He bought a ready-made settlement, so that the colonists had no sense of having built something for themselves. He took in anyone who came, and most of those who came had little or no commitment to his ideas or to the purposes of the colony. There was nothing to bind the members together. Each person was a law unto himself, and everyone disagreed with everyone else on the most fundamental principles and the most ordinary practices. No attempt was made to keep out rascals, cranks, or even, to judge from the record, the seriously mentally ill. Not only did most of the colonists not share Owen's ideas, but his attacks on religion and marriage antagonized many of the most valuable members, namely, the workers and farmers, and were shared by only a minority of the intellectuals. The employees at New Lanark, in Scotland, were just that, employees, and the ultimate discipline was the control of their job—they could be fired.

Owen's dictatorship of New Harmony was devoid of

power by his own wish. Questions of discipline were thrown into the general meeting, whose decisions were unenforceable. Many seceded from the colony or simply left, but few were expelled. There were lectures, concerts, dances, but there was nothing beyond these to bind the colonists together and to enforce commitment like the confessional meetings of the religious groups. Owen introduced a kind of dress-reform costume which was to be the uniform of the community, but only a minority of the people ever wore it, and there were no other techniques of enforcing group self-identification. By the time the Rappites had sold Harmony to Owen, they had become an almost self-sustaining closed economy with a surplus for the outside market which was making them rich. Owen had neither workers with the necessary skills to operate the Rappite plant nor a sure method for insuring that people did the work they were supposed to do.

Yet New Harmony was not a total failure. It certainly provided an example, though seldom heeded, of what not to do in the organization of a secular communalistic community. But it also introduced America to educational methods which would profoundly influence all public education, in the north at least, and which would help to make the Indiana school system for three generations the most progressive in the United States. Robert Dale Owen entered the Indiana legislature and was responsible for giving married women control of their own property and liberalizing divorce and inheritance laws as they affected women. The Owen brothers also made New Harmony a focus for early scientific activity. In 1839 David Dale Owen was appointed U.S. Geologist and established the headquarters of the U.S. Geological Survey in New Harmony, and was a founder of the Smithsonian Institute. From the colony's Workingmen's Institute and Library similar institutions spread

across the country—one still exists in San Francisco—and out of them grew the free public library.
Only two of the many daughter colonies of New Harmony were of historical importance: Nashoba, founded
by Frances Wright, and a succession of experiments
led by Josiah Warren. John Humphrey Noyes, the
leader of the Oneida colony, said of Frances Wright,
"She was indeed the pioneer of the strong-minded
women." Not only was she the leading woman in the
beginnings of secular communism, but she was essentially the founder of the secular anti-slavery movement
and women's rights. Even today she would be considered a radical feminist. Her interest in the Rappites at
Harmony preceded that of Owen's. She visited various
Shaker settlements and other communalist groups,
lived in the communities, questioned the leaders, and
studied their problems. She also traveled through the
southern states discussing her great plan with planters
and politicians. It was certainly an extraordinary one.
She hoped to establish a communist colony led at first
by white people and freed Negroes, but consisting
mostly of slaves, whom she proposed to purchase, or
who would be donated by slaveholders, and who would
be paid half of what they produced—with which they
would eventually purchase their freedom. She accompanied the Owens to New Harmony and took part in the
formation of the community and left in 1826, before the
disintegration. She purchased two thousand acres,
mostly marshy woodland on the Wolf River, thirteen
miles above Memphis, Tennessee, and settled it with
several Negro families, including fifteen active workers, whom she also purchased. Accompanying them
were a number of whites, amongst them D'Arusmont
from New Harmony, the family of George Flower, her
younger sister Camilla Wright, and a wandering communist, James Richardson.

At first there were only two cabins, one for slaves and one for whites with Frances and Flower the only white people, but in the course of the winter the others came down, bringing a former Shaker, Richesson Whitby. Frances spent the bad weather in Memphis and on good days went out and helped to clear land. As soon as it grew warm, it became apparent that the site was malarial. Frances, exhausted with manual labor, caught the disease and almost died. She went up to New Harmony for a rest and "the better air." New Harmony, of course, was also malarial. At this time she began her long off-and-on love relationship with Robert Dale Owen. Meanwhile she wrote and lectured on free love, a new enthusiasm. It was not long before the newspapers discovered her and linked her advocacy of free love with the interracial colony at Nashoba, and she became the priestess of Beelzebub. She and Robert Dale Owen went down to Nashoba where he hoped to live "a life of lettered leisure" while she visited her friend Lafayette in France. Owen was horrified at the poverty and disorder at Nashoba and decided to go to Europe with her. They solved the problems of Nashoba, as those at New Harmony were solved, by drawing up a new constitution. Lafayette, Camilla Wright, the Owens, the white people of Nashoba, and William McClure were made trustees and Frances gave them title to the estate, all her personal property, and the ownership of the slaves, and the others were invited to "invest" in the venture by donating money, property, or labor. The slaves were supposed to have the same rights as everyone else, but in fact they were still slaves. Noyes compared them to the helots of ancient Sparta, with the difference that they were continuously lectured about communism, racial equality, and free love.

Owen and Frances departed from New Orleans. George Flower left, disgusted, and Whitby took his place. Before embarking, Frances gave lectures in which she advocated both free love and miscegenation, and envisaged a creamy-colored race more suitable to the climate of the south than either black or white. The press raved, and audiences booed, but some took her seriously and listened. The fact that she was not mobbed or lynched is an indication of the open-mindedness of the American public in the 1820's, so different from a generation later. In New Orleans they also recruited several new members, including a creole of color, Mam'selle Lolotte, with several children, including a grown daughter, Josephine. Mam'selle Lolotte took over the school, such as it was, and all children were taken from their parents and placed under her management. This led to bitter resentment on the part of the slaves, who grew increasingly antagonistic to the free Negroes and to those of lighter complexion. Whitby and Camilla Wright got married and Richardson and Josephine began to live together, and Richardson gave a lecture on free love and miscegenation.

The extracts from the daybook of the colony, filled with this sort of thing, were sent off by Richardson to the abolitionist paper, *The Genius of Universal Emancipation*. American, British, and continental papers picked up the story and Nashoba became an international scandal. Camilla responded by publicly attacking marriage and stating that Richardson's conduct had the approval of all at Nashoba. Even Frances stated that Camilla and Richardson had been foolish. She returned from England bringing no converts, but accompanied by her friend Mrs. Trollope, who planned to tour the United States seeking a business opportunity for her husband, preferably in the west, possibly Cincinnati. Mrs. Trollope came to Nashoba for Christmas and was horrified at the tumble-down, improperly built cabins, the idleness, disorder, dirt, and disease.

Camilla, moreover, was seriously ill with malaria. When Mrs. Trollope left, Whitby and Camilla went to New Harmony with her, and Richardson said farewell to Josephine and joined them. Frances drew up a new constitution, hired a white overseer, and likewise departed for New Harmony. This time she and D'Arusmont fell in love, and Frances lectured in Cincinnati to packed houses. She was becoming a sensational lecturer, her ideas growing ever more radical as both New Harmony and Nashoba disintegrated. She and Robert Jennings went on a lecture tour of the country; and activities at New Harmony narrowed to publishing *The Gazette*, with Jennings, D'Arusmont, Frances, and Robert Dale Owen writing the copy and doing the printing. They eventually moved the paper to New York, and re-named it *The Free Inquirer*. Nashoba was hopelessly demoralized. Frances and D'Arusmont took the slaves to Haiti and freed them. The freed Negroes, including Mam'selle Lolotte, vanished from history. Frances went on to other adventures. She became a power in the Workingman's Party. Camilla's baby died, and then Camilla. Frances and D'Arusmont went to France and were married and a daughter, Frances Sylvia, was born. They returned to America and Frances, against the objections of D'Arusmont, resumed her lecturing and became the leader of the women's rights movement. They quarreled and D'Arusmont went back to France and eventually divorced her. In 1852 she slipped on the ice in Cincinnati and broke her hip and died, probably of pneumonia. She was only fifty-six and had led one of the most eventful lives of any woman in history.

16

Josiah Warren

Of all the remarkable people associated with New Harmony, the most remarkable by far was Josiah Warren. Had he been a general, a politician, or a capitalist, he would have been one of the most famous of all Americans. He was a genuinely universal man—a talented musician accomplished on several instruments, a craftsman skilled in several crafts, an important inventor, an economist, philosopher, and founder of American individual anarchism—as a movement at least, since Thoreau was too individualistic to be the founder of a movement.

Warren was born in Boston in 1798 of a well-known Pilgrim family. Not much is known of his early life, but in his 'teens he was making a living as a professional musician. At twenty he married and migrated to Cincinnati, the capital of the frontier, where he worked as an orchestra and band leader and teacher of music. Tallow and oil were in short supply, so he invented a lamp that burned lard and gave better light; soon he was running a lamp factory and became a moderately well-to-do-man. In 1825 he sold the factory and accompanied Owen and his first settlers to New Harmony, where he became the leader of the band and taught music in the school—the community's only two successful institutions. He also functioned as a general technical adviser and troubleshooter. Moreover, he was one of the few persons in the colony with any mechanical knowledge or skill. His philosophy had always been that the best way to understand a process was to learn to do it. At New Harmony he began his interest in printing. In 1827, as New Harmony disintegrated, he returned to Cincinnati. Of all the colonists, he was the only one, at least in a leading position, who seems to have learned anything. Most of them, like Frances Wright, were doomed to repeat the same mistakes and follies and end in the same disasters. Almost all critics of New Harmony have said that what it lacked was strong leadership, discipline, and commitment—strong government. Warren came to exactly the opposite conclusion. New Harmony had suffered from the disorderly exercise of freedom and the instability of Owen's authority. On the principle of like cures like, he was convinced that the basis of all future reform must be complete individual liberty. "Man seeks freedom as the magnet seeks the pole or water its level," he wrote, "and society can have no peace until every member is really free." But such a condition was not realizable under the existing organization and ideas of society. New views had to replace those of the past. For the future society new principles were needed. The first of these was "individual individuality." The sovereignty of every individual at all times had to be held inviolable. Everyone necessarily was free to dispose of his person, his time, his property, and his reputation as he pleased—but always *at his own cost.*

Warren had evolved a fairly comprehensive system of economics based on a labor theory of value, at first of the strictest interpretation, something like Marx's, or rather Engels' theory of labor power as distinguished from labor—all labor time was considered equivalent. Later, learning from what was in a sense a controlled scientific experiment, he came to believe in a limited scale of values based on skill. Warren's was the mind of a scientist and inventor. He immediately put the ideas he had evolved from his New Harmony experience into practical application.

On May 18, 1827, an historic date, he opened a little general store at the corner of Fifth and Elm Streets in Cincinnati. He called it the Equity Store, but as soon as people found out about it, this became the most popular retail business in the city, and was known because of its method of computing price as the "time store." Price was based on the principle of equal exchange of labor, measured by time occupied and exchange with other kinds of labor. All goods were marked with their cost plus overhead, usually about four per cent. It was, incidentally, the first self-service business. The customer selected what he wished, brought it to the counter, the clerk computed the time spent in service, and the customer gave a labor note, "Due to Josiah Warren on demand, thirty minutes in carpenter work, John Smith" or, "Due to Josiah Warren on demand, ten minutes in needlework, Mary Brown."

Customers left orders for their needs, and these were posted each morning. Craftsmen and farmers brought their goods in accordance with the list of needs and exchanged them for other goods or for labor notes, in accordance with a list of the cost and labor time for all staple articles. Beyond these simple arrangements there were practically no other rules and regulations. The store functioned automatically as a cooperative market for both buyers and sellers and as a labor exchange and employment bureau. The first week it did only five dollars worth of business, but in a short time the store was thriving. And the remarkable thing was that highly skilled craftsmen and professional men were willing to exchange their labor with others on a simple time basis, although later Warren would modify this arrangement somewhat. The store soon came to function also as an interest-free credit union, and loans in labor and commodities and eventually money, if absolutely necessary, were made without interest and no other charge than the labor cost of handling. Warren was eventually able to embark upon a moderate cooperative real-estate venture, based on the funds in labor and money of the time cost. All this was done when Pierre Joseph Proudhon, the generally considered founder of individual anarchy, mutual credit, and cooperative labor exchange, was still a schoolboy. Warren not only anticipated Proudhon, but he was a far clearer thinker and writer, and a man who believed in testing all of his theories in practice. Marx was right about Proudhon. He was a confused thinker and a confusing writer and far from being a practical man.

After three years of most successful operation of the Time Store, Warren decided that he had proved his point, the scientific experiment had justified the hypothesis, and in 1830 he closed out the business and went to New York to work with Robert Dale Owen and Frances Wright on *The Free Inquirer*. In about six months he returned to Ohio. In the next few years he attempted to found communes, which never got started, due to factors beyond his control. He ran another "time store" at New Harmony, and on the side, as it were, made several profitable inventions in printing machinery, culminating in the first rotary press. In 1847 he took over the leadership of a Fourierist phalanstery on the Ohio, about thirty miles above Cincinnati, which he renamed Utopia. It operated for about four years until the settlers sold out at a profit and migrated to Minnesota, where they disappear from history.

In 1850 Warren moved to New York City and joined forces with Steven Pearl Andrews, who became the chief propagandist for Warren's principles. These included the sovereignty of the individual, cost the limit of price, equitable commerce, and, eventually, mutual banking: in other words, the well-developed theory of individual anarchism or mutualism, which would survive as a small movement until well into the twentieth century, and which was certainly a much better worked-out general theory of free association than Proudhon's similar system.

In the same year Warren, Andrews, and others began the community of Modern Times, now called Brentwood, on Long Island about forty miles from New York. Due to Warren's principles, it is easy to confuse Modern Times with a cooperative real-estate development. Each family owned its own house and there was no regular form of government. Where New Harmony had failed, due to its open-door policy and the long struggle between Owen's authority and the factionalism of cranks and the parasitism of loafers, Warren's Modern Times solved these problems by ignoring them, by exercising no authority whatever. The cranks and loafers came, but in a short time eliminated themselves. Communism of consumption was insured by a "time store," but the colony was never able to achieve communism of production except in agriculture. There was never sufficient capital to start a successful manufacturing business. A paper-box factory was attempted and was quite successful for a few years but was wiped out in the financial panic of 1857. The colony never really died, but slowly withered away to become a model village suburban to New York. In his old age Warren moved to Boston and died there in 1874 at the age of seventy-six. For another generation the movement he founded was a small but significant factor in American radicalism. The principal voice of individual anarchism and mutualism was Benjamin R. Tucker (author of *In Place of a Book, by a Man too Busy to Write One,* the best exposition of individual anarchism), whose magazine *Liberty* lasted into the twentieth century; and Warren's principles of community organization were adopted in modified form by various communalist villages in both Great Britain and America. Mutual banking associations survive to the present day.

17

Brook Farm

During the 1840's, the commune movement reached a height it would not attain again until after the Second World War. Ventures at least calling themselves communal were started at the rate of from five to ten a year. Most of them were extremely short-lived, and many, for instance Amos Bronson Alcott's, were not really communes at all, but a kind of impoverished community boarding house occupied by a handful of eccentrics.

It was a decade of revolutionary ferment throughout the Western world, a time described by Marx and Engels in terrifying chapters on the primitive accumulation of capital. When the Satanic mills came into their full power, civilized human beings everywhere recoiled in wrath and horror at the consequences of primitive industrialization, and they were answered by economists and philosophers who said that unbridled individual freedom would guarantee that the misery of each would result in the good of all. In 1848 revolution swept Europe. It was suppressed, but the ruling classes were frightened; and movements of reform were permitted to gain a few of their objectives on a slow, piecemeal basis.

In the United States, it seemed for a while as though the American dream of a free cooperative society might win. That hope is most clearly embodied in the work of Walt Whitman. Amongst the New England Transcendentalists and on the fringes of the abolitionist movement the demands for widespread changes in society in clothing, sexual relations, government, economics, education, a total transvaluation of values, were universally the accepted commonplaces of America's first radical intelligentsia. (The founding fathers were radical intellectual gentlemen.)

From the panic of 1837 on, a series of economic crises established a cycle of boom and collapse that lasted until the Civil War. The economic instability and the growing struggle over slavery intensified the sense of crisis and alienation, not only amongst the intellectuals, but spreading to the general population. Louis Napoleon's Second Empire, with its primitive gestures toward a corporative State, aborted the revolutionary movement in France. In America the Civil War ended a time of revolutionary hope, but it is too often forgotten today that the intellectuals, the radicals, and the abolitionists not only went into the Civil War under the impression it was the revolution, but came out of it thinking they had won. Whitman was not the only person who had to learn slowly and painfully that the American dream was not going to be realized in his lifetime and possibly never at all. America has fought not two but three great wars, each the bloodiest in history, to make the world safe for democracy. It is important to understand that the radicalization of large sections of the educated population and the skilled working class was at least as intense and as widespread proportionately as the similar movement in the 1960's. Most of the ideas so popular in the latter period were part of the accepted ideology of the earlier.

Brook Farm owes its historical importance to the fact that it was not an experiment of obscure eccentrics, or what most people would call religious fanatics, but rather was a carefully considered attempt to secede from the dominant society by representative members of the intellectual elite.

In the summer of 1841, the Reverend George Ripley, who was an editor of *The Dial*, a member of the Transcendental Club, and a recent apostate from the Unitarian Church because he found even its vestigial dogmatism too confining, proposed in the circle of Boston Transcendentalists to found a communal society. The project would be financed by the sale of stock at a hundred dollars a share. Each shareholder would become a member. Ripley had been visiting the Shaker and other religious communities and had questioned closely former members of New Harmony and other secular communes. He hoped to avoid the mistakes that had led to failure and to incorporate on a secular basis those methods that had produced success. The colonists would combine in each member mental and physical work. Initially everyone would work on the farm and in the craft shop and at small manufacture, which it was hoped would be developed, and all would share in the domestic labor of cooking, housekeeping, and child care. One of Ripley's proudest boasts was to be that they had "abolished domestic servitude . . . we do freely from the love of it those duties that are usually discharged by domestics," a statement whose naïveté would indicate the class composition of its membership. All work was to be paid for at a rate of a dollar a

244 · | · COMMUNALISM

day to men and women alike, whether physical or mental. Housing, fuel, clothing, and food produced on the farm or cooperatively purchased was rationed at cost.

As in most secular communes, there was a strong emphasis upon the radical reform of education, with "perfect freedom of intercourse between students and teaching body." There were no rigid study hours and the children's time was divided between school and work in the fields or about the house. In the course of events, the colony attracted experienced farmers, carpenters, shoemakers, and printers, as well as several teachers, but initially the directors of agriculture were Charles A. Dana and Nathaniel Hawthorne, neither of whom knew anything about farming and who found the physical work so exhausting that it made intellectual effort impossible.

At first there were only twenty members. Most of the leading Transcendentalists, except for John S. Dwight, Minot Pratt, George Partridge, and Bradford and Warren Burton who were amongst the original shareholders, were skeptical; and Ralph Waldo Emerson remained antagonistic to the end, referring to Brook Farm as "a perpetual picnic, a French Revolution in small, an Age of Reason in a patty pan," a completely unjust statement. Most of the people had known one another before coming to the farm, and although the gospel of Transcendentalism—a combination of radical secession from Unitarianism and Universalism mixed with evolutionism, monism, pragmatism, humanism, and an interest in the just discovered mysticism of India—might seem to us to have been too amorphous a faith to inspire binding commitment, it did not seem so to them.

To the straight-laced puritan farmer in the neighborhood, Brook Farm was a secret iniquity, a Babylon set down in his midst. To colonists who came from straight-laced Congregationalist backgrounds, their fellow members seemed totally irreligious. They played croquet or went on picnics on the Sabbath, and the more abandoned female members even knitted and sewed. Ripley himself was an intensely religious man with a good deal of wisdom gained from his pastoral experience. He was imperturbably good-humored in the face of contentions and frustrations amongst his followers. In his quiet way he seems to have emanated a powerful charisma strong enough to hold the colony together and keep it on an even keel.

At first there were only twenty members and there were never more than eighty, but those who stayed worked together with enthusiasm and a surprising minimum of contentiousness. It could be said of Brook Farm that it was not a communist, but a cooperative enterprise; but the cooperative aspects were largely administrative, and the smallness, cohesion, and enthusiasm made it in fact a commune. Economically Brook Farm never became self-sustaining—even in agriculture—much less profitable; but the difference was made up by the school, which took in students from the outside, and which became not only successful and profitable but produced a number of moderately famous people, amongst them George William Curtis, Father Isaac Hecker, the founder of the Paulist Fathers and one of the first Catholic Modernists, General Francis C. Barlow, and a large number of well-balanced adults, who looked back on their school days at Brook Farm as amongst the happiest of their lives.

Although Brook Farm was on the border between a religious and a secular colony, and although its sophisticated members were far from being superstitious or "primitive" or dogmatic in their beliefs, the governing philosophy was certainly millenarian. In his early conversations with Channing, Ripley spoke of his failure as a minister because his congregation lived one life on Sundays and another, manifestly in defiance of Christian principles, on weekdays. He wanted, as it says of heaven in the ancient hymn, a society of perpetual Sabbaths. As plans for the colony matured, Ripley, Elizabeth P. Peabody, and Margaret Fuller began to speak in *The Dial* of Brook Farm in typical millenarian terms as an apostolic community modelled on the life of Jesus and his disciples. Further, it would come out of the doomed cities and establish a community of love to set an example to the world—in short, a saving remnant.

Hawthorne found the work too hard and left. He had come there hoping to find ample leisure to write. Others were offended by what they considered the irreligion or paganism. The colonists who stayed really seemed to have found a perpetual Sabbath. They worked hard part of the day and the rest of the time was spent in games and self-improvement. In the eveninig there was musical entertainment, discussions, and dancing, or people walked the nine miles from Brook Farm to Boston to attend concerts and lectures. Partly perhaps it was because of the abiding sweetness of temper, so uncharacteristic of most charismatic leaders, which emanated from George Ripley, that the Brook Farmers seemed to have had a continuous good time.

The colony was family-based and most of the personal relationships had been established beforehand. There seems to have been a certain amount of free love, as it would later be called, but very far from as much as its hostile critics imagined. Sexual problems never seem to have played much of a role. The members were also modified vegetarians. True Bostonians, they refused to give up a piece of pork in their baked beans, and they killed and ate the rabbits who invaded their crops. The men wore a little cap, a sort of blouse, and trousers, and the women short skirts and pantaloons.

In comparison with Owen's New Harmony, Brook Farm seems to have been free of the more outrageous cranks and eccentrics. Hawthorne's *Blithedale Romance* gives a false impression. It is obvious on the face of it that he was outraged by the feminism of the leading women members, most especially of Margaret Fuller, his character "Zenobia." Sexual equality probably antagonized more male intellectuals, visitors, and novices or postulants than sewing on the Sabbath antagonized females.

Even with the school, however, the colony always operated at a slight loss, made up by contributions and the purchase of additional shares by members and their friends. There was a marketable surplus of farm products, but it was not enough, and the projected "manufactures" never really got off the ground.

In 1844 Ripley became converted to Fourierism; and after prolonged discussion, the colony turned itself into a Fourierist phalanstery with a rigid, bureaucratized departmentalism envisaged by Fourier for a colony of some two thousand people, but totally unsuited to the seventy-odd Brook Farmers. Membership was thrown open to anyone who considered himself a Fourierist. The original membership slowly declined, to be replaced by the cranks and loafers who, fortunately, seldom stayed for very long. But for two years most surplus time and labor was devoted to the construction of the central building of a planned phalanstery with dormitories and apartments, class meeting-rooms and classrooms, an auditorium, and community recreation and dining rooms. On March 2, 1846, it was completed, and the colony and all its friends joined in a celebration. That night the building burned down.

Brook Farm never recovered. The disaster seems to have destroyed the morale of the colonists as well as ruined them financially. Brook Farm struggled for awhile, but "the enterprise faded, flickered, died down, and expired," and the land and buildings were sold at auction on April 13, 1849, contemporaneously with the consolidation of the power of Louis Napoleon in France and the dying out of the last embers of the Revolution of 1848 in Europe.

Emerson had been supercilious and Hawthorne embittered, but records indicate that almost all the Brook Farmers who stayed with the colony took a different view. They formed an association for ex-members and purchased a camp in the foothills of Mount Hurricane in the Adirondacks, which they called Summer Brook Farm, and every year they gathered to live again the Brook Farm life. Sixty years later the aged surviving members were still coming to the camp.

18

Fourierism

François Marie Charles Fourier was born in 1772 and died in 1837. His family had lost its modest wealth in the French Revolution and François' life as a result was conditioned by his sense of the injustice of the maldistribution of wealth. Behind him lay feudalism which in its best days had been functional, ordering society, but his life was to be spent in the demoralization and disorganization of the beginnings of the industrial age, Marx's period of the primitive accumulation of capital.

Fourier, more than any other utopian socialist, tried to solve all the problems of society by the construction of an elaborately detailed system in which every person, activity, and thing had its place, and every contingency was anticipated. He believed that the completely free development of man and the unrestrained indulgence of all desires and appetites would necessarily produce the good man in the good society, and that vice and evil

were results of restraints upon freedom for complete
self-gratification—the most extreme form of social optimism. Man was naturally good because he bore
within himself a fundamental moral harmony, the re-
flection of harmony in the universe. His "natural man"
was considerably more natural than Jean Jacques
Rousseau's, but he proposed to liberate him by means of
a most rigidly organized society. Of course, the assumption was that once a sample community of this society,
which only Fourier knew how to construct, was set up,
it would prove so immensely attractive that it would be
adopted universally within a very short time.

Society was to be divided into *phalanges*, or as they
were usually called in America, phalansteries or
phalanxes, each with a common building, housing from
sixteen hundred to eighteen hundred individuals on
about three square miles of agricultural land, divided
into fields, orchards, and gardens—Fourier was very
fond of fruits and flowers. The population would be divided into groups of at least seven persons, with two in
each wing, representing both the ascending and descending streams of taste and ability, and three in the
center for balance. At least five groups would form a
series, again with a center and wings. There would be a
series for every conceivable occupation, and the members could move freely from one to another. Each person might work no more than an hour or two in any one
series, so that all would find complete fulfillment. Unpleasant work like garbage removal would be performed by junior battalions of children, who would be
encouraged to find tasks like cleaning privies great fun.
Each family would have a separate apartment in the
phalanstery, which would also have a center and two
wings, and there would be theatres, concert halls, libraries, community dining rooms, counsel chambers,
schools, nurseries, and all public amenities. The fourth

side of the square would be closed by the barns, warehouses, and workshops, and on the center plaza the groups would be mustered each morning and marched to their work with music playing and banners flying. The phalanx would be financed by the sale of shares of stock, but every member need not be a stockholder, nor every stockholder a member. Work would be paid for and the worker would be charged rent and other expenses. At the end of the year the profits of the phalanx would be divided, five-twelfths to labor, four-twelfths to capital and three-twelfths to skill. Seven-eighths of the members would be farmers and mechanics, and the rest professionals, artists, scientists, and capitalists. There would be no discontent or discrimination, since all roles would be interchangeable. There would be a Chancellery of the Court of Love, and Corporations of Love, and an extraordinary system of organized polygamy. Not only sex, but food and all other sensual pleasures, would be organized to give maximum pleasure.

Fourier did not limit himself to reorganizing society. His utopia found its place in a fantastic cosmology. The stars and planets are animals like ourselves, he thought. They are born, mate, grow old, and die as we. The average life of a planet is eighty thousand years, half spent in ascending vibrations and half in descending; there are thirty-two periods of the earth, of which we are now in the fifth. When we reach the eighth, the Great Harmony will be consummated, and men will grow tails, with eyes on the tip. Dead bodies will be turned into interstellar perfume. Six new moons will appear. The sea will change into lemonade, and all fierce and noxious animals and insects will be transformed into sweet and gentle anti-lions, anti-rats, and anti-bugs. Then the phalanxes, numbering exactly 2,985,984, will spread over the earth, which will become one great Community of Love, ruled over by an Omniarch, three Augusts, twelve Caesarinas, forty-eight empresses, one hundred and forty-four Caliphs and five hundred and seventy-six sultans.

In his later years Fourier ran advertisements in the newspapers, saying that he would be home at a certain hour every day to meet with any capitalist who wished to invest in the future, found a phalanx, and possibly become a sultan or a caliph. No one ever came, but as time went by he gathered around himself a small group led by Victor Considerant, who in 1832 launched a Fourierist movement with a newspaper, *Le Phalanster*, which ran under various names until it was suppressed by Louis Napoleon in 1850. A community was established in 1832 near Paris, but failed almost immediately. There were no attempts of any importance after that in France. Fourier was patently mad, but Considerant was not. The Fourierists were careful not to emphasize the seas of lemonade and the men with seeing-eye tails. Instead they contrasted the combination of detailed planning and lives of joy, wonder, and sensual pleasure promised by Fourier's phalanxes with the frigid, hard-working, puritanical utopias of his competitors.

Associated with Considerant was the American journalist Arthur Brisbane, who returned to the States and began active propaganda of lectures and articles. In 1848 he published *The Social Destiny of Man*, a simple and logical exposition of the conceivably practicable ideas of Fourier, purging anything that might hint at Fourier's madness. The book attracted the attention of Horace Greeley, editor of *The New Yorker*; and in 1842, when Greeley became editor of *The New York Tribune*, he gave Brisbane a regular column in the paper and, in addition, considerable publicity for what Brisbane had christened Associationism in news and editorials. Greeley took to the lecture platform himself and finally pledged his property to the Association. Brisbane started a magazine, *The Phalanx*, which was absorbed in *The Harbinger* when Brook Farm was converted to Fourierism. The conversion of the Brook Farmers and their associates gave the movement prestige and intellectual respectability, which it had never enjoyed in France, where any expurgated version of its doctrines could be compared with the original works of the master. George Ripley, Charles A. Dana, John S. Dwight, William Henry Channing, T. W. Higginson, James Russell Lowell, John Greenleaf Whittier, Margaret Fuller, William Cullen Bryant, in fact, almost all the New England intellectuals and Transcendentalists except Emerson and Thoreau, wrote for *The Harbinger* and the other Fourierist papers that blossomed in the next few years.

The movement also gathered up many abolitionists and, at least for a while, almost all primitive socialists. Its cooperative industry was an answer to both chattel slavery and the increasing debasement of the working class by the industrial system. The advent of Fourierism in America happened to coincide with a long period of economic depression and with the increasing social tensions which would culminate in the Civil War. Fourierism became a craze which the leaders found difficult to control. Somewhere between at least forty and fifty phalanxes were started in the next few years. Of these only six survived more than a year, and only three for more than two years.

Often crowds of a hundred or more colonists trouped off with flags flying and music playing to the wilderness, or to abandoned farms for which they had paid high prices. The first day began with a picnic, and ended with dancing, drinking, and the fulfillment of Fourier's *parcours*, the concurrence of all sensual pleasures in perfect bliss. Within a few days, provisions began to run short, necessary skills were found to be in even shorter supply, and tempers were shorter yet. Soon competition for what little was available seemed worse than in the world they had left, and they began to quarrel and accuse each other of stealing. Some colonies lasted only a few weeks, and left the leading members seriously indebted. The tendency to buy as much land as possible and as heavily mortgaged was almost universal, and the purchasers were seldom able to distinguish malarial swamps and barren sand flats from agricultural land. Commitment to Owen's New Harmony had been weak enough. It was practically non-existent in the abortive phalanxes. Anyone was admitted who had become excited by reading the Fourierist press.

Almost all colonies began with a completely open-door policy. Not only was there no attempt to secure the balance of occupations, mechanics, and farmers necessary for any functioning community, but the phalanxes, like New Harmony, attracted a specific class, a caste of déclassés which had come into existence with capitalism itself—bohemians. Bohemians have been called people who would enjoy the luxuries of the rich without securing the necessities of the poor. The breakup of the old functions of society had produced large numbers of over-educated and under- or unemployed technical and professional people who were unable to find positions in society to which they fancied they had been called, and who had become increasingly alienated. They could not function with any satisfaction in the dominant society, and hoped to find a life aim and a significant role in an alternative community. But the demands of such a community were even greater than those of the dominant society, so they were, with few exceptions, foredoomed to still greater disappointment and demoralization.

The most successful Fourierist colony was the North American Phalanx, founded in 1843 near Red Bank, New Jersey. The founders were a group of Fourierists from Albany, New York, who had been discussing the possibility of organizing the community for some time and had thus become well acquainted. After considerable exploration, they selected a site of about seven hundred acres with pasture and woodland, but mostly under cultivation, and with two farmhouses. In August 1843 they called a convention, adopted a constitution, and raised an initial eight thousand dollars on shares. Although the constitution was largely an ideological manifesto, it also included a considerable amount of practical organization.

During the fall of the year, the first families occupied the farmhouses to capacity and began to build a large dormitory building for the main body which would come in the spring; in addition they went about doing all the necessary fall plowing and sowing. During 1844 about ninety people had settled in, planted and eventually harvested crops, built shops and mills, and worked out the details of practical organization. Membership was limited to what the project could support, and applicants were carefully screened and then underwent a probationary period of a year, preceded by a thirty to sixty-day visit. North American was anything but an open-door commune.

As time went on, the original joint-stock type of organization and the complicated system of paying wages and profits gave way to a more communal economy than even that of pure Fourierism. It took a while to work out the details of organization. One member said that the meetings of the first five years "were largely taken up with legislation." Unlike any other phalanx, they could afford the time. The members were far more united. They had money. They were not threatened by bankruptcy. At the beginning, the property was worth twenty-eight thousand dollars, with about ten thousand dollars in outside debt. In November 1852 the property was estimated at eighty thousand dollars, with an outside debt of about eighteen thousand dollars and about one hundred and seven dollars credited to each person, man, woman, and child, or some one hundred and twelve members. To reach this point they had worked hard. There was never time for the constant picnics, concerts, and lectures characteristic of Brook Farm. Life at North American remained spartan to the end. Partly this was due to the influence of Shakerism on some of the leaders.

In September 1854 fire broke out in the flour mill and eventually destroyed the warehouses and shops. There was only two thousand dollars in insurance and the members estimated the total loss at more than twenty thousand dollars. A meeting of the stockholders was called to raise new funds. Instead they voted to dissolve the colony. Most of the stockholders by this time had become absentee members. A few people lingered on into the next year, when the property was finally sold off.

Had it not been for the fire, North American could have gone on indefinitely. The attrition of the years had left a community of people who were content with a very low-level utopia of hard work, plain living, and almost no intellectual or aesthetic satisfaction. Members had not been admitted unless they were prepared to do unskilled or agricultural labor. Professional people were discouraged. The colony even turned down a skilled printer who wanted to establish a press, and they were never able to attract highly skilled mechanics, but forced to hire them as needed. In spite of this, most of the colonists, but especially the children, remembered their years at North American with pleasure.

Many of the members migrated to Victor Considerant's colony in Texas, which never really got started, and others distributed themselves over a variety of communes, all of them short-lived. The Wisconsin phalanx was almost as successful as North American. The original members, mostly residents of Racine County, Wisconsin, were exceptionally stable and practical men under the strong leadership of Warren Chase, who seems to have been—as were many other Fourierists, including many at Brook Farm—a Swedenborgian, and later a Spiritualist. The community started out free of debt, on ten sections of land near Green Bay. The first twenty pioneers spent the summer planting twenty acres of spring crops and one hundred acres of winter wheat, erecting three buildings, which housed eighty people, and putting up a saw mill, barns, and outbuildings. Within a year, they had joined the three buildings into a two-hundred-foot-long phalanstery, built a stone schoolhouse, a grist mill, dam and millrace, a large shop, a washhouse, a hen house, and a blacksmith shop, and they estimated their property as worth almost twenty-eight thousand dollars. Next year they had eight hundred acres in crops, but only admitted one new member.

The Wisconsin phalanx went from one success to another, very probably due to the solidarity and commitment of the members and the exclusion of eccentrics, cranks, and loafers—one new member out of hundreds of applicants. Everything was done systematically. The colony as a whole was incorporated and the phalanstery was incorporated as a town. Although they seem to have had far less bickering and factionalism, in December 1849, at the height of their success, the members voted to dissolve, and the property was sold off, mostly to members, in small farms and village lots, and the profits of the sale, which were considerable, were distributed. John Humphrey Noyes, summing up the brief history of the Wisconsin phalanx, said: "On the whole, the coroner's verdict in this case must be—'Died, not by any of the common diseases of Associations, such as poverty, dissension, lack of wisdom, morality or religion, but by deliberate suicide, for reasons not fully disclosed.' " Communalism and the ideas of Fourier seem to have been only a technique, for once eminently workable, by which a group of practical men and their families opened almost four square miles of good agricultural land on the frontier, developed it, and sold out at a profit.

19

Étienne Cabet

Étienne Cabet was born in 1788, a year before the fall of the Bastille. For the first forty years of his life he was the typical radical Jacobin of the post-revolutionary generation, untouched by the disillusionment of older men whose youth and young manhood was lived under the Terror, the Directory, and the Napoleonic Empire. In 1820 he gave up a law practice in Dijon and became a director of the French conspiratorial revolutionary organization, the Carbonari. In the Revolution of 1830 he was a member of the Insurrection Committee. Louis Phillipe appointed him Attorney General of Corsica, but he was dismissed for his attacks on the government in his book *Histoire de la révolution de 1830,* and in his journal *Le Populaire.* He returned to Dijon and was elected Deputy, whereupon he was arraigned on a charge of *lèse-majesté* and was condemned to two years' imprisonment and five years' exile. He went to Brussels, was expelled, and emigrated to England, where he became a disciple of Robert Owen.

In the amnesty of 1839, Cabet returned to France and in the next year published a history of the French Revolution, and *Voyage en Icarie,* a semi-fictional account of a communist society, which he considered a modern version of Thomas More's *Utopia,* as improved by the economic theories of Robert Owen. There is nothing particularly original or exciting about Cabet's plans for a new society, but like More's *Utopia, Voyage en Icarie* includes a devastating criticism of the contemporary social order—which was probably, for Cabet, its most important part. Its success must have amazed him. It became a bestseller, read or at least talked about by every radical working man and intellectual. For the next seven years in *Le Populaire* and a new journal, *L'Almanach Icarienne,* he built up a following which he claimed to number about half a million. At first, like Edward Bellamy, author of *Looking Backward* at the end of the century, it did not occur to him that people would wish to put his utopian ideas to practical application, but the great success of his movement finally persuaded him. His followers were demanding that he lead them into the commonwealth of the future, and he had already started a number of ill-conceived and abortive Icaries in France.

In 1847 Cabet issued a call, "Forward to Icarie." France was crowded, worn-out with a despotic government, and would never permit the establishment of modern communities, which soon would, by their example, revolutionize the society. In America it would be possible to build a communist colony of ten or twenty thousand people on the frontier, and in a few years millions would be converted. The response was tremendous. He was deluged with gifts, pledges, and recruits.

Since Cabet had neither picked a site nor made any

definite plans for settlement, he must have been a little frightened, and went to London to consult with Robert Owen. At the moment, Owen was enthusiastic about Texas, which had just been admitted to the Union and was anxious for settlers. A short time later, a Texas land agent in London persuaded Cabet to contract for a million acres on the Red River, "easily accessible by boat."

On February 3, 1848, the advance party sailed for Texas. In New Orleans they discovered that they had bought a hundred thousand, not a million, acres in the wilderness, two hundred and fifty miles from the river, alloted in checkerboard fashion, the alternate squares still in possession of the state; and by the terms of the agreement, they were obliged to build a log house on each of their sections before July. Furthermore, the Red River was not navigable beyond Shreveport, Louisiana, where it was blocked by an immense, permanent log jam.

Undaunted, sixty-nine enthusiastic Frenchmen, totally inexperienced in coping with the wilderness, stored most of their goods and set off overland with one wagon drawn by oxen. They did not even know how to manage the wagon and oxen. They broke down and became stuck in marshes. People began to get malaria. They ran out of food, but at last they reached the site of Icaria, and met the land agents of the Peters Land Company, who informed them that any land which was not occupied by a cabin and resident in each half-square mile would revert to the company, which would be glad to resell it at a dollar an acre. There was no possibility of fulfilling the contract, but the sixty-nine pioneers wrote a desperate letter to Cabet and set to work. Although many of them were skilled mechanics, almost none was a farmer or, curiously, a builder. They did not know how to plough, and the thirty-two cabins they were able to build were hovels. More and more people became sick, probably with malaria. Their doctor said it was yellow fever, but all of his diagnoses were for fatal diseases, and it soon turned out that he was insane. Most of the members became ill—the water was undrinkable, but few died. In the spring, ten more settlers arrived out of the five hundred Cabet had promised.

Meanwhile, back in France, the Revolution of 1848 had overthrown Louis Phillipe, and in the next few months revolutionary leaders like the poet Lamartine, Cabet, his friend Louis Blanc, and others of the left were discredited, partly by their own mistakes, but even more by the organized opposition of the right and the Bonapartists. On December 15, Cabet sailed for America with almost five hundred new colonists to find the shattered remnants of the pioneer settlement back in New Orleans. Cabet wished to return to Texas, but those who remained from the pioneer group rebelled. The winter was spent in bitter conflict, and eventually almost two hundred, mostly members of the group that had just come with Cabet, returned to France, and the others found temporary employment in New Orleans while Cabet shopped for a new site. In the spring he bought all the available property of the town of Nauvoo in Illinois from which the Mormons had recently migrated to Utah. For a down-payment and a large mortgage he got a variety of mills and shops, a distillery, a large community dwelling, numerous family houses, the ruins of the burnt-out temple, and fifteen hundred acres of land. Two hundred and eighty faithful Icarians went up the river with Cabet to their new home. Typical of the fate that dogged them, twenty died of cholera on the way.

Nauvoo would seem to have been ideal. Like Owen at

New Harmony, Cabet took over a completely equipped village, or rather, small town, which the Mormon Church had operated until driven out by persecution, not just successfully, but with such prosperity as to arouse the envy of their neighbors. For a while, the Icarians seemed to prosper too. Cabet had a tried-and-tested membership—tried, if not by fire, at least by mud, mosquitoes, disease, and hunger. Most of the people were experienced artisans, and soon the mills and craft shops were back in operation. Strangely enough, there were very few farmers, so much of the fifteen hundred acres remained uncultivated. During the year, new arrivals from France doubled the size of the colony. But the imbalance of craftsmen and farmers increased.

With all the immense amount of propaganda which Cabet put out in France, he never seems to have made the slightest effort to recruit specific kinds of workers to meet the needs of the colony. With fifteen hundred acres of some of the best land in the Mississippi Valley, Icarian Nauvoo did not, as similar unbalanced colonies had often done, hire farm laborers. Instead, they bought most of their food on the market. The work of the shops could not even begin to meet the steadily growing deficit, which was made up by the contributions of cash which Madame Cabet kept flowing from France. It does not seem to have occurred to Cabet that there was anything wrong with that. His letters and reports from the time are uniformly optimistic, in fact euphoric.

As usual, the colonists started a progressive school, with instruction in both French and English for their children and English classes for adults. They printed a newspaper and several pamphlets. They had an orchestra, a band, and a theatrical company, lectures by visitors and residents, and discussion and study groups. Cabet, however, was not content. He still hoped to found a utopian city, not a village, in which the habitations would be palaces, the labors of the people mere pastimes, and their whole lives pleasant dreams.

In 1852 the colonists who had left him at New Orleans sued him for embezzlement and he went back to contest the suit. The French courts acquitted him and he returned to a welcoming banquet in New York, a triumphant journey across country, and another celebration in Nauvoo. By this time, the colony was a modest success. Even the farming problem was on the way to being solved, and the deficit was steadily declining. To Cabet this was just the beginning. He went off to Iowa and purchased three thousand acres on a mortgage for the site of his dream city and communist Garden of Eden.

The government of the colony had been as vaguely conceived as its economics. While in France Cabet had been accepted as dictator for ten years, and this arrangement was renewed in New Orleans and again at Nauvoo. But in 1850, convinced of the success of the colony and its readiness for a pure communist government. Cabet gave up his dictatorship. A constitution was adopted in 1850 with a board of six governors, and a variety of administrative committees to take care of the details of the work and community life. Cabet was elected president each year until 1855. That December he proposed that the constitution be rewritten providing for the election of a president with dictatorial powers to appoint the members of the board of directors and all committees.

The constitution had provided for annual revision in March, so the community rebelled, and in the election of February 1856 elected J. B. Gerard president. This led to so severe a conflict that Gerard resigned and Cabet was re-elected under the old constitution for another year. For six months the majority of directors supported him, but most of the general assembly of the whole community opposed him. The principal reason for this opposition seems to have been Cabet's increasing eccentricity. He had forbidden alcoholic drinks in the community and insisted that the whole product of the distillery be sold outside. He then proposed to forbid all use of tobacco and began to try to enforce his own notions of diet and his eccentric but puritanical sexual morality. The fact of the matter is that Cabet was becoming an old man, impractical in his visionary schemes, rigid in his attempts at their application, and cranky in temperament—a typical product of a lifetime spent on the fringes of radicalism. At the summer election, he lost his majority on the board of directors and the colony broke down in chaos.

In no other communist community do we have records of such violent conflict. At first factions stopped speaking to each other, withdrew to separate parts of the dining room, and engaged in separate social activities. Work ceased in the mills and fields. The children quarreled with each other in school, and soon the members were literally fighting in the streets. At this point the anti-Cabet board of directors decided that those who did not work should not eat, and cut off the rations of the strikers on August 13. Cabet and the minority responded by petitioning the state legislature to revoke the charter of the community. The majority answered this move by voting unanimously to expel Cabet and his followers, who boycotted the meeting. Four weeks later, Cabet and a hundred and seventy faithful followers, many of whom had been with him from the beginning in Texas, arrived in St. Louis and, as they had long ago in New Orleans, sought individual jobs as mechanics. A week later, Cabet was dead.

Cabet's death was by no means the end of the Icarians. The majority at Nauvoo reacted with guilt and repentance. In the course of time, the memory of his faults and crankiness and the bitter factionalism of the last few years faded. Cabet became a kind of culture hero, the founder of a new civilization, like Theseus or Romulus in the opening pages of Plutarch, and selections from his wisdom were read at meetings, like the Gospels and epistles in church.

The St. Louis group established itself in three large cooperative houses and pooled all its resources. The members sent their children to public schools, but organized classes in adult education, especially in English, in which they were still deficient. They had been allotted a share of the large community library, and they added to it to furnish their large recreation and study room. Weeknights they continued to have music and theatrical entertainments, and on Sunday they met for instruction in the principles of Jesus Christ and Étienne Cabet. They also issued their own journal, the *Revue Icarienne*. Faithful to the end, they forswore the consumption of alcoholic drinks and tobacco in any form.

The movement in France recognized the St. Louis group as the legal Icarian community, and so it received steady income of contributions and periodic recruits of new members from abroad. The men found employment at good wages and the community was functioning as a quite successful urban commune, one of the very first of its kind. But they were not content.

They purchased a farm, the Cheltenham estate, a site now well within the city limits of St. Louis, and moved back to the land. Many of the members continued to go into their jobs in St. Louis, but the income from that source dropped considerably. The site was unhealthy —the whole Mississippi Valley seems to have been ridden with malaria in those days; and communist colonies seem fated always to find the most malarial sites.

There were still not enough farmers, so that the land did not even feed the community. There were no shops or mills, only a few log huts and one strong house. Within a year, the same faction that had split Nauvoo developed in Cheltenham. The majority wished to perpetuate the dictatorship established by Cabet. A minority insisted on complete democracy. Forty-two of the democrats withdrew, and the colony was unable to recover from their secession, since they comprised the majority of the skilled craftsmen and wage-earners. In 1864 only eight men, seven women, and their children were left. The French movement had withered and no money or recruits came any more from France. The mortgage was foreclosed and Icaria at Cheltenham ceased to exist.

After the secession of the minority, the community of two hundred and fifty at Nauvoo declined rapidly. Profits from the mills, shops, and distillery dried up, probably for lack of skilled workers, most of whom had gone to St. Louis. The Mormons, who still held the very considerable mortgage, threatened them with foreclosure. The plant was simply too large for the members to operate. They decided to migrate to the site in Iowa where Cabet had planned to build the palatial City of Utopia. They took over undeveloped land, far from any settlement, encumbered with a mortgage at ten per cent. In 1863 only thirty-five ill-fed, ill-housed, and overworked communists were left.

They were saved only by the outbreak of the Civil War. Settlers flooded into Iowa to save it for the Union. The colony found a ready market for its products at good prices, and they sold two thousand acres which they were unable to cultivate for ten thousand dollars. For twelve years they prospered, so much so that they bought back some of the land. They built decent houses, laid out orchards and vineyards, and began to go in for more intensive farming. Since they had had to learn by doing the art of agriculture, they probably had to work too hard to waste time in quarreling. At least, considering their past history, their personal relations were remarkably equable.

In 1876 there were seventy-five members. They had a dozen family dwellings on three sides of a square, a large central building with a community kitchen and dining room, used also for assemblies and recreation, a bakery and laundry, a dairyhouse, stables and barns and a large number of log outbuildings, all on a handsome site on a bluff above the valley of the Nodaway River; and behind them were two thousand fertile acres, seven hundred under cultivation with timberland, meadows, and pastures. They had six hundred sheep, a hundred and forty cattle, most of them milch cows, and raised corn, wheat, potatoes, sorghum, vegetables, and small fruits besides vineyards and orchards. All meals were taken in common, and many services like laundry were performed for the community as a whole. In the evening after dinner there was dancing, music, organized or spontaneous recreation, and on Sundays a service which included a lecture, singing of their own songs, and readings from the works of Étienne Cabet.

The disastrous blow dealt to the French radical movement by the Terror which followed the suppression of the Paris Commune in 1871 had brought them new recruits and had wrought changes, some obvious, some subtle but profound, in the ideology of the community. France itself has never recovered from the Commune, so it is not surprising that its effects were felt so far away from Paris, amongst a little community of French radicals in the midst of the Iowa prairies.

As the years had gone by, changes had taken place in the production economy of the colony. Except for grains and other large-scale crops, the produce of the individual plots attached to the family dwellings had come to dominate the food supply, produce, vegetables, and milk. Similarly the small craftsmen functioned as almost independent operators and commonly sold their products or took part-time jobs on the outside. The situation was not unlike that on the Russian collective farms before Stalin's wholesale purges. It was the older generation of revolutionaries who had pioneered with Cabet who insisted on this limited private enterprise. The young people, especially the refugees from the Paris Commune, demanded a complete communism of production. Many of them were disciples of Proudhon, Bakunin, Weitling (Weitling's own colony, Communia, had been in northeast Iowa, in Clayton County about fifteen miles from Gutenberg), or Marx, and the massacres and deportations that followed the suppression of the Commune had pushed them even further to the left. Communism had ceased to be generalized life philosophy, a sentiment or an attitude, and had become an ideology, or rather a number of mutually antagonistic systems.

The older members had learned that ideology was not enough and insisted on keeping the membership strictly limited. The younger members pointed out that the colony was poor and overworked, seriously understaffed with only eighty people, and demanded that as many members be admitted as the colony could support.

During the 1870's conflict became irreconcilable, and at last the younger group went to the courts and sued to revoke the charter, on the technicality that the colony was registered as an agricultural cooperative but engaged in manufacture. The court granted the suit, and the rebels incorporated under a new charter in 1879, while the older members were granted a thousand acres and several houses and other buildings—and no debt. The debts were assumed by the rebels. The older group, which ironically called itself the New Icarians, was modestly successful. The insurgents increased their membership, opened new industries, cultivated more land with improved agricultural methods, and more than doubled their membership. For the first time in the long life of the Icarian communities, women were permitted to vote and hold office. The colony was officially declared non-religious.

The economic expansion entailed an unmanageable debt, and the expansion of the membership soon resulted in the growth of new, irreconcilable factions. By the fall of 1881 the younger community was disintegrating and unable to satisfy its creditors. Efforts were made to move to California and combine with the Speranza colony at Cloverdale, but in the meantime the Cloverdale project itself collapsed, and the property was sold off to satisfy the creditors—some of it to the New Icarians.

The older party went on in their new community much as they had for many years. They planted orchards and vineyards, worked hard, ate simply, dressed poorly—they wore sabots to the end, and occupied their leisure with music and lectures by their members, and with their library of more than a thousand books, all of them in French. In 1883 they had thirty-four members. Their children left. They grew old. One by one they dropped away. By the end of the century a large proportion of the remaining members were in their eighties and unable to operate the property any longer, so it was sold off, all debts paid, and the very considerable remaining money divided pro rata according to the time of service. Each member got enough money to support him or her modestly to the end of life.

At least New Icaria ended in mutual good will and

financial solvency. Cabet's utopia had lasted, in one form or another, from 1848 to 1901, one of the longest lived of all secular communist ventures. Most remarkable, it lasted through incredible difficulties, suffering, and sickness, almost continuous factionalism, hard labor, much of it wasted due to lack of experience, and impractical and naïve financing, loss of money, and accumulation of debts. Life was always poor in the Icarian communities. Life at Brook Farm was sybaritic by comparison. At the end, the handful of survivors were still enthusiastically committed communists, although it is difficult to say what they were committed to. The theories of Cabet, where they were definite, were impracticable. Where they were not, they were vague and sentimental or, as in his position on sexual relations, women's rights, and the use of tobacco, destructive or irrelevant. Its charismatic leader was expelled early in the life of the colony and no one ever took his place. Yet Icaria endured, and even the dissidents and secessionists remained, most of them, convinced communists, and many of them migrated to other communes after Icaria was sold off.

20

Hutterites Again

We left the Hutterites in 1770, invited to settle in the Ukraine and the Volga region by Catherine the Great. In 1763 the Russian government issued a manifesto offering foreign settlers free land—as it happened, some of the best agricultural land in the world—complete religious freedom, their own schools, instruction in their own language, exemption from military service, and considerable tax exemptions, on the sole condition that they did not proselytize Russians of the Orthodox faith. Twenty-three thousand Germans, mostly Pietists or Anabaptists, had responded. Many more came in the following years. Until their settlements were broken up during the Second World War and they were exiled to Siberia or exterminated by Stalin, the "Volga Germans" were a small but significant portion of the population of European Russia.

In Rumania and Transylvania the Hutterites found

themselves, as absolute pacifists, at the mercy of the marauding troops of both sides. They appealed to the commander of the Russian forces, Count Rumiantsev, and he invited them to settle on his own estates near Kiev, under even more favorable terms than those offered by Catherine's manifesto. They arrived in the autumn of 1770, and before winter had already established the essential plant of the colony. They brought with them their craftsmen; and in a few years their village, known as Vishenky, had become a showplace, with a textile mill, a blacksmith's shop, distillery, and pottery. While they had been in the Austrian Empire their ceramics had become famous, and examples can be found today in the museums of Central Europe.

In 1796 Rumiantsev died and his sons attempted to cancel the old count's written agreement with the community. The Hutterites appealed to the new emperor, Paul I, who upheld the original agreement and granted them all the privileges given to the Mennonites who were migrating to Russia from Prussia by the thousands. After thirty-two years they moved from Vishenky to Radichev, eight miles away, on land granted them by the government. At this time they numbered a little more than two hundred adults.

Soon the Hutterites expanded their manufacturing enterprises and began to grow and weave fine linen and silk. They were probably the first to raise silk worms successfully in Russia. In these years, the life of the community differed little from that of the Hutterite settlements in the United States and Canada at the present time—except that there was far more manufacturing. Land was parceled out at a rate of about two and a half acres per family, only enough to feed the members. There was complete communism of consumption. They ate in a community dining room, men and women at separate tables. They wore clothes issued to all alike.

They were permitted a minimum of personal possessions. Their children were raised in nurseries. The day
began and ended with religious services, and Sundays
were spent mostly in their stark, unornamented chapel.
Their communism of production, which they had
practiced from the beginning, had the curious result of
making them amongst the very first pioneers of the factory system. The manufacture of products such as pots
was broken down into a series of separate operations,
each performed by different individuals. However, people were permitted to change their tasks, and even their
occupation, to avoid monotony. The reports of Russian
officials who visited were enthusiastic, as well they
might have been. Around the Hutterite settlement were
villages of Russian peasants, inefficient, disorderly,
and filthy, virtually unchanged since neolithic times.

By 1840 the land had ceased to be able to support the
increased population, and in 1842 the Hutterites were
moved by the government to the Mennonite settlements
in the Crimea, where they were granted land as individual farmers; and an effort was made, both by the
government and by the administration of the Mennonite communities, to break up their communist mode
of life. Some were absorbed into the Mennonites, but
within a few years, most had re-established the old
communal patterns and were prospering. Although
many of their manufacturing enterprises continued on
a small scale, it was in these years that the emphasis
shifted to agriculture.

In 1864 a law was passed putting all the schools in
the entire empire under the supervision of the State,
and making the Russian language the exclusive and
compulsory medium of instruction. The government
also announced that military service would be made
compulsory within ten years. The Hutterites, unanimously, and most of the Mennonites, decided to emi-

grate. Members of both groups were sent to the United States, Canada, and South America to find suitable land and governments which would permit them to preserve their way of life. At the last moment the Russian government, anxious to retain such valuable citizens, offered to grant most of the original terms of settlement, but only a very few Hutterites, although a considerable number of Mennonites, remained behind. Those who persisted in practicing communism were exterminated by the Bolsheviks during the Civil War and World War II.

The first group of Hutterites, one hundred and nine people, left for Nebraska in 1874, and soon moved from there to southeastern South Dakota to the James River Valley. They were followed in the next three years by all the others who wished to migrate. In those days the Dakota Territory was scarcely settled. The Indian Wars were still going on. Custer's defeat in 1876 and the Black Hills Gold Rush began at the same time. But in 1872 there were only twelve thousand people in what later became North and South Dakota. Each colony as it came in spent its first Dakota winter in sod huts, but in the spring immediately began work on stone houses and barns, and by the second winter were decently housed. The colonies were far out of the way. The world ignored them and they ignored the world. At last they were able to return to strict orthodoxy, discipline, and uncompromised communal living; and due to their isolation they necessarily became almost entirely self-sufficient. They spun and wove their own clothes, made their own shoes, did all their own blacksmithing and iron work, and made their own simple farm machinery. However, except for these absolutely necessary crafts, the Hutterites became purely agricultural colonies in America. They were never to return to the craft and manufacturing enterprises of the first hundred years.

The leader of the first colony, Michael Waldner, was a blacksmith, hence *Schmiedenleute,* the Blacksmith People. The leader of the *Dariusleute* was Darius Walther. And of the last group to arrive, the leader was Jacob Wipf, a teacher, hence the *Lehrerleute,* the Teacher's People.

Left to themselves, the colonies flourished. By 1915 there were over seventeen hundred members in seventeen colonies, fifteen in South Dakota and two in Montana. The increase was almost entirely natural. They made practically no converts. But they had, and still have, one of the highest birth rates of any group in America. By 1917 they were no longer isolated. Montana and the Dakotas were states, and the colonies were surrounded by settled farms, and there were towns nearby.

The United States entered the war and the draft laws made no provision for conscientious objectors, even on the part of members of the historic peace churches, or even, as in the case of the Hutterites, though the government had originally promised that the settlers, whom they were so anxious to attract, would be forever exempted from bearing arms. The pacifist Secretary of War, and author of the draft law, Newton D. Baker, advised all young men from the historic peace churches to join the army, go to camp, and ask the commanding officer for noncombatant service. As might be imagined, this advice resulted in imprisonment, torture, inspired persecution, and mob violence.

The Hutterites were absolutists and refused to have anything to do with the draft or with war work. Besides very few of them spoke anything but German. They went to prison, and in prison were subjected to relentless persecution. Two Hutterite boys died under the torture of prison guards. Once again the Hutterites were forced to migrate. Not only were their young men im-

prisoned as draft evaders, but mob violence and arson
and wholesale theft of their livestock by the neighboring
farmers was steadily increasing. The state of South
Dakota revoked their incorporation, with the announced objective to "absolutely exterminate the Hutterites in South Dakota." Delegations were sent to the
Canadian government in Ottawa, and the provincial
governments of Alberta and Manitoba, and arrangements were made with the Canadian Pacific Railway.
The State agreed to respect their pacifism and refusal to
vote or hold office. In fact, the Canadian government
had been trying to get the Hutterites to come since
1898. In the fall of 1918 the entire body arrived and was
soon distributed on new settlements, the *Schmiedenleute* in Manitoba, the *Darius* and *Lehrer* in Alberta.
Within ten years they had bought back the old South
Dakota sites and established new colonies in Washington, Montana, North Dakota, and Saskatchewan.

The Canadian government had never deliberately
provoked anti-German feeling against its own citizens,
as had Wilson's propaganda machine, directed by the
liberal intellectual George Creel. The war ended soon
after the arrival of the colonists in Canada, and for several years they were more than welcome, and once
again prospered. However, their high birth rate continued, and the colonies were continuously budding off
into new land, which they farmed far more successfully
than did their Gentile neighbors. They ceased to do their
own weaving, although most colonists still make their
own shoes, and all knitwear. Blacksmithing is largely
confined to horseshoeing and machine repair. The old
one-man ploughs, scythes, and cradle-scythes are a
thing of the past. Unlike the stricter Amish, the Hutterites believe in using all the latest farm machinery.
In fact, they have often been criticized for over-
capitalizing their farms. Since they still live lives of

strict austerity and spend no money on entertainment or domestic utilities, except refrigerators, which they usually get from the Amana Colony, and since radios, televison, musical instruments, and all but the simplest clothing are completely forbidden, and their farms are uniformly successful, they have little else to do with their money except to spend it for farm machinery. Only in recent years have the Hutterites permitted a very few carefully selected members to continue their education beyond the legal minimum, although there is now a growing feeling that they should produce their own doctors and teachers. In the past, a rare member has withdrawn from the community, obtained a college education, returned, repented, and served the community as a resident professional. Since they do not believe in ever going to court, they at least do not need to produce their own lawyers. They have always trained their own midwives and nurses.

Although the Hutterites have often adopted the policy of buying less desirable land than that of their neighbors, they have always made more money out of it, and soon improved it to the point where it was better than anything around. Their dress is odd, although nowhere near as odd as the stricter Amish. They speak a bygone German dialect amongst themselves, although they all speak English. Like the Quakers, they never haggle over prices. They buy almost all outside goods wholesale, and even the heaviest farm machinery is often bought for several colonies at once. They do not drive automobiles for pleasure—women, incidentally, are forbidden to drive them at all. They are a "peculiar people," and in all contacts with Gentile society conspicuously practice the apostolic virtues. Hence they are hated and envied. Canadian prejudice against the Hutterites has steadily grown. It has never reached the fantastic degree of persecution suffered by the

Doukhobors, but simply because the Hutterites have only responded by turning the other cheek. Unlike the Doukhobors, they do not believe in confrontation or nonviolent demonstrations. They do not burn down their own buildings or take off their clothes, parade naked through towns, or when their men are locked up surround the prisons with a crowd of hymn-singing, naked women. Canadian prejudice and pressure has so far operated under the guise of legality. Abusive gossip and malicious myth-making are to be expected amongst competing farmers in the barrooms of the neighboring towns. But what is astonishing is prejudice amounting to a rigid refusal to see anything good in the Hutterites, and a kind of sniggering contempt amongst educated professional people, including professors in Canadian universities, among them scholars in the sociology of religion.

On the other hand, the Gentile Dakotans seem to have learned their lesson; and although the Hutterites may be envied, they are rather admired. The brutal fact of the matter is that, as was prophesied by its founder, a strictly lived Christianity inspires hatred and fear in "the world." The Roman State persecuted the early Christians because they refused to burn incense to Caesar. The general populace hated them because they were seclusive, dressed differently, supported each other economically, were honest and direct in their dealings, and did not attend the gladiatorial combats in the circus, except as unwilling participants.

The Hutterites form by far the oldest communist society in the world—or in history, except for pre-literate tribes still more or less in the condition of "primitive communism." It is over four hundred and fifty years since Jacob Hutter in 1533 joined the Anabaptist communities, gathered together from Switzerland, Bohemia, Moravia, and the Austrian Tyrol, and per-

suaded them to adopt a completely communal life. In
the golden age of the Moravian settlements, there were
over twenty thousand members in more than ninety villages. Today in Canada and the United States, there are
more than a hundred and fifty colonies, yet the number
of surnames is amazingly small. All existing Hutterites
are descended from the few families that survived centuries of migration, persecution, and desertion.

It has often been pointed out that one of the principal
factors in the failure of most nineteenth-century communes, particularly the secular ones, was the lack of
discrimination in the acceptance of members. The contemporary Hutterite communities are the end-products
of the most rigorous selection imaginable. They have
survived both martyrdom and prosperity, and migration
to and through the most incongruous political environments, although their physical environment has
remained remarkably uniform, the ecology of the
Ukrainian blacklands, the long grass prairie, and the
Danubian basin. At the beginning they deliberately recruited members with the necessary skills, both craftsmen and successful peasants. In Moravia, and for a
while in Russia, they were settled on large manorial
estates, where the self-sufficiency of the economy of a
feudal community survived, and which they were able
to perfect. To this day they still profit from lessons
learned in centuries of a manorial way of life. Although
modern liberal Christians might call them fundamen-
talists, the Hutterite confession of faith is in fact more
flexible, less strict and, what is most important, more
capable of etherealization than that of most Anabaptist sects of the past or millenarian and pentecostal
contemporary churches. In fact, the chiliasm and millenarianism have died away.

The Hutterites do not look upon themselves as a remnant set apart to be saved out of a world of evil at the

Second Coming and the Last Judgment. They simply consider themselves Christians, living the kind of life which self-evidently follows from the words of Jesus and the narratives of the apostolic life in the Gospels and Acts. Since the Gospels and Acts and the words of Christ are also, if read without preconceptions, marked by a dramatic eschatology, the expectation of the imminent arrival of the fire and the kingdom, this adjustment is comparable to that of the larger, respectable Christian sects. The group which most resembles the apostolic Christians is probably Jehovah's Witnesses.

But unlike Jehovah's Witnesses or the Black Muslims, the Hutterites are not a garrison society. If a community builds a sufficiently impenetrable wall around itself, it will be broken down. The Hutterites are almost as open to the Gentile world as are the Quakers. They quietly accept their religious beliefs and their way of life as distinguishing themselves from the rest of the world, and are content. They do not use cosmetics, or watch television, but such practices amongst the Gentiles do not arouse them to a holy fury. They not only accept their relationship to the world, but the world's to them. This is very important. Had they been combative and indulged in massive confrontation, as a tiny minority in the midst of a world which was often bitterly antagonistic, and at the best indifferent, they would have long since been destroyed. Hutterite society is truly a peaceable kingdom.

Most communal movements have depended on the charisma of one individual leader, a Robert Owen or a John Humphrey Noyes, and have succeeded in a measure to which that leader was also a practical administrator and a man of many knowledges, as Noyes was, and Owen was not; or, at times, on the ability of the charismatic man or woman to raise up a practical leader to share the governance of the colony. We are dealing with a very ancient polity, the priest-king and war-king of the transition from the neolithic village to the town. The constitution of the Hutterite communities was carefully adjusted to raise up out of each commune individuals with just sufficient charisma and practicality to insure the cohesion of the community and the efficiency of its economic life. Perhaps it is carefully controlled charisma which has helped the society to endure. The spectacular personalities lie back at the beginning of Hutterite history—the founders and their immediate successors, Jacob Widemann, Hans Hut, Jacob Hutter, Peter Riedemann, and Andreas Ehrenpreis—and their influence overrides that of any leader since, let alone of any contemporary. Their writings are still read in church and their hymns are still sung.

Actually, the Hutterite community owes its cohesion to a diffused charisma, of which each member is the bearer. The community, like the mystical Israel, or the Church as the Bride of Christ, is the pentecostal person. The Hutterites are well aware of this fact, but such awareness seems to mark the limits of etherealization. We know little of the interior life of the devout Hutterite, but there never seems to have occurred a mystical hypostatization of the community. There are no visions of the Shekinah as amongst the Hassidim. The round of work in the fields and kitchens, nurseries and shops, and the congregational work seem to be charged with a consciousness of mystical glory sufficient unto the needs of the very practical-minded Hutterites. There may be a contemplative life, especially amongst older people, that Gentiles never know anything about; but at least viewed from the outside, the Hutterites would seem to be a society of Brother Lawrences.

Unlike many, perhaps most, communal societies, secular or religious, the Hutterites are governed more by custom than by written law, and they have seldom found it necessary to make serious constitutional changes. At the head of each colony is a *Diener am Wort*, the Servant of the Word. When a new leader is to be chosen, the heads of other colonies are invited to a meeting and they, together with all the given colonies' male members, vote for one of a list of candidates submitted by the community. After prayer, from those who receive more than five votes, one is chosen by lot. After a probationary period of two years or more, he is then ordained by the laying on of hands of two or three other leaders. He does not eat at the community table, and in many small ways lives a more individual life in his own home.

Most leaders are comparatively young when chosen—between twenty-five and forty—and serve for life or until incapacitated by sickness or old age. They are the spiritual leaders of the community, and formerly the general administrators, although it has become more and more common to elect by simple majority a practical administrator for the economic affairs, known as a *Haushälter*, the Householder. As colony steward he oversees the work, assigns tasks, takes care of the finances and bookkeeping, and himself takes turns at various jobs, even the most menial. It is important not to think of the *Haushälter* as "the colony boss." He is more of a coordinator. Under him is a farm foreman, and if the colony has other important activities, as very few do, other foremen.

There is considerable rotation of tasks. A man may be a cobbler one year, a beekeeper the next, and a farmer the third year. In the course of time, most people settle down into a regular occupation, but often switch, even late in life. There is a similar hierarchy amongst women—a *Haushälterin*, who supervises the kitchen, the sewing room, the garden, and the kindergarten.

There are also women who specialize in midwifery, and most of the women are competent practical nurses. Although the doctrinal constitutional documents of the Hutterites insist rather strongly on the submission of women to the governance of men, observers are unanimous in their reports that Hutterite women seem to be extraordinarily happy, working together in a state of cheerfulness verging on euphoria. And of course, due to the nature of "women's work," if it is done cooperatively by a large number of women, it is decidedly easier than the chores of the single farm housewife.

Hutterite families live in separate homes or apartments with their children, and are assigned larger ones as the family grows. In the past children were sometimes raised in cooperative nurseries, but this practice has been dropped—except that babies and very young children are cared for cooperatively while the mothers are working. Family relationships are even stronger than those of the old-fashioned German patriarchal family. Questionnaires submitted to children attending public school away from the colony reveal practically none of the alienation, generation gap, much less "Oedipal conflict" typical of modern youth. In spite of the lures of the outside world, with its commodity culture, conspicuous consumption, and over-stimulating entertainment, Hutterite young people almost all seem to want to be just like their parents and the five hundred years of communist ancestors behind them. Those who leave in late adolescence, usually do so to marry a Gentile spouse. They return on holidays and weekends to the colony, often settle nearby, and frequently the spouse is converted, baptized, and the couple are returned, with rejoicing, to the fold.

There is far less desertion of the Hutterite way of life than there is even of similar but non-communist sects like the Amish, Mennonites, or Mormons, or the communists of Amana. One reason for this probably is that there is nothing in the Hutterite creed so improbable as to demand a drastic effort of etherealization on the part of a person educated in modern schools. Very few Hutterites go on to college, although more do under the direction of the colony than used to, to provide professional services and further insure the self-sufficiency of the community. Those who do, almost without exception, return to the colony.

Furthermore, the twentieth-century movement imitating the original Hutterites, the Brüderhof, founded by German and English intellectuals, and still made up largely of college-educated and quite sophisticated people, has never come in conflict with the birth-right Hutterite communities over matters of faith and morals. The disagreements have been basically about customs and folkways of two radically different classes. This was probably one of the weaknesses of the Shakers. As time went on, it became harder and harder for people to believe in Shaker doctrines, especially since they involved celibacy. So the Shakers were almost never able to hold the orphans they raised, and eventually were unable to recruit new adult members.

In practice, the result of almost five hundred years of practice, the governance of the Hutterite community is remarkable for its elasticity. The modest hierarchy of administration can always rise to an emergency. Its flexibility makes it earthquake-proof, and the general governance of the entire movement is similarly flexible. Both colony and general councils, like the Quakers, try to avoid action without unanimity; and since the Hutterite way of life is the end-product of almost every conceivable testing, this unanimity is usually easily arrived at. "Not the rule of men, but the administration of things," as Marx said.

An interesting and possibly significant detail is that the Hutterite colonies, like many villages of primitive people, practice a limited exogamy. Couples choose one another from nearby colonies more often than from within a single colony. This, of course, creates a web of cohesive family relationships, radiating out from the original settlements, and preserves a wider hereditary range, a bigger "gene pool." The gene pool is small enough as it is. Outsiders are always saying "Hutterites all look alike." In 1965, there were only fifteen surnames of the *Haushälters* of all one hundred and fifty-five colonies. The Hutterites may all look alike, but they certainly do not look like what is commonly meant by "inbred." Hereditary diseases and dysfunctions are practically unknown amongst them. They suffer less from such things than the general population.

Epilogue –
Post-Apocalyptic
Communalism

It would be possible to go on describing nineteenth-century American communes indefinitely, but such work would be little better than a dictionary, and there is little point in devoting space to what were really cooperative farms or boarding houses or to abortive colonies that lasted only a few months. There were in the nineteenth century and still are today communal religious cults, most bizarre in their doctrines and despotically ruled by a leader who is the keeper of special revelations. It is a mistake, however, to classify these as communes. They are actually rackets, large-scale collective confidence games operated at immense profit to their leaders. Their history is an entirely different subject and merits another book.

Earlier we referred briefly to a most significant movement in the early history of communalism, the

Jesuit settlements in Paraguay. There is amazingly little literature on this subject in English. Still the best book is R. B. Cunninghame Graham's *A Vanished Arcadia,* published in 1924. When the Jesuits entered the territory in 1607 it was still "wild," almost completely untouched by Spanish or Portuguese influence. In the course of time their communities came to dominate much of the eastern watershed of the River Paraguay. Their villages were really reconstituted tribes, provided with as much of the technology of Europe as they could absorb; and ruled, or rather guided, by a handful of priests, whose instruments of government seem to have been almost exclusively the sacraments of penance and communion. The Indians were harried by slave raiders from São Paulo and the Jesuits were almost as badly harried by ecclesiastical jealousy. Yet they survived until the expulsion of the order in 1767, when most of the Indian villages were destroyed. Their fields reverted to the wilderness, the Indians were scattered and returned to a savage mode of life, or were enslaved, and their immense herds of cattle roamed wild over the pampas.

The Jesuits did not establish their villages as communes deliberately. They simply adapted the social organization of the Indians. The little societies were rather highly structured. Status derived both from offices in the community government and from eagerly sought-after roles in the various ceremonials. Life must have been very like that in one of the more communal pueblos of the American Southwest—Zuni, for instance—but in an environment far more bountiful and therefore permissive of much greater leisure, much of which was devoted to ceremonial—Catholic, much modified by aboriginal elements. Contrary to popular belief, the eminently successful missionary activity in Paraguay was closely watched by the Church, and at-

tempts were made to found similar communities elsewhere in Spanish America, notably by the Jesuits in
Arizona. Had the order not been suppressed just as it
was entering California, the story of the California Indians would be quite different. The Franciscan missions were far from being communes. The Indians were
little better than slaves, and the turnover due to mortality was appalling. After the Americans took over in the
Gold Rush, the Indians were hunted down like jack
rabbits, California grizzlies, coyotes, and condors, until
almost none of them was left in the arable parts of the
state. In Paraguay a few villages founded by the Jesuits
survive to this day. The social and economic relationships are those of free enterprise, but the memory of the
communities of three hundred years ago lingers on. In
many ways the Jesuit "reductions," as they were called
in Paraguay, are one of the best organizations of society
ever to exist, either in theory or in actuality. The Indians were certainly happier than anyone would be in
Plato's Republic, or St. Thomas More's Utopia. Life was
an almost uninterrupted ritual, a kind of group contemplation suffused with joy. The extraordinary thing is
that nothing like it has ever happened at any other time
in history, certainly not since the neolithic village.

At the opposite pole from the Jesuit "reductions" was
the colony of Topolobampo, founded in 1872 on the Gulf
of California. This was the scheme of a professional
land developer, Albert K. Owen, who seems to have believed that the most profitable way to develop a remarkably valuable site on a sheltered, deep-water bay
was to organize a settlement as a cooperative colony
and joint-stock company. The initial plans were certainly communalist, but in a very short time the colonists split into private-enterprise and communalist
factions. Separately, they did an immense amount of
work in opening up the country, digging by hand an

irrigation canal eight miles long, one hundred feet wide and fifteen feet deep, and many miles of ditches. The colony was open to anyone who would buy stock, and in fact to anyone who managed to get there. Owen's schemes for a great port and commercial center came to nothing. The Mexican government reneged on its promises. The colonists rapidly declined from six hundred to two hundred members, most of them private enterprisers. A few descendants of the colony survive in the area today, married into Mexican families. Topolobampo may be the only example of communism as a form of capitalist business enterprise. Considering the scale on which Topolobampo was planned, and the number of people involved, both colonists and non-resident stockholders in the corporation, which was known as the Credit Foncier, there is an extraordinary lack of information. *A Southwestern Utopia* by Thomas A. Robertson, whose childhood was spent in the colony, was published in 1947, with a new edition in 1963 by Ward Ritchie in Los Angeles. The book is folksy and anecdotal, and unfortunately Robertson's family were members of the group that chose private enterprise, so there is very little about the commune. The book has neither bibliography nor index.

One of the colonists at Topolobampo was Burnette G. Haskell, whom Robertson places there in 1887, with his wife and family, and who, one would judge from Robertson's note, also died there. As a matter of fact, in those years Haskell was editing the anarchist magazine *Truth* in San Francisco and busy founding and leading the Kaweah Kooperative Kommonwealth in the foothills of the Sierras, in what became Sequoia National Park, above the town of Three Rivers. Haskell seems to have been an unstable, brilliant, and highly emotional person; and apparently he and James Martin, a socialist and practical labor leader, quarreled from the

settlement's beginnings. Haskell and a man named
Buchanan, who led the great Kansas Railroad Strike,
claimed to have presided over an organization which
was the legitimate successor of the First International
after it was split between the followers of Marx and
Bakunin, and moved by Marx to America. At immense,
in fact incredible effort, the colonists built a road from
Three Rivers into Giant Forest, where they named the
largest Sequoia, now known as the General Sherman
Tree, the Karl Marx Tree. The federal government in-
validated the land claims of the colony under the pressure of the railroads and lumber companies, but the
latter were disappointed. The whole area and the high
country behind it was declared a national park. Haskell
must have gone to Topolobampo after this time.

Another even more famous revolutionary connected
with American communalism was Wilhelm Weitling,
the working-class leader and theoretician, who in the
1840's had a much greater influence than Marx and
Engels, who borrowed liberally from him in their early
days. Weitling evolved a rigid system, secular but with
a heavy millenarian and apocalyptic emphasis. His
communism really involved a rejection of industrialism
and a return to a cooperative handicraft system of production. The apocalypticism of Marx and Engel's
Communist Manifesto reflects the influence of, and
competes with, Weitling. After the failure of the revolutionary movements of 1848, Weitling migrated to
America and ran a newspaper and founded a workers'
association which provided insurance, financial aid,
and pensions to its members, what Marx called a "coffin
club." In 1851 he became interested in Communia, one
of the many small colonies founded, mostly by German
émigrés from the Forty-Eight, into which he poured
much of the money of his *Arbeiterbund.* Quarreling
and plain laziness soon bankrupted the colony and

ruined Weitling. This failure seems to have affected him far more than the failure of the 1848 revolutions. He became a crank and evolved a universal system from cosmogony to economics, and his last years were spent in profound eccentricity. Weitling is too little regarded in the history of revolutionary thought. Quite independently of Hegel, and before Marx, he developed a theory of human self-alienation as the primary evil of capitalist production, and some years before Marx or Proudhon he was an avowed communist. In a sense, Marx and Engels joined *his* communist movement and took it over. His only monument is the large building on the site of Communia, which still functions as a social center and dance hall.

There is a temptation to go on and on describing at least briefly colony after colony. Many of the religious ones were bizarre in the extreme but most of them differed from communities like Oneida or the Shakers in that the founders and leaders were obviously religious racketeers, in it for the money. Many of these people seem to have realized that the more outrageous their gospel, the more dupes they would attract. The will to believe things because they are impossible was not confined to Tertullian, but is a widespread failing of the human race. Most of these movements held all things in common, but always excepting the leaders who led lives of vulgar, ostentatious luxury. Such groups therefore probably should not be called communes. The end in view was always to get the members to give their life savings and from then on work hard without pay.

What are the conclusions to be drawn from a survey of the long history of communalism? They are pretty much the conclusions that were drawn by intelligent leaders when nineteenth-century communalism was at its height—by John Humphrey Noyes of Oneida and

Frederick Evans of the Shakers—and with few exceptions the colonies were open to the criticisms of Marx
and Engels.

To take the Marxist criticism first, what they called
utopian socialism always represented a return to an
earlier, more primitive form of production and social
relationships. With few exceptions, communalist colonies were revivals of the neolithic village with more or
less modern technology. This is still true today. Communalism has been haunted by a gospel of "back to the
land" and in so many instances the colonies have failed
because the members have insisted upon basing their
economy almost exclusively on agriculture, even
though the colonists knew nothing about farming, least
of all what hard work it was. In some instances, they
even determined upon limiting themselves to the most
primitive agricultural technology, although this is more
true of the communes that have proliferated after the
Second World War.

Secular communes have almost always failed in very
short order. It is astonishing that Robert Owen's New
Harmony should bulk so large in the history of communalism. It lasted so short a while and managed to do
everything wrong. A simple belief that all men should
live together as brothers is not sufficiently well defined
to inspire a strong commitment. And where the community is open to anyone who wishes to come and enroll
himself as a member, disaster is certain. Commitment
is weak at best, but such colonies attract the redundant
individuals cast off by the dominant society—idlers,
cranks, and those who cannot get along with anybody
at home or on the job, and who therefore think themselves qualified to get along with the delicately balanced extended family of a commune. An open-gate
policy also admits sociopaths and criminals who, at the

worst, seize power or split the community, and at the least run off with whatever cash and movable assets they can lay hands on.

Almost every commune has tried to be self-sustaining and to achieve both communism of consumption and production. Only the Hutterites have managed to be financially successful agriculturalists, and in their earliest days they too were primarily craftsmen. Ideally, a community should have sufficient land to feed itself, and in addition have some specialized manufacture which can compete in the market place because of its high quality. Oneida, Amana, and in the twentieth century the *Brüderhof* are good examples.

Not only have the longest-lived colonies owed their cohesion and commitment to supernatural sanctions, but they have also been governed by individuals of powerful charisma. In some instances the leadership has been divided exactly as it was at the end of the neolithic, between the religious leader and the practical leader, the priest king and the war king, the apostle and the business manager.

A certain degree of interpersonal tension seems to further the cohesion of a colony. The celibacy of the Shakers, which in their ceremonials verged on orgies without sexual intercourse, and the group marriages and special techniques of sexual intercourse and eugenics of Oneida, are really two forms of the same thing, two faces of the coin of generalized erotic tension.

It should be emphasized again that communal living in theory is very advantageous to women. Most of the work of a housewife or mother can be divided and distributed. Children can be taken care of in a nursery by one or two women. Cooking, sewing, laundry, housecleaning, all the tasks that were considered "women's work," can be distributed so that each woman has considerable leisure. This, of course, is why Mormon polygamy was more popular with women than with men. Thousands of women walked from St. Louis to Salt Lake to take part in it.

However, just as today in many hippie communes the only work done seems to be done by women, so in the history of many of the secular communes of the nineteenth century. Women rebelled, because all the work was shifted to them, while the men sat around, drank whiskey, chewed tobacco, and discussed communism, the equality of the sexes, and the freedom of women.

Communism as such does not seem to have been a factor in the failure of most colonies. Many, perhaps most that fail, do so for economic reasons. Commonly, they bought too much land on expensive mortgages and were unable to use it profitably. Many enjoyed a considerable income from non-resident members. Even the Kaweah Kooperative Kommonwealth received money from a non-resident membership, both in the United States and Europe. The secular colony Icaria, which persisted longest, received very considerable funds from France until the final schism. Its special mistake was undertaking to farm too much land, but it is difficult to understand why throughout the lifetime of the Icarian movement the community life was one of desperately hard work and involuntary poverty.

Wherever there existed powerful forces for commitment and cohesion, a carefully screened membership, and intelligent leaders with wide practical experience, communism proved to be, economically, extremely successful. The model in this regard is the Hutterite colony. Their principal problem today is the envy inspired by their uniform success and prosperity.

It is difficult to relate the thousands of groups that call themselves communes that have sprung up all over the world—except in the Communist countries—since the Second World War. Many are not communes at all, but cooperative boarding houses in university towns of the sort which have always existed. These are the groups that have attracted the most attention from journalists because they are most accessible. Just because their members smoke marijuana and sleep with each other indiscriminately does not make them fundamentally different from the Greek-letter fraternities. Some open-gate rural communes are in fact outdoor "crash pads." Three hundred adolescent hitchhikers bivouacking on three hundred acres which the more or less permanent members do not bother to farm does not constitute a commune. Here again, sensationalist journalism has had a field day. It is true that for many, perhaps most, contemporary groups that call themselves communes, sex and drugs have taken the place of chiliasm and charisma. Even so, a large number have managed to organize themselves as genuine communes—of consumption, and a very few, of production.

The modern communalist movement is held together by a secular version of the old millenarianism. It began with the dropping of the atom bomb. The fire and the judgment ceased to be a matter of faith and became not too distant facts. A "saving remnant" began to withdraw from the centers of population, and in many instances from the northern hemisphere. In the early years of the Cold War the apocalypse did not seem to be very far away and at least twice, once at Dien Bien Phu and again during the Cuban Missile Crisis, it was imminent. People no longer talk very much about the bomb. It has been taken for granted. However, a number of opinion surveys have shown that a majority of college students do not expect to be alive in the twenty-first century. Shortly after Nagasaki and Hiroshima, Alex Comfort said that if the Americans had not invented the atom bomb, the modern capitalist State would have secreted it as a kind of natural product. Just so, modern warfare has also produced an immense number of totally alienated people, who matter-of-factly regard Western civilization as having come to an end in August 1914.

It is this pervasive and absolute alienation that takes the place of religion or ideology amongst contemporary communards; and the modern communalist movement is a direct attack on human self-alienation as such, discarding the roundabout maneuvers of socialism or communism. "After all," as someone once said in a meeting of the Italian Communist Party, "we have had socialism over one-sixth of the earth for fifty years and over an additional area and over twice as many people for twenty-five, and human self-alienation has not declined but increased. What are we doing?"

Marx thought that the industrial process would teach the working class class-consciousness, by which he meant Marxism. This is not particularly noticeable in Detroit or Gary. But the breakdown of Western civilization has taught an immense number of people, not all of them young, an almost instinctive response both to the dominant society, as enemy, and to their peers as comrades, which greatly resembles the Communist anarchism of Bakunin and Berkman, of whom few of them have ever heard. It is remarkable how all-pervasive this is. Highly authoritarian groups like the Black Muslims, the Black Panthers, Jehovah's Witnesses, the *Brüderhof,* and the Jesus People may be defiant of the outside world and present to it a highly structured exterior, but within each movement a communal ethic has developed. This is true even of neo-Bolshevik organizations like the Trotskyites or Maoists, which can no longer enforce the old Leninist rigid organizational forms, and which also constantly spin off guerrilla grouplets, whose interpersonal relations are as communist-anarchist as Kropotkin could have wished, and whose relations to the dominant society are those of the terrorist-anarchist groups in France at the end of the nineteenth century. Grouplets like this are born totally without ideology—except that of total alienation. Modern secession is a continuum which stretches from the Manson Family and the Symbionese Liberation Army to the religious anarcho-pacifists' commune whose members spend at least two hours a day sitting in meditation.

One of the factors making for cohesion is cult. Medieval monasticism, with its continuous round of Mass, Divine Office—the chanting of psalms, hymns, canticles, and prayers every few hours throughout the day and night—and the continuously varying rites of the year, so involved the monk or nun and so identified him or her with the community that it was difficult even to think of breaking away. In America in the nineteenth century the Shakers undoubtedly had the most highly developed cult. But even the successful secular communes originated a ceremonial life, although doubtless the members did not think of it as such.

Another factor often part of the ceremonies of the community was confession, a powerful binding force in the Shakers and surviving today in many communal groups, the most famous of which, in this regard, is Synanon, where the harshest group criticism of the members and the most abject confession have been elevated to a governing principle in the community. Any technique which systematically attacks the least appearance of egocentricity obviously increases group cohesion, except of course that it runs the danger of pushing the individual to the breaking point where he simply leaves. Only the religious communities, and not all of them, have been able to hold their children. This seems to be no problem at all to the Hutterites, who now can safely risk sending selected young people away to college. One of the most important functions of the Shakers was their care of orphans and abandoned children in a day when the orphanages were few and bad. The children were raised in the Shaker life, but almost none of them remained in the community. On the other hand, many secular communities survived principally as "progressive schools." With all its disasters and follies, this was the principal contribution of Owen's New Harmony; and the anarchist colony at Stelton, New Jersey, soon became a cooperative suburban "development," except for the school, which kept the community alive until it was overwhelmed by spreading suburbia (it is now almost entirely a Negro district). Some twentieth-century communes have been primarily schools, the best example being Commonwealth College in Mena, Arkansas. It is doubtful if Black Mountain College could be called a commune. Antioch College, however, is the ultimate descendant of a number of converging communal groups, some of them spun off from New Harmony.

In all the many books which have been written about the communalist movement in America in the nineteenth century, there is little disagreement as to the factors that make for success. They are:

A religion, or at least a powerful ideology which all the members of the group accept, which should include the belief that the dominant society fails to provide sufficient value for a happy life, and is sick, or doomed, or dying, or, nowadays, already dead, and that the commune is a saving remnant plucked from the burning. A leader with powerful charisma and, even more important, the ability to persuade people to his will, and also with considerable equanimity. Noyes, for instance, seems to have been blissfully unruffled by any of the contentions that developed at Oneida. Such a personality can be extremely authoritarian and coercive. About fifty per cent of the people attracted to a communal life seem to be characterized by an extreme social masochism, and they have little trouble finding communities ruled by small tyrants. The other fifty per cent are strong individualists and require the leadership of a highly skilled manipulator, able to persuade them that his ideas originated with themselves. All the charisma in the world cannot make up for a wide range of talents. Noyes, again, was a truly universal man, who apparently could do anything well; and the Hutterite leadership commonly revolved through most of the tasks of the community in their lifetime. If one leader has only charisma, he has to have a business manager, and this dual leadership has not been uncommon.

There should be an accepted method of assigning and rotating tasks, with both sexes sharing the boring jobs of housekeeping. The laundry has traditionally been the focus of discontent amongst women. And of course the members should be responsible—the tasks should be done. Many contemporary communes, urban and rural, are characterized by disorder, filth, and undone jobs.

Farming is very hard work. It is hard work even for experienced farmers. It is not just the concentration of capital which created American agribusiness. For over a generation it has been impossible to hold the sons on the small, two-hundred-acre or so family-run general farm. And all over the semi-tropical and tropical world peasants desert their little farms and move to the slums of the cities, where mostly they starve in squalor. Farming today in America on a small marginal or worn-out general farm is a nearly impossible proposition, and of course the acreage cannot sustain much capital investment in machinery. A large truck garden and a couple of milch goats and some chickens can provide a considerable proportion of the food for a medium-sized commune, and leave ample work time free for some easily distributed specialized manufacture. This is the only solution for a big-city commune, although some of them rent land for garden plots on the outskirts of the city. "Back to the land" and "contact with Mother Earth" are part of the mystique of most contemporary rural communes, whose members find it more desirable to work hard and inefficiently for small returns than to shift the economic base to crafts or manufacture. To each his own.

There is a certain unreality, moreover, about an old mansion or a twelve-room Riverside Drive apartment occupied by lawyers, professors, psychiatrists, and social workers who share expenses, play musical beds, and call themselves a commune. The nearer a community comes to being potentially completely self-sustaining, the nearer it approaches its ideal of a saving remnant, the nucleus of a society which will survive when the dominant society perishes. There are a few urban communes which operate with a communism of production as well as of consumption. They seem to be mostly religious and under extremely authoritarian leadership. Of course, in the apocalypse the urban communes will perish along with the cities, which is the best final argument for establishing communities in remote parts of the country. The only trouble is that the war-making State has the same idea. The New Mexico communes are in the midst of the original centers for atomic warfare, and even the Hutterite colonies in North Dakota are within range of the silos for intercontinental ballistic missiles. Sunburst Farms near Santa Barbara, one of the most successful agricultural communities, is in the direct line of a blast on Vandenburg Air Base, and the San Francisco Bay area is liberally dotted with atomic-war installations and communes on a sort of share-and-share-alike basis.

A complete "Do as thou wilt shall be the whole of the law" total individual anarchism simply does not work. A good many contemporary communes operate on this basis, but they seem to have an average one hundred per cent turnover every year. The commune persists, essentially, as just an address. Most groups of this sort have come together to share drugs and sex, and they are held together, insofar as they are, by the enmity of the dominant society. All the contemporary methods making for group cohesion exist in one community or another. Group sex, encounter groups, group confession and criticism—many communes practice them all, and each group has its antecedents, not just in the nineteenth century, but in the radical Reformation.

Finally, a community can endure as an immense "crash pad" with a completely open-gate policy, but it cannot endure as a commune. Selectivity is the first law of communalism. Even the most anarchistic, where nobody believes in laws, must at least believe in anarchism. The communes that are most successful today either do not allow visitors at all, or do not allow them to stay more than overnight, and prospective members are subjected to a searching novitiate. In the early days of the post-World War II movement, when every hitchhiker was welcomed with open arms, the communes not only filled up with loafers and sociopaths, but they all faced serious problems with abandoned dogs and abandoned children, left behind by wandering

communards. The Rule of St. Benedict has a chapter
devoted to the menace of such people at the beginning
of Western monasticism. Abandoned dogs and abandoned children are social problems, but there is an
aesthetic, even ecological problem. Most rural hippie
communes are approached by a dirt road lined with
dead and abandoned automobiles, which make great
playground equipment for the scrambling, naked children, but which are nonetheless an eyesore, and ultimately an expensive disposal problem.

Index

307